Y0-BDZ-178

Binational Human Rights

PENNSYLVANIA STUDIES IN HUMAN RIGHTS

Bert B. Lockwood, Jr., Series Editor

A complete list of books in the series
is available from the publisher.

BINATIONAL
HUMAN RIGHTS

The U.S.-Mexico Experience

Edited by

William Paul Simmons and Carol Mueller

CABRINI COLLEGE LIBRARY
610 KING OF PRUSSIA ROAD
RADNOR, PA 19087

PENN

UNIVERSITY OF PENNSYLVANIA PRESS

PHILADELPHIA

JC
599
.M6
B56
2014

#8807577777

Copyright © 2014 University of Pennsylvania Press

All rights reserved. Except for brief quotations used
for purposes of review or scholarly citation, none of this
book may be reproduced in any form by any means without written
permission from the publisher.

Published by
University of Pennsylvania Press
Philadelphia, Pennsylvania 19104-4112
www.upenn.edu/pennpress

Printed in the United States of America
on acid-free paper

10 9 8 7 6 5 4 3 2 1

Library of Congress Cataloging-in-Publication Data
ISBN 978-0-8122-4628-5

CONTENTS

Binational Human Rights

Introduction

The news of the ongoing and widespread human rights crises in Mexico is shocking even to hardened human rights workers. Over 60,000 people were killed in the drug war in the years 2006–2012. Hundreds of these killings involve beheadings or other gruesome mutilations and tortures often paraded prominently on the Internet. The well-known feminicides in Ciudad Juárez, despite unprecedented international pressure over the past fifteen years, have not declined but have reached record rates, with over 1,500 young women and girls killed since 1993 (Gupta 2011). Journalists covering the drug war are routinely targeted, with over thirty killed since 2006. Not surprisingly, they increasingly exert widespread self-censorship out of fear of the drug cartels. One Juárez newspaper even declared the cartels "the de facto authorities" of the city and asked what they would like to have published (Committee to Protect Journalists 2011: 104). Migrants from southern Mexico and Central America are routinely victimized (robbed, raped, kidnapped, and killed) on their way to the United States. The Mexican Human Rights Commission reported that in the first six months of 2010 more than 11,000 Central American migrants were kidnapped in Mexico (BBC News 2011c).

Amnesty International (2010) reports that approximately 60 percent of migrant women are sexually assaulted along the journey, while Simmons and Téllez's chapter in this volume cites on-the-ground workers who place the number closer to 100 percent. The terror faced by immigrants and the way they are treated as commodities or objects by the cartels and others is perhaps exemplified by the seventy-two migrants mostly from Central America who were killed "execution-style" in San Fernando, Tamaulipas, when they reportedly refused to work for the cartels as assassins.

These tragedies are fueled in part by widespread impunity and corruption in the legal system. Dozens of cases are reported of authorities aiding the cartels because of threats or bribes. Major prosecutors have been arrested for receiving hundreds of thousands of dollars (U.S.) in bribes. And Mexican law enforcement officials who refuse to be corrupted are routinely targeted by the drug cartels and gangs. Two officials, including a police chief, investigating the Tamaulipas massacre were gunned down less than a week after the crime. Under such pressure, entire police forces have resigned or have been fired and replaced by military units. In an especially poignant example, in Praxedis G. Guerrero, a small town in the northern part of the state of Chihuahua, the cartels tortured and killed the mayor and police chief, leading most of the police officers to resign. Marisol Valles García, a twenty-year-old criminal justice major at the University of Guadalajara, became police chief when no one else was willing to serve. After receiving numerous threats by the drug cartels, she and her family have now fled to the United States, where they are seeking asylum.

This list increases exponentially when we consider the related human rights abuses occurring regularly at the U.S.-Mexico border, especially in our home state of Arizona, where U.S. policies have funneled tens of thousands of undocumented migrants. Thousands have died crossing the U.S.-Mexico border since 1998, with an average of more than 200 dying in the Arizona desert each year since 2002, including a near record 253 confirmed deaths in the Tucson sector in 2010. Add to these the enormous human costs inflicted by the U.S. government's deportation procedures, including the routine separation of family members, frequent migrant sweeps or round-ups, streamlined removal procedures, long-term detentions without legal representation, and the broken and overwhelmed immigration court system. Migrant workers on both sides of the border, especially the undocumented, also endure abysmal working conditions and exploitation.[1] The scope and breadth of these abuses expand farther when we consider the closely related human rights abuses in Central America, most notably brutal gang wars, widespread violence against women including the feminicides[2] in Guatemala (Fregoso and Bejarano 2010, Center for Gender & Refugee Studies 2005), staggering amounts of domestic violence and sexual assault, the exploitation of street children, and rampant poverty.

Some of these abuses, especially the gruesome killings in the Mexican drug war, receive extensive, often overly sensationalistic coverage by the national and international media. Others, like the feminicides in Ciudad Juárez, formerly received a great deal of attention (Staudt 2008) but have been overwhelmed by recent events. Yet others, such as the migrant deaths in the U.S. desert and the failed detention and deportation system, have become routine and are mostly ignored by policymakers and the media. Indeed, these human rights abuses have slipped from, or evade, the consciousness of the public and elites in Mexico, the United States, and around the globe. They grind on, year after year, abuse after abuse.

Localizing Human Rights Across Borders

This book focuses primarily on three of these abuses—the feminicides in Ciudad Juárez, the drug war in Mexico, and the plight of migrants trying to come to the United States from Mexico and Central America. While each of these occurs in a specific, mostly Mexican context, we argue that they need to be understood in a broader binational context. Neoliberal trade policies, especially the North American Free Trade Agreement of 1994 (NAFTA), have led to unprecedented movements of Mexican peoples from rural areas to urban areas, and also to large-scale emigration, especially to the United States. With the crackdown on drug cartels in Colombia and across the Caribbean, Mexico became the number one transit region for drug shipments to the United States and one of the largest producers of illicit drugs in the world. Estimates are that 90 percent of all cocaine shipments to the United States cross Mexican territory, and Mexico is a "major supplier of heroin and largest foreign supplier of marijuana and methamphetamine to the U.S. market" (U.S. Central Intelligence Agency 2012). At the same time, immigration policies in the United States, at both the national and local levels, heavily influence the movement of people throughout the region, as well as the actions of drug cartels and other organized crime groups in Mexico.

After decades of rather stale debates about cultural relativism and universalism in human rights, a consensus is beginning to emerge that there is a need to localize human rights (Merry 2006). That is, human rights may possess universality, but they cannot be divorced from, or made sense of without considering concrete conditions in specific, complex, and multifaceted contexts. However, in a globalized world, the context in one country cannot be understood in isolation, without considering the actions or inactions of other states and transnational actors. Human rights must be localized, but simultaneously understood in a transnational context: we call this approach "localizing human rights across borders."

Localizing the current human rights crises that center on Mexico and its borders is a difficult enterprise, as the situation is large, complex, and ever changing. The geographic area of concern is vast. Mexico is the 15th largest country in the world with the 13th largest population, and the U.S.-Mexico border is the longest border in the world between a developed nation and a developing nation, while Mexico's border with Guatemala is extremely porous. A large number of actors, both governmental and nongovernmental and on both sides of the border, directly affect the human rights situation. And the context continuously shifts over time as issues evolve, but also as media, policy, political, NGO, and academic agendas change. For these reasons, in this volume we have brought together leading scholars, government officials, and human rights activists from both the United States and Mexico.[3]

The U.S.-Mexico relationship is often studied, especially its historical, economic, and political aspects, or lately with a focus on criminal justice issues (war on drugs, etc.) or environmental issues (Grayson 2010; López-Hoffman et al. 2009). The binational relationship surrounding human rights, however, has been relatively neglected. This is striking when we consider how strongly U.S. and Mexican government policies have a direct effect on the human rights situation in the other country. Human rights activists from both sides of the border are acutely aware of this and have adapted to address these problems binationally, often partnering with organizations across the border. And yet, policymakers in both countries, but especially the United States, often dictate human rights conditions in the other country with little forethought about the human rights consequences in the other. Consul Escobar Valdez writes the following in his chapter (this volume) on immigration, but his words apply equally to other human rights issues: "In the case of Mexico and the United States, two nations that share one of the longest borders in the world, I find it incongruous that we are partners in economic matters and antagonists when it comes to the immigration issue." He goes on: "Also I would like to point out that the Mexican immigration is by all means a binational affair, in terms of causes and consequences, because it implies nationals of one country that has a labor supply, moving to some other country with a labor demand. Nevertheless, decisions are being taken unilaterally and this unilateral handling of the immigration issue occurs always in response to the U.S. interests."

Mexico as a Human Rights Outlier

Many human rights workers around the globe are likely, at least at first, envious of Mexico's objective conditions for human rights. Mexico ranks highly on many of the variables that scholars have shown are significant for creating a positive human rights record. Mexico has made significant strides in democratization with the end of one-party rule in 2000 and significant judicial reforms,[4] and is developing economically (with the highest income per capita in Latin America, an economy ranking 13th in size in the world, and a growing middle class). Its people, in general, possess good health with a life expectancy of 75.1 years and high education and literacy levels.[5] Mexico is deeply enmeshed in the global economy with strong connections to its neighbors through social, cultural, and economic exchanges. Mexico has an increasingly well-developed civil society with dozens of international human rights NGOs having a significant presence in the country, as well as hundreds of domestic human rights organizations. Since the 1990s, Mexico has become increasingly involved with regional and international human rights bodies. Mexico acceded to the jurisdiction of the Inter-American Court of Human Rights in 1998 and has been party to several significant decisions. The country has ratified every major international and regional human rights treaty. Mexico also has a structurally autonomous national human rights commission (Comisión Nacional de los Derechos Humanos, CNDH) that conducts numerous investigations and issues several important authoritative reports each year. In addition, each state of Mexico has its own human rights commission, which operates with more or less effectiveness. Finally, the human rights abuses in Mexico are well documented and well known nationally and globally. Major films, books, music, and theater productions have been used to raise global awareness of the human rights issues in Mexico. As a consequence numerous transnational actors closely monitor the human rights situation.

Despite these advantages, the human rights situation in Mexico is worsening. In addition to the examples cited above, the country rates poorly on a number of critical human rights indices. It ranks 18th in Latin America and 96th in the world on Transparency International's corruption index. Its gender gap score ranks 91st of 134 countries, and it has one of the lowest scores among upper-middle-income countries, ranking particularly poorly on economic participation and opportunity for women. Mexico's score of 4 on the Political Terror Scale is very high, equal to that of such notorious human rights offenders as Zimbabwe, Eritrea, Algeria, Central African Republic, Iran, and Haiti. This rating means that "Civil and political rights violations have expanded to large numbers of the population. Murders, disappearances, and torture are a common part of life. In spite of its generality, on this level terror affects those who interest themselves in politics or ideas" (Gibney, Cornett, and Wood 2011).

So, with mostly good objective conditions, why is Mexico suffering from such massive human rights abuses? Mueller, in this volume, examines the confluence of forces in time and space that have led to the human rights abuses of women in the sprawling border city of Ciudad Juárez. Many of those same factors can be applied to the country as a whole. This "perfect storm" has offset Mexico's relatively advantageous human rights context. The storm includes numerous structural factors, such as vast income inequality between the rich and poor, and between the richer northern and central regions and the struggling southern states. The country continues to democratize, but its democracy is built on a traditional authoritarian political culture that historically fuels widespread corruption and failure to provide social services. Mexico's culture is heavily misogynist, with high rates of domestic violence and entrenched traditional roles for women (Staudt 2008). This perfect storm of income inequality, little chance for upward mobility for large sectors of the population, corruption, patriarchy, vast displacements of peoples, and relatively large segments of society involved in illicit activities has led to widespread human rights abuses that have affected vulnerable populations disproportionately.

Structural Violence, States of Exception, Cauterization, and Vulnerability

Following recent social philosophers such as Giorgio Agamben (2005), several authors in this volume use the term "state of exception" to help explain the mechanisms by which this perfect storm leads to such widespread human rights abuses. A state of exception is usually marked by lawlessness, but it can also be caused by hyperlegality, especially when the law is applied selectively and arbitrarily. In either case, governmental or nongovernmental actors possess great discretionary power over vulnerable populations. In a state of exception, the law, with its guarantees to rights and freedoms for all citizens, is suspended in the name of a national emergency.[6] Conditions of hyperlegality, such as heavy militarization, also can lead to a state of exception, where institutions that usually provide oversight of governmental agents are lacking, leaving vulnerable populations with little recourse when rights are abused. When law is ever present, those acting in the name of the law are also given free rein. Endless examples from history, from slavery to apartheid and Abu Ghraib, attest to the fact that both the absence of law and its omnipresence often lead to massive human rights violations.

Lawless zones exist throughout Mexico and its neighboring regions. Migrants kidnapped by gangs of bandits and held at gunpoint in a drop house are at the mercy of their captors. Migrants caught by border patrol agents in the remote deserts depend in large part on the agents' professionalism to protect their few rights. Mexican towns that have been taken over by the cartels have little opportunity for formal complaint. Undocumented workers have little recourse when their wages are withheld by exploitative employers. The unprecedented movement of people, the steep growth in the power of organized criminal networks, and the inability or unwillingness of the Mexican and U.S. governments to gain control of the situation have led to states of exception where already marginalized peoples are made even more vulnerable and are subject to numerous human rights abuses.

Their plight is made worse by a generalized lack of concern for the victims. Simmons (2011) has coined the term "cauterization" to describe the comprehensive way that marginalized groups are exploited and their suffering ignored. The three stages of cauterization correspond to the term's three interrelated meanings (see *Oxford English Dictionary*). The first meaning comes from its roots in the Greek verb *kauteriazein*, "to burn with a *kauter* or a branding iron." Such branding historically marked a slave or criminal as beneath humanity, below those who deserve rights. In the U.S.-Mexican context, vulnerable people are branded as commodities by the cartels and gangs; while in Mexico, the prevailing ideology brands indigenous peoples and Central American migrants as inferior, and in the United States, unauthorized migrants are branded as "illegals" and therefore deserve little or no protection or social services from the government. Second, cauterization refers to a medical procedure in which burning is used to seal off or remove part of the body. This procedure is most often used to stop bleeding, but it can also seal a wound to stop the spread of infection. In the human rights context, those who are deemed inferior or rightless are sealed off from the polis or the courtroom—their voice treated, in effect, as an infection that must be stopped from spreading. The migrants and other victims have little or no voice in Mexican or U.S. policy debates, and those who advocate on their behalf are shouted down with simplistic slogans such as "What part of illegal don't you understand?" In both countries, the victims are ignored, and the rhetoric of war (on drugs, on terror, on illegals) has drowned out advocacy for them. Finally, in its most metaphorical meaning, cauterization refers to the deadening of feelings, making one callous to the suffering of another. Those with rights, the full members of the polis, deaden their feelings toward the suffering of those who are branded rightless.[7] As the death toll continues to rise, the public, especially in the United States, have taken the suffering of others in stride as if these victims were beneath them or deserved their fate. Although exposed regularly to the statistics of migrants dying in the desert, the kidnapping of large groups of migrants, the increasing death toll in the drug war in Mexico, and raids on drop houses down the street, the public is not spurred to action. How is such grand suffering cauterized by generally caring people who are mere miles away?

U.S. Immigration Policies and the Plight of Immigrants: An Example of Structural Violence, States of Exception, and Cauterization

The structural violence that creates these states of exception and the cauterization of suffering also affects government policies on both sides of the border. Policies that will aid the victims are rarely adopted or even seriously considered. Instead, policies prevail that view human rights abuses as collateral damage in the war on terror or the war on drugs. Policy proposals that further arm the Mexican government or further secure the U.S.-Mexican border are enormously popular, while programs that give legal empowerment to vulnerable groups are rarely considered.

Precious few policymakers seriously consider that their policies, supported by invisible ideologies such as nativism and racism, are fueling these human rights crises. As an example of how binational policies exacerbate the states of exception where marginalized peoples are made more vulnerable and then victimized on a grand scale, we will briefly consider the U.S.-Mexican borderlands. Failed U.S. immigration policies for nearly two decades have been marked by simultaneously sanctioning, at least unofficially, large-scale immigration for economic benefits and increasing border enforcement aimed at preventing immigration. As a result, tens of thousands of individuals migrating across the Arizona-Sonora border face a shadowy world of *coyotes*, unscrupulous smugglers, drop houses, a militarized Border Patrol, expedited removals, immigration sweeps, and temporary and not so temporary detention facilities. Years of policy inaction by the federal government has led states like Arizona to pass such controversial measures as SB 1070 in April 2010, which further criminalizes migrants and drives them even farther underground.

Immigrants paradoxically face both a state of exception where law is mostly absent and a place of militarization and hyperenforcement where law is everywhere present. When law is absent it gives free rein to those with power, be it the power of force, coercion, patriarchy, or money.

Those crossing the border are victimized by both state and private actors. The silencing of their voices by mainstream media or in policy debates and academic circles further victimizes them. The states of exception along the borderlands are not neutral. Yes, a state of exception could allow some officials and nongovernmental organizations (NGOs) discretion to seek to improve human rights. Nonetheless, the states of exception along the border are embedded in a pattern of structural violence, whereby vulnerable individuals, especially women, are exploited by state and nonstate actors, and their suffering goes basically unnoticed (see Guidotti-Hernandez 2011). This structural violence includes racism, misogyny, and the glorification of criminal activity. On a broader scale, the border crossers are already victims of a larger structural violence. They take these risks because of the immense poverty in Mexico and countries farther south. This poverty is a predictable outcome of natural disasters and neoliberal policies such as structural adjustment programs and NAFTA. To better their lives, everyday citizens take the hazardous step of leaving home knowing that they could be exploited on the journey. Few are completely oblivious to the risks, and yet they are drawn to the border with all of its possibilities and the lack of viable alternatives.

The conditions faced by migrants have worsened because of border enforcement and drug interdiction policies. As the U.S.-Mexican border was increasingly militarized, it became much more difficult to cross as hundreds of thousands of migrants had been doing for years with the aid of small-scale "mom and pop" organizations. As "push factors" continued to drive them north, organized crime networks saw yet another lucrative opportunity and took over the task of ferrying migrants past the high-tech surveillance equipment and thousands of armed officers. In addition to the traditional forces of Border Patrol and local law enforcement, we now have military personnel, the national guard, and private militias such as the Minutemen. As the border became more militarized, criminal organizations responded by becoming better armed and increasingly treated the migrants as another cargo or commodity—like drugs or guns—to be transported solely for profit. Indeed, the migrants are often used as "burros" to carry drugs or other contraband across the border.

Criminal networks not only transport the migrants but also exploit them in many ways, including robbery, assault, and sexual violence. Increasingly migrants are kidnapped by their smugglers or others and held for ransom until family members on either side of the border pay for their release. Drawing on the increasing pervasiveness of violence, a new group, called *bajadores* or bandits, has appeared near the border; groups of armed men who often ambush groups of migrants, basically stealing them from the *coyotes*. These ambushes often occur in the desert once the group has crossed or, increasingly, in the drop houses where migrants are kept in Phoenix or Tucson. Bajadores have determined that it is more lucrative and less risky to steal a group of migrants from a *coyote* than to lead the migrants across the border themselves. Since the *bajadores* rarely harm the *coyotes*, they might be allies who have found yet another method for exploiting the migrants.[8] The cartels are much less forgiving of the *coyotes* when migrants are not delivered intact to their destination.

The migrants, whether led by *coyotes* or by *bajadores*, are picked up in vans and trucks at the border and moved to safe houses in southern Arizona. Most migrants then make it the 150 miles or so to the Phoenix area where they are often kept in drop houses (Simmons, Menjívar, and Téllez, Forthcoming). It is not unusual for them to be kept in these houses, often foreclosed properties, against their will, until family members agree to pay additional monies for their release. They get taxed for housing and food, and smugglers continue to add on costs, so that it takes longer and longer to pay off the debt. The conditions in these drop houses are often brutal, with violence and terror used to keep order.

With increased militarization, and increasing cartel control of migrant traffic, many migrants experience constant vulnerability, where they are at the mercy of *coyotes*, gangs, cartels, and *bajadores*. They are often become disoriented along the journey, fearful of being left behind, split from family members or friends, and held against their will. They are often threatened with weapons, attacked by gangs and others, or exploited by other migrants. They experience, not one, but a series of states of exception where those with the guns or a monopoly on other forms of coercion are in control. Counterintuitively, where law is ever present, it is both present and absent. There are few checks on the power of law enforcement officials, especially in Mexico; and, if detained in the United States, migrants are confronted with such controversial practices as expedited removals, group hearings, and indefinite detention. If the migrants decide to apply for asylum in order to stay in the United States, they experience what is aptly termed "refugee roulette" (Ramji-Nogales et al. 2007), where their fate is determined by a bewildering bureaucracy overburdened by an immense case load. In both states of exception—lawlessness and hyperlawfulness—migrants are exceedingly vulnerable, and thus susceptible to every kind of victimization.

The perfect storm of structural violence, cauterization, and governmental policies that create states of exception has also hindered the human rights activists and humanitarian workers seeking to help the victims, and those advocating for policy change.

The Rise of Transnational Advocacy Networks and Democratization amid Economic Crises

While Mexican civil society organizations dealing with human rights have become quite robust and have developed close ties with transnational NGOs, it is important to understand that, somewhat paradoxically, the human rights culture and the human rights abuses arise from common factors. Understanding the common causes of these phenomena goes a long way toward understanding Mexico's current status as a human rights outlier. In this section we argue that transnational economic factors that had put pressure on the ruling party, the Partido de la Revolucionnario Institucional (PRI) and created an opening for human rights organizations and discourse, also led to the disintegration of the PRI hegemony, which left a political vacuum in many areas of the country that could be exploited by more ruthless elements, leading to increased human rights abuses.

Yes, the international community has increasingly responded to the expanding crisis of human rights abuses in Mexico (see Anaya Muñoz, this volume), but this is not merely because violations of human rights have become more serious (which they have), but because the ongoing transitions in Mexico have opened up opportunities for domestic human rights organizations. Threats to the authoritarian system that sustained the seventy-year dominance of the PRI led to increasing violence in Mexico following its "dirty war" against the Left of the 1960s and 1970s—even before the South American drug cartels began to move their operations overland through Mexico. Thus, it was only with the "success" of democratization that human rights abuses became serious enough to create a domestic human rights community that could attract attention from a growing network of transnational human rights activists. Nonetheless, the NGOs have not been able to keep pace with the human rights crises, and they often are only able to address the consequences of abuses, a sort of triage, while not being able to effectively address the structural causes of these abuses. To better illuminate this paradox of an increase in human rights abuses going hand in hand with increasing democratization and electoral competitiveness, we look to the severe economic crises that shook Mexico in the 1980s and 1990s.

Transnational Activism, Democratization, and Human Rights in Mexico

The period following World War II and the creation of the United Nations with its Universal Declaration of Human Rights (UDHR) saw the gradual emergence of an international civil society concerned, among other things, with human rights (Smith, Chatfield, and Pagnucco 1997; Boli and Thomas 1999). While Moyn (2010) points to the discontinuities in the creation of a transnational human rights community, NGOs increasingly developed linkages and campaigns across national boundaries. By the 1970s, when human rights began to flourish with the strengthening of NGOs like Amnesty International and the surprising support of state actors for the Helsinki Accords, these linkages would be identified as "transnational advocacy networks or TAN(S)" (Keck and Sikkink 1998; J. Smith 2004).

Human rights abuses by authoritarian dictatorships in Latin America were a major focus of the emerging networks with Amnesty International winning the 1977 Nobel Peace Prize for exposing the widespread disappearances perpetrated by the Argentine junta during its "dirty war" (Bouvard 1994). Faced with such dramatic atrocities further south (and even serving as a refuge for political exiles from Chile, Argentina, and Central America) Mexico, with its formal democracy, hardly seemed to warrant serious attention from the growing human rights network (Lutz 1993; Sikkink 1993). Thus, despite long years of one-party rule supported by a nationwide system of clientelism, stifled media, and widespread corruption, Mexico's human rights record escaped the network's scrutiny for decades (Fox and Hernández 1992; Moralaes-Moreno 2004).

This began to change in the 1980s. Keck and Sikkink (1998), two of the foremost scholars on transnational advocacy networks, argue that increased attention to Mexican human rights abuses resulted from an increased human rights consciousness within Mexico and the growth of domestic NGOs concerned with human rights, such as the Mexican Academy for Human Rights, formed in 1984. Internationally, they contend, as democratization swept the region, TANs could turn their attention to more ambiguous human rights situations, such as that in Mexico.

While they point to several important factors, Keck and Sikkink neglect the increasingly precarious situation of the Mexican economy, which brought into question the competence of the PRI and contributed to undermining its control of the Mexican political system (Morales-Moreno 2004). Other observers of the rocky path to increasing Mexican democratization place more emphasis on the economic crises that weakened Mexico's ruling party, the PRI (see, for instance, Lutz 1993; Binford 1999).

As a result of unfavorable trade imbalances throughout the post-World War II period, Mexico repeatedly borrowed money from the International Monetary Fund (IMF) and the World Bank. Growing indebtedness led to a debt crisis in 1982 that opened the PRI to international pressures from creditors, to domestic party opposition, and, increasingly, to the current human rights abuses. Mexico was compelled to accept the structural adjustment programs or neoliberal economic policies of the IMF: that is, to reduce state subsidies, privatize government enterprises, and open its markets to foreign direct investments. Thus, the debt trap and resulting IMF policies reduced the PRI's ability to support the wide array of subsidies that, coupled with the selective use of violence, had supported its successful clientelism for over half a century. These economic changes eroded the position of the once hegemonic PRI and contributed to growing political opposition at both the federal and municipal levels, increased the leverage of the Federal Congress, supported the increased independence of the media, and fostered the creation of an autonomous electoral monitoring body (Morales-Moreno 2004: 111).

With the PRI unable to fulfill obligations to its multiple clients, a disgruntled splinter group developed that supported Cuauhtémoc Cárdenas, who ran a close campaign against PRI candidate Carlos Salinas de Gortari in the presidential election of 1988 (Lutz 1993). Two of Cárdenas's top advisors were killed on the eve of the election, and more violence followed when

Cárdenas and his supporters brought accusations of electoral fraud. The Cárdenas group created the Partido de la Revolución Democrática (PRD), drawing off the most economically marginalized former supporters of the PRI. With the loss of PRI hegemony and the disruption in the PRI's traditional patronage and client networks came a rise in rural homicides over the 1990s (Villareal 2002). More than one hundred deaths of PRD party activists were recorded between 1988 and 1994 (Eisenstadt 2004), and by 2004 this number had risen to 660 (Morales-Moreno 2004, 264). These murders were disproportionately located in states where there was strong competition between the PRI and the emerging PRD (Schatz 2008: 265).

The Rise of Human Rights Advocacy After the 1988 Election

The increased violence in the aftermath of the close election in 1988 was ironically matched by growing attention to human rights issues by the PRI government. Facing widespread accusations of violence and human rights abuses associated with the 1988 election, a highly critical report by Americas Watch, as well as an impending visit by U.S. President George Bush to begin negotiating a North American free trade agreement, in 1990 President Salinas announced the formation of a National Human Rights Commission (CNDH). This marked the beginning of an explicit human rights policy on the part of the federal government. The longtime opposition party, the Partido Acción Nacional (PAN), was emboldened to start running candidates in state and local elections and brought three separate charges of election fraud against the PRI at the Inter-American Commission on Human Rights (IACHR) of the Organization of American States. These cases were decided in favor of the PAN, and, for the first time, the PRI had to deal with what it regarded as a loss of sovereignty in the realm of human rights (Morales-Moreno 2004).

The creation of the CNDH was followed by a series of reforms that "gradually transformed Mexico's electoral laws and institutions" facilitating the development of a multiparty system (Anaya Muñoz 2009: 36). For instance, in 1991, the Mexican Academy of Human Rights and the Potosino Center for Human Rights mobilized three hundred people to observe the gubernatorial elections in San Luis Potosi (Aguayo Quezada 1995). At the same time, the Arturo Rosenblueth Foundation and the Council for Democracy deployed several hundred volunteers in the Federal District to monitor the Mexico City election. These efforts culminated in the creation of the Civic Alliance by 1994, a coalition of hundreds of NGOs, labor unions, and social movements concerned with transforming the electoral process. Thus, it would appear that increased economic vulnerability led to growing electoral competitiveness and accusations of election fraud followed by an increasing number of concessions from PRI political leaders on human rights.

While the end of the 1980s may have marked the beginning of a human rights regime in Mexico, Anaya Muñoz (2009c) argues that it was under Ernesto Zedillo (1994–2000) and Vicente Fox (2000–2006) that the government's approach to human rights shifted significantly. This "involved Mexico's opening to international monitoring and assistance, the ratification of important international instruments, the promotion of constitutional and legal reforms, changes in government institutions, and the elaboration of a National Human Rights Program" (37).

Increased participation from civil society, which followed from increased violence and the electoral crises of the late 1980s, which were fueled by earlier economic crises, also led to the increased attention to Mexican affairs on the part of transnational human rights advocacy networks. This attention is shown by high-profile reports by Americas Watch in 1984 and 1990 and Amnesty International in 1986. In addition to international NGOs, both the U.S. Congress and the IACHR held hearings or considered cases of Mexican human rights abuses by 1990. By 1992, the UN Committee against Torture condemned the gap between Mexico's progressive laws and the abusive practices of its law enforcement apparatus (Lutz 1993). These responses stood in sharp contrast to the silence that greeted the 1968 killings and disappearances of hundreds of students following their peaceful demonstrations in Mexico City (Keck and Sikkink 1998: 110). One estimate indicates that in the period from 1988 to 1993, the number of active NGOs had grown from 4 to over 200 (Lutz 1993).

In addition to increased interest in the election process on the part of groups like the Civic Alliance, the Chiapas insurgency of 1994 dramatized the severity of Mexico's human rights situation. With a particularly savvy leadership taking advantage of traditional as well as new media (Froehling 1997), the grievances of indigenous peoples at the margins of society were broadcast to the world on January 1, along with the bloody response of the Mexican government. The crisis in Chiapas was not only a humanitarian catastrophe, but also a public relations disaster for the Mexican government, and it "shook the political system to its roots" (Aguayo Quezado 1995: 161).

Not by accident, the uprising coincided with the launch of the neoliberal policies of NAFTA.

In response to internal and external pressures as well as to the popular insurgency in Chiapas, the Zedillo administration reluctantly instituted a major human rights offensive. In the next few years, the government invited the IACHR to send a special *in loco* mission to Mexico (1996), as well as the UN special rapporteur on torture (1997), secretary general of the UN (1998), and UN special rapporteur on extrajudicial, summary or arbitrary executions, and the high commissioner on human rights (1999) (Anaya Muñoz 2009c). President Zedillo also recognized the jurisdiction of the Inter-American Court of Human Rights (1998) and signed a "memorandum of intent" with the Office of the UN High Commissioner on Human Rights (UNHCHR 1999). Finally, both the constitution and supporting legislation were reformed to give the CNDH greater autonomy.

Vicente Fox, the first president elected by a party other than the PRI in seventy years, dramatically strengthened the human rights commitments of his new administration. Domestically, a Unit for the Promotion and Protection of Human Rights was created in the Ministry of the Interior in 2001; the next year, the Ministry of the Interior was authorized to lead a Commission on Governmental Policy on Human Rights Issues (Anaya Muñoz 2009c). Within this Commission, the government articulated a National Human Rights Program in 2004 to promote human rights values throughout the federal bureaucracy and appointed both a Commission (2003) and a Special Prosecutor's Office (2005) to investigate the killings of women in Ciudad Juárez. In 2002, Fox commissioned the CNDH to investigate human rights abuses committed during the "dirty wars" of the 1960s and 1970s. Their 3,000-page report named at least seventy-four officials from thirty-seven government agencies who "were involved in a campaign of disappearances, torture, and executions of leftists in the 1970s and 1980s" (2). Fox publicly supported the report's findings, although few prosecutions followed. The government was also unsuccessful in getting an ambitious legislative agenda for human rights through the Congress, in which the PAN failed to achieve a majority.

Internationally, from 2001 until 2003, fourteen special human rights agencies of the UN and the OAS visited Mexico (Anaya Muñoz 2009c). In 2002–5, Mexico ratified two UN Conventions and three Optional Protocols and was very active in the UNHCHR. Zedillo's restrictions on visas for foreign human rights observers were also lifted. A permanent office for the

UNHCHR was established in Mexico, and, in 2003, it published a diagnosis of the human rights situation in the country with cooperation from Fox's administration. The president publicly supported its recommendations, although very few substantive changes were enacted.

The Juárez Feminicides and the Limits of Transnational Activism

While Anaya Muñoz places the peak of general transnational advocacy for Mexican human rights in 1998, on more specific human rights issues, like the feminicides in Ciudad Juárez, the peak of attention occurred later. For almost two decades, Ciudad Juárez has been the scene of one of the worst feminicides in the history of the Americas, and the limited results of sustained pressure on the government to address these abuses mirror the limits of human rights advocacy throughout the country.

Early efforts by family members and human rights activists protesting the indifference and hostility of local law enforcement eventually caught the attention of a transnational advocacy network of human rights activists within international governmental and nongovernmental organizations (Aikin Araluce 2009). These networks had already been alerted to serious abuses in Mexico from the time of the 1988 election fraud and the Chiapas uprising. With the help of the network, marches, demonstrations, and protests spread across the border, and delegations from international governmental and nongovernmental organizations paid visits to both Juárez and Mexico City. Their reports served to bring international attention to the issue, which culminated in a celebrity-studded march from El Paso, Texas, into Ciudad Juárez on Valentine's Day, 2004. The march included thousands of families, activists, movie stars, and college students from both sides of the border and garnered the most media coverage of any protest event on this issue.

International attention subsided after the march (Staudt 2008), and yet the murders continued. Nonetheless, while the attention of activist networks may rise and fall, this does not mean that nothing is accomplished. It is clear that the efforts of the TAN initiated a process of socialization to international norms regarding violence against women by the Mexican government, particularly the Federal Attorney General's Office (PGR) (see Aikin Araluce 2009). Although Mexico had signed the Convention on the Elimination of

All Forms of Discrimination Against Women in 1981 and the 1988 Inter-American Convention on the Prevention, Punishment, and Eradication of Violence Against Women it did not apply these "criteria, language or standards" (151) to the problem in Ciudad Juárez. Instead, both local and federal authorities continued to characterize the problem in official terms of "crimes of passion" or "girls gone bad."

However, Aikin Araluce notes the gradual abandonment of a policy denying governmental responsibility.[9] Over the period of growing TAN activity, the PGR acknowledged that the Juárez murders were not just a local problem; it created the Joint Investigative Agency for the Homicide of Women in Ciudad Juárez; in 2004, it created a Special Prosecutor's Office to address the murders; and, gradually, the PGR accepted the language of "femicide" and "violence against women" to characterize the murders and accepted the premise that violence against women is based on gender discrimination. In addition, the Fox administration proposed a constitutional amendment that would have given the federal government greater leverage in local human rights issues such as that in Ciudad Juárez; and, in 2007, the Mexican Federal Congress passed the Law on Women's Access to a Life Free of Violence. While this activity at the federal level did not stop the impunity in law enforcement on the border, nor did it slow down the feminicides, it did represent a long and sustained period of adapting the framing of the issue of violence against women that was initially foreign to it.

Urgent Needs Resist Comprehensive Solutions

After thirty years of active engagement by networks of transnational activists dedicated to human rights norms, many observers optimistically held that increasing electoral competitiveness in the Mexican political system with at least a tacit embrace of international human rights norms meant that Mexico was well on its way to thorough democratization and a positive human rights record. The accounts in this volume suggest that there is still a long way to go, for the habits of a pervasive authoritarian system die hard. Long years of local autonomy in which the PRI ruled through payoffs to patronage networks, particularly in rural areas, have left behind remnants of local strongmen or *caciques* whose allegiance has shifted from the PRI to a new generation of more lethal drug cartels. With the militarization of the drug war by the second PAN president, Felipe de Jesús Calderón Hinojosa, in 2006, violence reached unprecedented levels as states of exception proliferated throughout Mexico. These included zones of lawlessness where intercartel rivalries and cartel-government battles erupted, and zones of lawfulness where either the cartels or the military assumed complete control, leaving vulnerable citizens without recourse to legal remedies.

In addition, the consequences of neoliberal policies throughout Mexico and Central America have unleashed wave after wave of migrants who seek, in vain, to elude these predators. Since their final destination is frequently the United States, attempts to describe their plight in terms of human rights abuses fall prey to the vitriol of anti-immigrant rhetoric there. This obstacle has proven too great for transnational advocates, who face not the vulnerability of an increasingly dependent Mexican state, but more formidable political adversaries in the United States. It now appears that the growing influence of an increasingly mobilized Hispanic voting bloc in presidential elections may succeed where human rights approaches have failed. Additionally, several chapters in this volume hint at a new form of grassroots activism largely independent from traditional transnational actors that seeks to address, or at least cope with, the massive human rights abuses. The concluding chapter will analyze the prospects of such organizations.

Overview of the Book

The contributors to this volume work in several fields both within and outside academia and analyze human rights issues with a variety of methodologies, including ethnography, qualitative interviews, personal reflections, and participant observation. Each chapter builds on the central argument that the binational context, especially but not solely U.S. policies, has created states of exception that exacerbate existing structural violence to render vulnerable individuals more susceptible to human rights abuses. Furthermore, organized crime syndicates, acting rationally in response to governmental policies such as the militarization of the U.S.-Mexico border and President Calderón's drug war, have further commodified migrants, women, and other vulnerable populations, worsening the human rights crises. These chapters lay bare the mechanisms that have led so many to be treated as worthless bare life, in the terms of philosopher Giorgio Agamben. Throughout, the reader is introduced to a number of little-known stories of human rights victims, and human rights heroes who are responding to these crises despite enormous obstacles.

Part I focuses on the plight of migrants from Central America and Mexico to the United States, showing how failed immigration policies and other factors have led to a range of human rights abuses. All three chapters document the human costs of sharply increased immigration enforcement along the U.S.-Mexico border. Consul Escobar-Valdez, drawing on years of working at Mexican consulates in the borderlands and extensive study of these issues, provides a critique of U.S. unilateral immigration policies as well as his personal reflections on the hundreds of migrants who have died in the Arizona desert. He ends with poignant anecdotes of the suffering of female migrants who have died in the blazing desert and their children who are left behind. The chapter by Simmons and Téllez reports on one of the most extensive studies yet conducted on sexual violence against migrant women and children. It documents the high prevalence of sexual victimization and concludes that sexual violence is not an event for these women and children, but more of a condition. Simmons and Téllez place these abuses in the context of the recent psychological literature that shows how difficult it is to address trauma stemming from multiple forms of victimization. To make matters worse, the same structural factors that make migrants especially vulnerable also further hinder efforts to address their suffering. Dunn's chapter steps back and analyzes these human rights tragedies from the perspective of a "clash" between two competing rights frameworks: national sovereignty/citizenship and human rights. He argues that while economic and cultural globalization has led to a denationalization process, as predicted by several prominent sociologists, where the nation-state has shrunk in importance, in the areas of national sovereignty, especially citizenship policies, there has been a renationalization process. As a result, the migrant victims are often seen only as an unfortunate and justifiable tragedy in the name of upholding national sovereignty. While there have also been a number of important episodes of resistance by local groups and governmental bodies against anti-immigrant measures and heightened border enforcement, suggestive of some movement toward human rights and "denationalized citizenship," this process is "asymmetrical" in favor of policies favoring renationalization and national sovereignty. Dunn ends with a rethinking of national sovereignty from a human rights perspective "as a means to promote the well-being of the people residing in a nation."

Part II shows that analyses of the states of exceptions the migrants face cannot be divorced from the rise of the drug war. Indeed, similar dynamics frame both of these issues. Just as increased border enforcement has strengthened organized crime groups and created more states of exceptions, so has President Calderón's cartel war in Mexico. Also, both of these policies are embedded in, and exacerbate, preexisting forms of structural violence.

Murphy Erfani's chapter provocatively concludes that the "war on drugs" is a series of "drug war crimes" perpetrated by drug gangs aided and abetted by the U.S. and Mexican governments, as well as transnational corporations. The governments and the U.S. private sector, acting within frameworks of states of exception, have contributed to the military clout of drug warlords, especially the Sinaloa cartel, by directly and indirectly arming and assisting them. Calderón's drug war has served to move public and media attention from what was a burgeoning popular insurgency against his administration to a "criminal insurgency" fought against the cartels. Thus, effectively, Calderón governed through a state of emergency, which gave his government almost limitless power in a variety of contexts while allowing it to maintain a veneer of democratic governance. In other words, the state has effectively employed the drug war to shore up its own shaky legitimacy. Murphy Erfani employs the "theoretical lens of necropolitics that holds that the right to kill is the ultimate form of sovereignty," and claims that "the number of actors who have the right to kill has expanded exponentially, and therefore numerous groups, both governmental and nongovernmental, can claim sovereignty."

Arriola Vega's contribution shows how U.S. security policies are "externalized" all the way to Guatemala and beyond. The Mexico-Guatemala border, which has long been the site of mostly benign illicit trade is now a major corridor (*plaza*) for smuggling guns, drugs, and migrants. The region has become contested turf among cartels, including the Zetas, and the violence, especially against migrants, has increased exponentially.

Taken together, the two chapters of Part III offer a case study of the violence against women in Ciudad Juárez, especially the structural violence that fuels the feminicides and hinders local groups seeking to address the situation. Mueller lay out the intersection of factors that led first to the feminicides, and then to Juárez becoming a major battlefield in the cartel wars. A sprawling border town, Juárez expanded rapidly as mostly young women came from the Mexican countryside to work in the maquiladoras. The rise in maquiladoras, Mueller cogently argues, is a response to the neoliberal policies imposed on Mexico by the United States and the IMF in response to the Mexico debt crisis and the devaluation of the Mexican peso. Also, the success of massive efforts to interdict the drug supply from Colombia through the Caribbean led the cartels to an overland route through Mexico, especially the Juárez-El Paso corridor, which became the largest transfer point of drugs into the United States. This rise of narco-trafficking overwhelmed the anemic and often corrupt local law enforcement efforts. Of course, this rise would not be possible without the rampant use of illegal drugs in the United States and the ready availability of U.S. weapons smuggled into Mexico.

Jusidman, from her participant observation with civil society organizations in Juárez, shows how they developed organically as activists mobilized to address the needs of the huge influx of migrants from other parts of Mexico. In response to the feminicides in the 1990s, these groups formed coalitions that were successful in raising attention locally, nationally, and globally. Jusidman argues, though, that the efforts of the civil society organizations were stymied by the calculated decisions made by wealthy business owners, influential members of the Catholic Church, politicians, and other elites. She sadly concludes "that not even such commitment and love for the city, nor the effort, intelligence, and service of civic activists, has been able to counter the greed, evil, lack of humanity, and violence in the city."

The chapters in Part IV analyze the effects of transnational advocacy networks (TANs) on change in human rights in Mexico. Staudt, who has long been at the forefront of the study of the Juárez feminicides, examines how various transnational actors have responded and how successful their efforts have been. At the same time, her analysis provides an evaluation of prevailing theories of transnational activism. While the TANs have successfully shamed the Mexican government and brought much attention to the feminicides, real change has proven elusive. Staudt argues that traditional theories of TANs need to place more emphasis on regional contexts and political structures. The Juárez feminicides are shaped in large part by macrolevel binational policies, especially drug policies, which have proved resistant to change. Furthermore, the decentralized and nascent political structures in Mexico are difficult to navigate, and many governments at the subnational level are so corrupt that they have failed. Further, the Mexican government has been quite resistant to legalized gender equality. While it has embraced the rhetoric of democracy and human rights, its functioning still "privilege(s) men and wealthy classes and render(s) the economically marginalized majority of women irrelevant to policy priorities." The very institutions that dominate the Juárez landscape and would be necessary for any resolution to the feminicides—the military and law enforcement—have been most resistant to adopting such a perspective.

Anaya Muñoz compares the role of TANs across three examples of human rights abuses in Mexico: the feminicides, the drug war, and the civil disturbances and subsequent government crackdown in Oaxaca starting in 2006. He shows how Mexico, despite its democratization, has continued to attract the attention of numerous international organizations, such as the NGOs Amnesty International and Human Rights Watch, intergovernmental actors like the UN and the OAS, and nations such as the United States and those in Europe. These actors have undertaken formal fact-finding missions to Mexico, issued authoritative reports, and put other pressures on the Mexican government. He shows that the feminicides have attracted the most attention because of the amount of evidence that was available, they involved systematic bodily harm to vulnerable individuals, and violated clear human rights norms. While the development of TANs has not ended the feminicides and other human rights abuses, Anaya Muñoz points to some very concrete changes, including the strengthening of local NGOS, the reform of the Mexican judiciary, the adoption of numerous laws aimed at protecting human rights, and the development of a human rights discourse in the country.

Since the drug war intersects with the other major human rights violations discussed in this book and since each of the analyses points to a major U.S. role in the human rights abuses, it is fitting that the last full chapter explores the use of U.S. pressure in its funding for the drug war. Meyer begins by discussing the important reforms undertaken by the Calderón administration, and often neglected by scholars, including changes in law enforcement policies and constitutional reforms. However, she argues that the drug war has dominated Mexican policy, and that this war is being funded in large part by the United States through the Mérida Initiative, which has provided military hardware including helicopters but also funds softer initiatives such as judicial reform and anticorruption activities. Since portions of the funds are conditional on Mexico's human rights record, several NGOs have seen the Mérida Initiative as an opening to put political pressure on Mexico indirectly through lobbying the U.S. government. They have prepared reports and lobbied members of the U.S. Congress to withhold these funds until Mexico's human rights record is improved. These efforts have put some pressure on Mexico and brought added attention to the abuses through the media and the U.S. Congress, but the funds in general have not been withheld.

Simmons examines the prospects for substantive change in the volume's concluding chapter. While he shares much of the pessimism of the other contributors, Simmons also agrees with Meyer and Anaya Muñoz that some structural and rhetorical changes are taking place, and these will be integral to any reversal of human rights abuses. Furthermore, the new grassroots movements outlined in several of this volume's chapters point to a new force that could exert pressure in new forms and could possibly make headway in the face of seemingly intractable obstacles. Nonetheless, in the short term, binational policies and structural violence appear likely to overwhelm human rights norms and actors. But the foundation is being laid for when the "perfect storm" subsides. When and how that will happen remains to be determined.

PART I

Migration to the United States
in Binational Context

CHAPTER 1

Reflections on Immigration, Binational Policies, and Human Rights Tragedies

Miguel Escobar-Valdez

The fundamental premise of migration is economic. And the variables of the immigration equation between Mexico and the United States are an affluent and industrialized economy on one side and an undeveloped nation with a considerable labor supply on the other side, leading to a salary asymmetry that fuels migration.

Migration is a fact of life in our modern societies and a characteristic of the globalization that permeates all aspects of life, with over 200 million human beings migrating all over the world (IOM 2010). The interaction of market forces with communications and technology promotes migratory flows from south to north and from east to west, reversing the courses followed by other migrants and conquerors five hundred year ago when Europeans traveled southward to Africa and America and eastward toward the Orient, in order to subjugate other cultures. I would call this reversal of directions a sort of poetic justice. The truth is that we cannot think in terms of global integration with global communication without global migration. Poverty, the lack of development, natural disasters, political instability, inequity in the distribution of wealth, and the very understandable human yearning for a better life—all these factors are closely interconnected with migration.

When it comes to Mexican migration to the United States, some specific elements add to the complexity of the phenomenon, including a long tradition of migrating from south to north and extensive social and family networks. In the case of Mexico and the United States, two nations that share one of the longest borders in the world, I find it incongruous that we are partners in economic matters and antagonists when it comes to the immigration issue. And this creates tensions because on the one hand we have an expanded and unimpeded flow of capital, goods, and services, and on the other hand labor flows encounter all kinds of legal restrictions as nations try to shape and impose new forms of state sovereignty. It is lamentable that immigration agendas are subordinated to issues of terrorism and drug dealing. It is also worrisome that national security agendas trump socioeconomic and political considerations. We need to break out of the enforcement box. Such priorities promote serious violations of the fundamental rights of migrants—the loss of life of undocumented crossers being the most tragic—and provoke various manifestations of radicalism, intolerance, and xenophobia. In this chapter I trace the failure of current immigration policies and attempts at reforming the immigration system in the United States, and conclude by bearing witness to the human side of this failure.

The *Mexican* Migration

An Anglo-American speaking of "the border" almost always refers to the one shared with Mexico, rarely the one with Canada. For U.S. citizens the divisive border is to the south, with Mexicans, who have a different culture and a different way of life. U.S. citizens may identify with Canadians but they differentiate themselves from Mexicans. For an Anglo, to say "Mexican border" would be pure redundancy.

In a similar way, Mexicans, when they talk about migration, always mean migration north, to the United States, the most important destination nation, actually almost the only one for Mexican nationals. According to a report of the Pew Hispanic Center (Passel, Cohn, and Gonzales-Barrera 2012), "the U.S. today has more immigrants from Mexico alone—12.0 million—than any other country in the world has from all countries of the world." During the first decade of the new millennium, half a million Mexicans on average migrated every year to the United States. That is why, from my perspective, immigration remains one of the main issues in the always complex bilateral relation between Mexico and the United States. And that is why Mexico has, besides its embassy in Washington, D.C., a total of fifty-one consulates in the United States, the greatest concentration of consular offices of any nation in the United States

It is pertinent to add that this trend, according to the Pew Hispanic Center report, has seemingly come to a standstill as, indeed, "the net migration flow from Mexico to the United States has stopped" due to a combination of many factors, including a weakened job market, particularly in the construction industry, severe border enforcement, increased deportations by U.S. authorities, greater risks associated with border crossing, a declining birth rate in Mexico and Mexico's recent economic improvement.

Having said that and being realistic, we should recognize that Mexican migration north will not disappear in the next few years, not with the prevailing growth rates in Mexico, not until the nation arrives at that magic annual increase in GDP of 6 or 7 percent, not while asymmetries in salaries persist. So, notwithstanding the current standstill in immigration, I would predict the continuation of *el flujo de migrantes*, "the flow of migrants," in the near future, as the U.S. economy recovers.

Also, I would like to reiterate that Mexican immigration is absolutely a binational affair, in terms of causes and consequences, because it involves nationals of one country with a labor supply moving to another country with a labor demand. Nevertheless, decisions are being taken unilaterally and this unilateral handling of the immigration issue almost always occurs in response to U.S. interests. Two effects of this unilateral approach to immigration stand out: first, the social perception that immigrants are undesirable individuals, almost "criminals"; and second, that the "problem" of undocumented immigrants, being a "domestic" one, should be addressed by means of unilateral policies, because of its negative effects for the United States. Reality, however, points out that a bilateral approach is needed to address a phenomenon that, by definition, is bilateral.

The Effects of Increased Border Enforcement

A debate has been raging in the last few years about the effectiveness of heightened enforcement against unauthorized immigration to the United States. For instance, those who propose that it is better to establish enforcement at the border and to talk later about possible immigration reform often cite Yuma as an example, claiming that the U.S. Border Patrol Yuma Sector is the ideal model to be followed for the rest of the 2,000-mile border. It is boasted that in this sector there is "operational control," defined by the Border Patrol as "the ability to detect, respond and interdict border penetrations in areas deemed as high priority for threat potential or other national security objectives," and that in this sector, the illegal apprehensions have diminished significantly (Rosenblum 2012). Mark Krikorian (2005), director of the Center for Immigration Studies, an anti-immigrant think tank, points to the decrease in the number of unauthorized crossers detained by the Border Patrol, as proof of the success of the enforcement policies. In addition, he claims that the sum of a number of heavy-handed measures against irregular migrants forces a sort of "self-deportation" and that the policy of "attrition through enforcement" is actually the solution to illegal immigration.[1]

I would argue that a crucial issue to consider in any judgment of the effectiveness of border enforcement is the human cost. The strict enforcement along the border—the overflowing cornucopia of human and material resources—clearly had "unintended consequences," as stated by Doris Meissner, commissioner of the (now extinct) INS, at a press conference in Phoenix. Lost in these claims of effectiveness are what Meissner's identifies as "unintended consequences": the appalling rise in the number of deaths (see Eschbach, Hagan, and Rodriguez 2001) *en circunstancias de cruce*, "in crossing circumstances"—the phrase used by Mexican consulates when they report these deaths.

To be fair, both arguments have some merit. Even if the flows of migrants to the United States have been dwindling in the last few years, as reported by the Pew Hispanic Center, I do not believe immigration from the south—from Mexico and Central America—will stop in the short term. Wayne Cornelius, director of the Center of Expertise on Migration and Health at the University of California-San Diego, rejects the idea of increased return, saying that migrants that have made it to the United States and found employment are hanging in there and riding it out.

The bottom line is that enforcement along the border has had quite evident effects in some areas. Numbers of apprehensions are down for the time being. Having lived and worked along the border in Arizona and California for fifteen years, I can say that the combination of walls of different types, advanced technology, more Border Patrol agents, raids at work sites, mass deportations, and various U.S. policies such as Operation Streamline, Lateral Repatriation, Quick Court, and Mexican Interior Repatriation, are making things very tough for people who are just trying to find their place in the sun, people looking for jobs. Is the recent decrease in border crossings a consequence of the increased enforcement along the border? Not totally. The lower apprehension numbers have to do with a combination of factors, enforcement being, of course, just one of them. The most important factor, in my opinion, is the persistent financial crisis, which has taken a heavy toll on the entire population, but especially on immigrants who suffer from severe unemployment. It is important to remember the immigration equation: Low GDP + High Unemployment = Migration.

Another factor to be considered and another "unintended consequence" of border enforcement strategies has been the increased number of irregular immigrants settling in the United States. With so many "Migra" (Border Patrol personnel) and the risk of apprehension and even death, migrants often refrain from returning to the old country to visit their families. Facing the myriad ordeals of another border crossing they just decide to stay put in the United States. And thus, the traditional "circularity of the flow," *la circularidad del flujo*, has disappeared. As Jiménez and López-Sanders (2011) argue, all the state-of-the-art technologies, the increase in Border Patrol agents, the wall, and other enforcement methods "keep migrants in, not out."[2]

Has the economic crisis that pummeled the United States and most of the rest of the world provoked a mass exodus of the millions of undocumented Mexican migrants living in the United States? So far we have not seen that predicted avalanche. Migrants will just pinch pennies, hope for better times, and make use of social and family networks, so strong among Mexicans, to help weather the storm. That said, a minority of immigrants are returning to Mexico in a form of self-deportation. These are the immigrants who are getting fed up with living in the shadows as nonexistent human beings, who are tired of being harassed. They reason that as long as they are going to be facing economic hard times, they might as well ride out those hard times in Mexico.

Immigration Reform

The issue of immigration in the United States is of course extremely divisive. The only point on which both factions, pro- and anti-immigration, agree is in the failure of current immigration policies. "The system is out of control" is the oversimplified and stereotyped characterization. The bipartisan initiative regarding *una reforma migratoria integral*, "a comprehensive immigration reform," as it was being called, was rejected by the U.S. Senate in June 2007. And in 2013 a reform bill passed by the Senate was rejected by the U.S. House of Representatives, controlled by a minority of radical conservatives. The last initiative's failure closed the doors to the regularization of millions of human beings living in the United States in conditions of near apartheid, stigmatized by the cardinal sin of lacking *papeles*, "papers."

What was really violently and passionately rejected was the regularization of the unauthorized immigrants living in the United States, a regularization that was equated with "amnesty," a word that is anathema to the extreme Right. The concept was hammered incessantly by right-wing radio and television personalities. Thus, the main stumbling block to achieve some kind of consensus is what to do with the 11.7 million unauthorized immigrants, half of them from Mexico, already living in the United States. In spite of what some on the political right say, it is next to impossible to deport these immigrants, and to hope for "self-deportation" is unrealistic. Having said that let me also state that a record number of immigrants *are* being detained and deported at a rate of 400,000 annually, by the Obama administration which has deported nearly two million immigrants. So, there has to be more than enforcement in any strategy to fix immigration problems. Congress and the president, the business sector and everybody else should be involved in devising a comprehensive immigration reform that includes a path to legalization for those irregular immigrants living in the shadows, programs for temporary workers, workplace enforcement and, yes, security at the border. Nevertheless, it should be very clear that there is no way immigration reform could become reality unless it includes a path to citizenship or at least some sort of legal status.

Immigration reform was not a high priority in the first Obama administration especially in difficult financial times, promises notwithstanding. The floundering of banks and big business, unemployment, the economic stimulus, budgetary wars, health care reform, Afghanistan and other domestic and foreign policy matters were deemed more pressing priorities. Everything, it seems, but immigration reform was more pressing. All that changed after the 2012 presidential election. President Obama was reelected, in large part thanks to the Latino vote.

Then comes 2013 and again, when we thought that there was a good chance of finally concluding the elusive reform, there was Syria, the shutdown of the U.S. government, the fight over the federal debt ceiling, and the unthinkable possibility that the leading global power was losing its capacity to govern. So, at a time when political rhetoric had turned into increasingly dysfunctional political actions, no one was thinking of immigration reform. Immigration is right now at the back of the line and the issue will probably not come up again seriously for months. If the highly contentious issue surfaces in 2014, members of the House will be voting in the middle of a Congressional election year. So if Congress does not conclude the reform before spring, when the primaries will start, the issue might be delayed until after the November elections, a possibility that could take us all the way to 2015.

The reality of undocumented immigration has to be recognized by everybody, especially politicians. It is very difficult to keep confronting the issue with such profound ambivalence: the United States requires the labor of immigrants and at the same time efforts are being made to maximize enforcement of the border and in working places. The bottom line is that both nations require a new approach to immigration, more rational, more ordained, and more humane, so that migration becomes a matter of a personal decision, not one of necessity. That is the challenge.

Other nations understand that any proposal for immigration reform must include up front the issue of security at the border. And they can live with that tenet. And they are quite aware that preventing terrorism is one of the main priorities of the U.S. government. But I can tell you, there are no terrorists among the millions of irregular immigrants, whose main concern is only to put food on the table. It is understandable also that *el muro*, "the wall," being highly visible, responds to a necessity of internal politics. Nevertheless, it has not stopped the migrants, or the narco-traffickers, and it most likely will not stop well-funded and better-organized terrorist cells. So what is keeping the United States and Mexico, two good neighbors, from dealing with the migration phenomenon?

I am not being naïve. I am conscious of the role that the U.S. Congress plays in this complicated process. And I do understand the differences between the trade and immigration issues in terms of perception. Trade is perceived as an issue of external politics in which Congress tends to authorize fast-track negotiations for the president. But immigration is viewed as a domestic issue, of unilateral interest, under the control of Congress. Yet discussion of immigration should be bilateral, because it concerns the human rights of Mexican nationals, rights that cannot be taken away by their immigration status.

Now, the U.S. Senate proposes to spend forty-six billion dollars to secure the United States border with Mexico in order to persuade the radical members of the House of Representatives to approve the comprehensive immigration reform package, a sort of ransom to be paid to liberate the bill. The unintended consequences of this idea include the outrage, consternation, and amazement generated among Mexicans who wonder if we are at war with the neighboring country. And yet, Mexico and the United States are supposed to be "friends and neighbors," besides being trade partners. As Univision news anchor Jorge Ramos said, "neighbors don't do this to each other." This "surge" includes an addition of nearly 20,000 Border Patrol agents, roughly double the current force, funding for the completion of 700 miles of border fence, 24-hour surveillance flights by drones, complete and mandatory implementation of E-Verify for all U.S. business, etc. All of this has contributed greatly to reinforce a long-held opinion among Mexicans that U.S. border policy, which relies mostly on enforcement, is an insult to their nation. And of course there are unintended victims of this perception: the Peña Nieto administration, labeled as "passive and negligent" for not speaking out more forcefully. There are grounds for this critique, as the Mexican regime opted to stay out of the immigration debate raging north of the border, feeling perhaps that any intervention might be construed as unwarranted meddling. So, the U.S. will keep on adding more "Migra" (Border Patrol officers), more miles of "Muro" (wall), more of everything to seal the border. Mexican intelligentsia like to recall the words of President Reagan when he demanded, standing in front of the Berlin Wall at the Brandenburg Gate, "Mister Gorbachev, tear down this wall." Things have changed. Now dividing two nations that are friends and partners, we have a wall seven times larger than the Berlin Wall with four times more agents to keep people out.

The Human Rights of Migrants

The stigmatization of the immigrant, be it in the United States or the European Union or anywhere else, degrades the dignity of the human being who migrates out of necessity. Stigmatization leads to intimidating attitudes during detentions, indifference when it comes to the obligation of the consular notification, unsafe and disorderly repatriations, racism, and so on. And the deaths "in crossing circumstances" should be treated as authentic violations of the human rights of the victims, because these migrants, who have been directed to places of high risk by unilateral immigration policies, have an inherent right to life.

We should understand that migration is a modern phenomenon, not a crime. Therefore, the human rights of all migrants must be recognized and respected, and unjust and discriminatory treatment rejected. This is of particular importance in the United States, where "the nativists are restless."(*New York Times* 2009). The United States has experienced lately, in large sectors of society, a disturbing trend toward radicalization of political and social positions. There is a toxic rhetoric when it comes to topics like immigration, an extremism that generates an undeniable potential for violence. Notable among the many manifestations of this xenophobic nativism is the proliferation of extremist bills generated by state legislatures. SB 1070, signed into law in Arizona in 2010, as well as the multitude of bills considered by the Arizona State Legislature in the past few years, are classic examples. Unfortunately, the Arizona model has been spreading, with highly publicized bills introduced in several other states, such as Alabama and Tennessee.

Despite nativist rhetoric and policies, nations of origin and nations of arrival have to approach the immigration phenomenon ethically, understanding the structural causes of the massive displacement of people. To migrate is not a crime. Crimes are causes of migration. We are bound by the ethical duty to recognize the right of minorities to "freedom and the pursuit of happiness," and to be different, because difference enhances the great richness of the human race of which we are a part. Difference begets tolerance. And tolerance has to be understood in its most positive sense, as the explicit will to accept the other one, and to recognize him or her in his or her different ways. This state of mind has special significance when we accept and recognize those who are excluded by reason of ethnicity, religion, politics, or social status. The General Assembly of the United Nations in the Universal Declaration of Human Rights (Article 3) proclaims that "Every individual has a right to life, liberty and safeness as a person." It would be worthwhile if all of us would respect these rights.

Deaths "in Crossing Circumstances"

If there has been a sharp decline in net migration from Mexico since 2007, according to the Pew Hispanic Center report, why do we not see the same trend in the number of migrant fatalities? A decrease in the number of apprehensions should imply fewer unauthorized crossings and a congruent decrease in the number of deaths in the unforgiving deserts of Arizona. And yet, while undocumented crossings have dropped dramatically in past years, hundreds of bodies are still found annually on the border. Since 1994 at least 5,513 migrants have been found dead along the border with Mexico, including 463 in fiscal year 2012 (Rodríguez 2013). The Border Patrol reports that in fiscal year 2010 there were 118 known deaths per 100,000 apprehensions in the area covered by the Border Patrol Tucson Sector, up from 88 known deaths per 100,000 apprehensions in 2009, and 57 in 2008. Indeed, in 2004 the rate of deaths per 100,000 apprehensions was only a third as high, just 39 (McCombs 2011). In view of the historic buildup of agents, fences, roads, and technology along the Arizona-Mexico border, the urgent question is: whatever happened to the Border Patrol mantra that "a secure border is a safe border"?

I had a Jesuit teacher that used to say that concepts can be more easily understood by the use of examples. Anecdotes tend to clarify the points we are trying to make. It is in that context that I include narratives that might help us better understand the drama and, all too often, the tragedy of the undocumented Mexican diaspora.

Death Has Witnesses

How horrible to die in the desert! Even more horrible if a ten-year-old child watches, as a terrorized witness, the death of his own mother.

At dawn, July 18, 2007, a tracker from the Tohono O'odham people in southern Arizona discovered the lifeless body of a thirty-three-year-old woman, María Reséndiz Pérez, from San Juan del Río, in the central Mexican state of Querétaro. The unfortunate woman was found dead a short distance from Highway 24, forty miles west of Tucson, Arizona. Her ten-year-old son Luis Daniel was found, terrified, next to her body.

María, Luis Daniel, and other undocumented people had entered U.S. territory in search of the American dream by crossing the unforgiving desert located to the north of Sásabe, Mexico. Their dream, though, turned into a nightmare. In scorching temperatures of more than forty degrees Celsius (104°F), the woman collapsed from heatstroke. As her symptoms got worse her friends improvised a stretcher to carry her until she died in front of her small child.

In a macabre coincidence, twenty-four hours after this tragedy, during the morning of July 19, another undocumented woman, Lucía Sebastián Diego, a forty-seven-year-old Guatemalan, fell victim to the extreme weather conditions. And her son, Baltasar Mateos Sebastián, who had just turned ten, witnessed her die.

A U.S. Border Patrol agent spotted the Guatemalan boy walking about a mile north of the border on the Tohono O'odham Indian reservation, in an eerily similar scenario to the one in which María had died. Lucía and

Baltasar had traveled through Mexico by bus to cross the border and join their husband and father, who lived and worked in Indiana. The woman and the child, together with other immigrants, entered Arizona guided by a *coyote*, but the woman slipped and fell in a hollow, hurt her back, and struggled to keep pace with the rest of the group. Lucía must have perished of dehydration before dawn only a day after María's death. The boy told the uniformed man that his mother had died and led him to the site of her corpse.

On August 23, again in the deadly summer of 2007, Border Patrol agents from the Nogales station discovered, on the grounds of a ranch just west of Interstate 19, the corpse of Blanca Carpio Ruiz, a thirty-year-old woman, who like María was from San Juan del Río, Querétaro. Standing beside the dead body of her mother was Itzel Saavedra Carpio, six years old. She told the agents about Mrs. Carpio's stepson Antonio Barrón López, a seventeen-year-old adolescent who was found later.

We can go on and on. Another undocumented woman was found the afternoon of July 29 at a desolate site near Three Points, Arizona, a short distance from Route 86. She was suffering from the effects of dehydration and heatstroke and was transported by plane to a hospital in Tucson. She died on her way to the hospital. Then there was another Guatemalan woman, Lilián Ramírez García, only twenty-three, whose body was discovered July 22 the same year, in the foothills of the Huachuca Mountains, south of Sierra Vista, Arizona.

In this drama of the migrant woman, which is inscribed in the larger drama of undocumented migration, there are also collateral damages. That is the case for Carmen Ortiz, a woman from Guerrero, twenty-something years old, who was seven months pregnant when she attempted to cross the desert in the last days of July 2007. When she had the first symptoms of labor, the trafficker abandoned her at the parking lot of a shopping center in Tucson. The labor took place there, and by time the woman got medical attention her premature newborn had already died. Mrs. Ortiz was assisted by the Mexican consulate in Tucson. Before she was sent back to Mexico, she gave instructions to have her baby cremated and have the ashes sent to her.

Migrant Women's Plight in Summer

Much could be said about the terrible summer of 2007 in the desert between Sonora and Arizona. Actually it would be redundant to qualify that summer as "terrible," since on this border, every summer of every year is terrible. The statistical records constitute a sharp cry indicting the dehumanizing approach to irregular migration.

But let us emphasize that too many women are dying while crossing the desert in the summer, particularly in July. The *Arizona Daily Star* database reports that women constituted 22 percent of all undocumented people who died while crossing Pima, Cochise, Santa Cruz, and Pinal Counties in the period between 2004 and July 2007, and are 2.87 times more likely than men to die while crossing the desert as a consequence of the deadly combination of high temperatures and the unforgiving sun. Apart from the fact that it is unquestionable that every day more women cross the desert, alone or accompanied, the gender issue is indeed significant but rather neglected.

Why do so many women lose their lives while trying to cross in the summer (see Rubio-Goldsmith et al. 2006)? Melissa McCormick, of the Binational Migration Institute of the University of Arizona, argues that women, less strong than men, are more susceptible to the brutal heat. They are not as accustomed to high temperatures as men, who work outside in the agricultural and construction fields. Furthermore, many of them cross the border accompanied by their young children, who delay them on the lengthy walks. A mother will always protect her little ones, and if the children are small, even carry them in her arms. In addition, a mother needs to carry food and water for her children. When liquid and food become scarce, she will save them for her children, even when this action puts her own survival at risk. And of course, there are cases of women who dare to cross while pregnant. If unable to keep up with the fast pace imposed by the *coyotes*, they are abandoned as the classic aphorism of every *coyote*: "El que se rezaga se queda," "Those who cannot keep up are left behind." In the desert, especially during the summer, that is the equivalent of a death sentence.

This outcome is clear from the above-mentioned anecdotes from the tragic summer of 2007 at the Sonora-Arizona border. That particularly scorching summer saw thirty-seven consecutive days in which temperatures in the desert area between Sásabe and Tucson reached triple digits. For instance, the undocumented Guatemalan woman started walking in the desert on July 18, when the thermometer indicated 104 degrees, and died on July 19, when it reached 110 degrees. That month, of the total forty-six migrants found dead in Arizona, sixteen, or 35 percent, were women. That is the same percentage of women found dead every July between 2004 and 2007 (36 percent), more than double the percentage of women who died during other months.

Undocumented migrants in general, but specifically women, have a greater chance of survival crossing high risk sites if they are accompanied by others when they suffer any contingency that weakens them, such as extreme weather. However, if migrants, especially women, are abandoned, their possibilities of survival are minimal. Although almost everybody agrees that the *coyote* is the proverbial evil who abandons those in trouble without remorse, it should also be said that the spirit of solidarity is not always present among migrants. Frequently, they follow the example set by their guide and abandon their fellow men and women if they foresee any possibility of continuing the journey without being apprehended. Luckily, to confirm our faith in humanity, there are those who sacrifice their personal interests to help others in need of assistance.

There are all kinds of people in the Lord's domain.

"Mamá Is Dead"

The little girl maintains her composure. She clenches her jaw and somehow manages to hold back her tears. Her little brother is sitting on a bed in the emergency room at the Copper Queen Hospital in Bisbee, Arizona, his skinny legs dangling over the edge. He stares at his sister, who stands before him, trying to understand what she, deliberately, slowly, enunciating each syllable, with terrifying clarity, is saying:

"Mamá is dead."

Carlos Enrique Bazán Miranda, five years old, hears the words but does not understand. But he suspects that something terrible has happened to his mom.

Ana Laura Bazán Miranda, eleven and carrying a tragedy the size of the whole world on her shoulders, swallows hard, puts her hands on Carlos Enrique's thighs, and with infinite patience, repeats:

"Mamá—is—dead."

The scene in the sterile room is witnessed in absolute silence by doctors and nurses, by a psychologist called in to provide professional assistance, by the social workers of the Child Protective Services of the state of Arizona, and by this chapter's author, at that time the Mexican consul in Douglas. All of them, dismayed by the scene, make desperate attempts to keep their emotions in check.

The little girl is aware of the presence of strangers at a time when she would prefer to have privacy; she puts her arms around the child's neck and pulls his little head toward her and begins to whisper what seems like a long monologue in his ear. The witnesses watch as Carlos Enrique gives in and reality penetrates his small capacity for understanding and somehow registers in the small store of knowledge accumulated in his scant five years. What is clear is that the child now cries for the first time.

He cries in silence, without sobs, or hiccups, or facial contortions, solemnly, the big tears coursing through the layer of dirt on his cheeks. Finally he too takes his sister by the neck and holds her close.

Everyone else feels as if they are intruding; they hang their heads and pretend to be looking for something that has fallen to the floor.

Rosalía Bazán Miranda, a single mother of thirty-three, born in Mexico City and living in Coacoalco, in the state of Mexico, accompanied by her two small children, Ana Laura and Carlos Enrique, leaves home heading for the northern border on August 2, 2000, full of dreams. She arrives at Agua Prieta, Sonora, early the next day. At midmorning she enters the United States, and that very afternoon she dies of sunstroke and dehydration in the desert west of Douglas, Arizona.

Thus, in a few hours, the dreams of a Mexican family have disappeared—instead of a new life and a promising future, they came face-to-face with death and abandonment.

Jubilation prevails in the compact family nucleus composed of the mother and the two offspring during the course of the journey of more than a day on board the bus that takes them to *la frontera norte*. The family is headed for—Delaware!—on the northeastern coast of the United States, a destination that for all practical purposes, given its distance from the Sonoran border, might as well be Outer Mongolia. Rosalía has relatives in Delaware whom they can stay with and who will surely help her find work.

The day they arrive in Agua Prieta, around 10:30 a.m., the three undocumented family members cross the border to the west of Douglas. Three neighbors from Coacoalco, two men and a woman, cross with them. The hot August morning gives a taste of what will be: an inclement sun and a temperature that tops 100 degrees before noon. The migrants take to the road. The small troop walking along the bottoms of the dry arroyos trying not to be seen by the "Migra" (U.S. Border Patrol) march without the guidance of a *coyote*, and it seems with no idea how to arrive at their initial destination, Phoenix? Tucson? It is clear at least that Rosalía and her kids do not even know where the sun rises or sets in that harsh desert with its intolerable heat, all so different from the welcoming lands and benevolent climate of the Mexican highlands.

Were they planning on walking from the border until they came to Highway 80, where they could find a ride? Had they planned to rendezvous with some vehicle that was to transport them? Would they fly from Tucson or Phoenix, if everything went well, to the Baltimore airport, or perhaps Wilmington?

So many questions, most of them left unanswered.

What is clear is that a little while after they entered the United States, the group separated. The three neighbors went ahead, saying they would try to ascertain the whereabouts of the Border Patrol, and promised to return shortly. The pair of men and the woman disappeared. Señora Bazán and the little ones continued on their way under the blazing sun.

Since leaving Agua Prieta, Rosalia has carried a plastic gallon container of water. They have now endured four or five hours of hard walking under the blazing sun, and the woman drinks frequently, but when she sees that there is only a little bit left, she saves it for her little ones. At one point the woman says she is very tired; first she sits down, and then she lies on the ground, "as if she were sleeping," as the daughter would later say. Time passes, Rosalía does not react. The little ones take fright because they cannot "wake her up," and now, terrified, Ana Laura takes Carlos Enrique by the hand and heads for a nearby dirt road to look for help.

Just then, a gas company truck goes by, and the driver is surprised to see a couple of scared-looking kids in the middle of nowhere and calls the Border Patrol on his radio.

The Border Patrol arrives at 3:40 p.m. and finds the lifeless body under the sun and renders immediate first aid, to no avail.

Rosalía Bazán Miranda is declared dead at 4:26 in the afternoon.

And in that inhospitable spot, fifteen miles west of Douglas, the "American dream" ends for the young single mother and her family.

The afternoon falls, the shadows lengthen, and the silence becomes eternal. Seated at a table in the empty hospital cafeteria, the consul of Mexico in Douglas and Ana Laura watch each other. The former tries to find some common ground to allow communication, because he desperately needs information about the events: what happened, how it happened, who they crossed with, where they are from, where they were going. He also needs the names and addresses and telephone numbers of family members to contact, to give them word of the tragedy and offer them the assistance of the consular representation for the repatriation of the remains to Mexican soil, because Mexicans always want to bring their loved ones back to bury them in the maternal womb of the native soil, and . . .

And this information can only come from the dark, skinny little girl, barely eleven years old, who picks at her plate, without eating any of the food the good souls of the cafeteria prepared for the children who have eaten nothing since the day before. There are no other witnesses to the tragedy, the authorities know nothing, and there is no way of interrogating the five-year-old who does eat, and heartily. Carlos Enrique sits at the table as a silent presence and does not participate in the laconic exchange of questions and monosyllabic responses between the man with the serious face and his sister. Ana Laura, then, is the only source of information; very reluctantly and fully aware of how unpropitious the moment is, the consul steels himself and continues to question her.

The child shows extraordinary intelligence; the tragedy that just made her an orphan has matured her far beyond her eleven years. Her physical and mental strength surprises the Mexican official. The little woman left Mexico City yesterday, traveled on a bus all day and all night, woke up today in Agua Prieta, crossed the border, walked for hours under the terrible sun, saw her mother die that afternoon, and is now alone and responsible for her younger brother, in a new place among strangers, does not know what is going to happen to them, and—lo—her stoic demeanor, her inscrutable face, her serene look. The man, awed, asks himself, where do these child-adults get their strength?

Little by little, bits of information emerge, which are passed on to the deputy in charge of the investigation for the Cochise County Sheriff's Department, and somehow the consul's compassion and his feeling of pain begin to permeate the wall the girl has erected around herself, and Ana Laura asks timidly, "What are they going to do with my mother?"

The children are under the temporary custody of the Child Protective Services while the consular office locates their relatives. Next comes the telephone call that sooner or later every Mexican consul abroad, especially those on the border, has to make to the relatives of some unfortunate *paisano*— and the sequence of disbelief, anger, and emotional crisis, in that order, on the part of the relative at the other end of the line, and then finally acceptance of what cannot be changed.

"Hello, Señora Lucía Bazán? Are you the sister of Rosalía Bazán Miranda? Señora, I am very sorry to have to inform you that . . ."

The coroner's verdict was just what they expected. Exposure. Rosalía died as the result of extreme heat, which provoked dehydration and sunstroke.

A brother of the deceased came to Douglas to pick up the orphans. The dike finally broke when the little girl of iron saw her uncle inside the consulate and let loose a river of tears. Hours later, the three boarded a bus headed back to the state of Mexico.

Rosalía also returned to her native land. Her mortal remains traveled from Douglas to Tucson, to Houston, and finally to Mexico City, on August 8, 2000.

She was buried the next day, a week after she left, dreaming of a new life.

CHAPTER 2

Sexual Violence Against Migrant Women and Children

William Paul Simmons and Michelle Téllez

> You know, I've been really surprised at the high percentage that I come across working here. I never dreamed it would be this high. The more people get comfortable with me the more that they end up divulging. I think almost, it just surprised me, close to every girl that I've come across that I've interviewed has been sexually abused. Usually by a *coyote* on their trip, some point throughout the trip. Especially the older ones. It's sad [about] those seven or eight year olds, but the older ones almost always experience abuse on their trip here, not to mention what happens in their own countries. I think it's shocking, and something that isn't well publicized, people don't know here.
>
> —Phoenix social worker

This chapter narrates another little-told story of human rights abuses along the U.S.-Mexico border: the sexual violence experienced by women and girls as they migrate into the United States, especially into Arizona through the northern Mexican state of Sonora. The increasing militarization of the border and the growing power of organized crime have interacted with and exacerbated the structural violence—poverty, nativism, racialization, misogyny—endemic to the region (Segura and Zavella 2007). This has led to a state of exception that has put thousands of individuals in extremely vulnerable situations, especially the growing numbers of women and children crossing the Sonoran desert. Our research reported here, based on fifty qualitative interviews in the Sonora-Arizona corridor, reveals that this vulnerability leads to numerous horrific incidents of sexual violence.

A number of factors, including underreporting, fear, and little to no accountability on the part of law enforcement on either side of the border, will prevent us from ever having an accurate number of those who have been victimized. However, it is clear from scattered media accounts and from our research that significant percentages of women and children are sexually assaulted as they migrate to the United States. Also, since significant percentages of migrants are likely to cross the border multiple times throughout their lives, the risk of exploitation for any given woman or child migrant is probably quite high. In addition, our research shows that most of those who suffer sexual violence suffer in silence, with little formal or informal assistance. The numerous tragedies that women and children experience when crossing into the United States merit immediate and heightened attention from the media, human rights organizations, and policy makers at the local, state, and federal levels.

The sexual assault and terror women and children suffer while migrating to the United States are only part of a series of attacks they face. Our findings suggest that "victimization is more of a 'condition' than an 'event'" (Finkelhor, Ormrod, and Turner 2007 on victimized children in the United States). Or, as Ruiz Marrujo (2009: 31) writes, "along the U.S.-Mexico and Mexico-Guatemala borders sexual violence has become [a] fact of life for migrant women." Women and girls are victimized and revictimized over time in a number of ways. Many of the immigrants are victims of sexual abuse by family members and acquaintances in their home country before they ever consider migrating. Throughout their journey, not just at the U.S.-Mexico border, they suffer exploitation. The exploitation continues in the border crossings and at drop houses in cities such as Phoenix and Tucson. And it is not uncommon for the exploitation to continue once the women and children are reunited with their families or when they reach their final destinations. Migrants who are apprehended by law enforcement officers and subsequently detained are also at risk for abuse, both in the United States and in Mexico. The physical, psychological, and social effects of these abuses are complex, iterative, and long-lasting.

Recent research has shown that this form of multiple victimization or polyvictimization is especially pernicious, with each abuse having a

cumulative effect on the victim's physical and mental health (Turner, Finkelhor, and Ormrod 2006; Finkelhor, Ormrod, and Turner 2007).[1] Unfortunately,
social services set up to protect and serve these victims are overwhelmed by
the sheer number of cases and are mostly ill prepared to deal with multiple
victimizations. In addition, the structural violence that renders migrant
women and children vulnerable in the first place creates considerable additional obstacles to adequate provision of services.

After a brief survey of the scholarly literature on this topic, we outline
our study's methodology, and then provide an overview of the journey many
women and children migrants experience. We conclude with a discussion of
the multiple effects of this polyvictimization, and possible solutions in the
context of both international law and alternative practices for local service
providers.

Literature Review

Very few systematic studies have been conducted on the experiences of women
and children crossing the border and the attempts to provide them with
social services once they arrive in the United States. Occasionally, the media
have reported on victimization of migrants, and some human rights groups
have published reports chronicling victimization during a particular stage
of the journey. For instance, Amnesty International and the UN Special
Rapporteur on Migrant Rights (UNHRC 2008) have written about abuses in
long-term detention facilities, and the Arizona-based migrant aid organization No More Deaths (2008) has written about systematic abuses suffered
during short-term custody (less than seventy-two hours) along the Arizona-
Sonora border. However, very little scholarship has been produced about the
sexual violence migrants routinely face, despite the increased academic work
recently done on migration from Mexico to the United States.

Ruiz Marrujo (2009) has conducted an important exploratory study of
sexual violence against migrant women focusing on the Tijuana-San Diego
corridor and part of the Mexican-Guatemalan border in Chiapas. She delin-
eates many of the structural variables that make women and girls in these
areas especially vulnerable: patriarchy and the general domination of women
in society, vestiges of colonialism, class inequalities, the acceptance of violence, the proliferation of sexualized popular culture that commodifies
women, and the tendency to categorize some people as native and others as

Other, especially along international borders (39). Ruiz Marrujo is especially helpful in outlining and navigating tensions between the way the women themselves might conceptualize sexual violence, cultural and social definitions of appropriate sexual behavior according to which the women are raised, and international norms of human rights. These tensions need to be balanced in order to identify the scope of the problem, but also in tailoring solutions to the problem such as in providing services (46–47). For example, Ruiz Marrujo points out that the act of a migrant woman taking birth control pills in fear of being sexually assaulted on the journey may not be seen as a form of sexual violence by the woman herself, "but from the standpoint of human rights, it is difficult not to see it as such" (34).

Falcón (2007), drawing from Enloe's (2000) work on militarism's effects on women, argues that the increased militarization of the U.S.-Mexico border has reproduced "hyper-masculinity, colonialism, and patriarchy" (203–4), through which women's bodies are targeted for sexual assault and other attacks. She then outlines how militarization and structural violence served to fuel several high-profile cases of sexual assault by Border Patrol and INS officers.

Several studies have reported on women and children being trafficked into the United States through Mexico and sent to migrant labor camps where they serve as prostitutes for migrant laborers (see Ugarte, Zarate, and Farley 2003; Hernandez 2003). In their discussion of general societal causes underlying the sexual violence, Ugarte, Zarate, and Farley focus on the subordination of women and the high prevalence of sexual violence in Latin America in general. Rape and domestic violence are often treated as minor crimes and are rarely investigated, let alone prosecuted. The authors argue that large numbers of abusive homes lead to tens of thousands of homeless youth who are at extreme risk of prostitution and trafficking. This is exacerbated by the culture of rape resulting from the civil wars in Central America in the 1980s and the militarization in Chiapas in the 1990s. The women themselves often feel that they are to blame for the sexual assault because they did not do enough to resist or they were forced to consent because of their poverty or other vulnerabilities. This sense of shame further prevents women and children from coming forward to authorities or seeking social services.

Ugarte, Zarate, and Farley then lay out case studies that show the enormous variety of services needed to address the "multiple layers of trauma" experienced by survivors of trafficking and prostitution. "The healing process is lengthy since survivors suffer psychological damage from captivity, terrorization, physical violence, and brainwashing and in many cases a long history of family and community violence" (161). One girl required assistance from more than twenty different agencies (151), including a battered women's shelter, law enforcement on both sides of the border, health clinics, family services, consulates, legal groups, hospitals, and human rights groups. Ugarte et al conclude that these myriad social services must be linguistically and culturally appropriate and must address race, class, and gender issues in a sensitive way.

Data and Methods

Our study builds on this previous research to better understand the prevalence and experiences of sexual violence against migrant women throughout multiple stages of their journey (before, during, and after crossing the border). In spring 2009 we conducted a systematic qualitative study based on fifty interviews, some with multiple interviewees present, in southern and central Arizona with social workers, humanitarian groups, local and federal law enforcement, consulate staff, and victims' advocates who have significant direct contact with migrant women and children who were victims of sexual violence. In total over sixty individuals were interviewed, about evenly divided among three geographical regions: the vast Phoenix metropolitan area (approximately 120 miles from the border), the Tucson metropolitan area (approximately 60 miles from the border), and Nogales (a border town) and the surrounding areas in the Sonoran desert.[2] We interviewed law enforcement, social workers, humanitarian groups, and consul staff from each of these three geographic areas. Law enforcement included Border Patrol agents, Immigration and Customs Enforcement (ICE) officials, and local officials. Consul staff included consuls as well as those working more directly with migrants, such as "protection officers." In all interviews but one, which involved undercover officers, we recorded the interviews using digital recorders and took copious notes. Several interviewees also provided us with official and unofficial reports from their organization and other data we consulted in drafting this chapter.

The interviews were semistructured with a short set of general questions that we asked all respondents, and ranged in length from approximately thirty minutes to over two hours. We conducted the interviews in the language that the participant was most comfortable using, which in approximately one-fourth of the cases was Spanish. The recordings were transcribed and translated into English, if necessary, and then triangulated with our field notes. Through a thematic analysis and coding of our interviews, we captured a general, but multilayered, account of the experiences of migrant women and children. Not surprisingly, considering the contentious nature of the immigration issue and the often sharply divergent roles of our interviewees, there were some stark differences in their accounts.

The Journey to the United States

This section describes the experiences of sexual violence among migrant women and children as we have come to understand it from our interviews. We will share unsettling details here, not to be voyeuristic or overly detached, but to begin to provide a snapshot of what is happening to migrant women and children—a complex story that is known in fragments at best. Here, we lay out the stages of migration and what happens in the in-between spaces of the journey.

Prevalence of Sexual Violence

Some sources found it impossible to give even ballpark estimates of the prevalence of sexual assault, but among those who offered a response, estimates ranged from a few sexual assaults a year to almost 100 percent of the women who crossed the border.[3] These estimates seemed to vary based on the population of migrants with which the interviewees worked, where they encountered them, and in what capacity. Those interviewees who worked along the heavily patrolled border area and were involved in law enforcement reported rarely encountering victims of sexual violence. This can be explained by the fact that the crossing at the border itself has to be done with extreme haste because of the massive buildup there of law enforcement officials and surveillance equipment. Agents at the border have the task of interdiction and quick repatriation. If migrants are to be detained they will be handed off to ICE officials very quickly, with little in the way of interviewing. On the other hand, those who assist migrants who become lost in the desert for several days suggested the prevalence of sexual assault was much greater, especially among migrants who were most vulnerable. One migrant aid worker said:

"if a woman is by herself in a group in the desert we assume 100 percent of the time that she was sexually assaulted." Similarly those who work with migrant women who have been kept in drop houses in Phoenix against their will, a form of kidnapping or trafficking by itself, reported widespread sexual violence. By the same token, social workers who counsel women and children who may have been trafficked, and those who have a chance to ask the migrants to reflect on their experiences, reported high prevalence. One said: "I would say they *all* are [victims of sexual violence] because they're coming with a perpetrator, they're coming . . . with the person who is trafficking them. So yeah I would say almost all of them." There also appeared to be a gender component to prevalence estimates, with female interviewees generally reporting higher rates. A female law enforcement official working near the border reported very few incidents she personally dealt with, but conjectured: "I wouldn't be surprised that 100 percent of the women coming through the desert are sexually assaulted."

Those who interview the women about their whole journey from the place of origin, including their journey through Mexico, offered the bleakest picture, reporting that several of the women and girls they interviewed have been victimized multiple times over their lifetimes. Several interviewees reported similar stories, such as this one from a law enforcement official in Tucson: "Unfortunately women are sexually assaulted multiple times . . . I recall a case of a young girl who is a juvenile and she had been raped from almost the time she left her home in El Salvador and through Mexico, and then raped at the border, crossing the desert she was raped several timed by the guides, [she] entered the drop houses and the assaults continued."

Origins: Rural Mexico/Central America

The journey for most migrants to the United States through Arizona often begins in rural Mexico or rural Central America. Our interviewees reported that some hire guides in their hometowns, while others travel in small groups with friends or family members. The migrants leave looking for a better life and to escape immense poverty and often abusive homes. Those who travel alone are most vulnerable, but we heard numerous accounts of guides being hired in their hometown that then turned out to be traffickers and would later abuse the migrants. Those who speak only indigenous languages were also reported to be more vulnerable, as they are unable to easily communicate with other migrants and law enforcement officials if necessary.

We talked with one social worker who works mostly with girls who have made the journey from Guatemala. She reported that nearly all her clients had problems in their home communities or homes:[4] "They were very vulnerable at home, and raped at home, and physically abused at home, and also abused while on the journey." Another social worker said most of the physical and sexual abuse was perpetrated by family members, with some by neighbors, others from the village, or members of their extended families. The abuse in the sending country is not limited to girls. Several interviewees told stories of young boys being abused, often brutally:

> I have one boy that was gang-raped by a bunch of boys, in the neighborhood that were older boys. He was a little boy, just seven, six or seven. There's just . . . every story is so unique it's really hard to, to generalize. But, I know, I had one boy who really was abandoned and he was taken in by an aunt and an uncle. And so the uncle—him and his sister were taken in by that aunt and uncle. And so the uncle sexually abused him and the sister. And he was like a witness to the sexual abuse too of his sister.

Unaccompanied youth, not surprisingly, appear to be at significant risk for sexual violence and trafficking. The following is a compilation of the accounts of two social workers who work closely with unaccompanied youth that have migrated to the United States. A girl seeking to escape abuse at the hands of a family member, such as the father, uncles, or often a brother, "finds this person that's promising them all these good things and it's so easy to go." She is lured by a new "boyfriend" who is a friend of a friend or an acquaintance, with the promise of a job in the United States. The girl is then "groomed" by the "boyfriend" in the hometown or during the early parts of the journey. "A young male, many times good looking and young . . . gets her to have sex with him on the journey and that kind of just starts." The promised job in the restaurant turns out not to materialize, but she is then forced into prostitution. The connection to the village increases the vulnerability of the girl, as the trafficker can threaten: "if you say anything, if you do anything, if you report it," we know where your family lives back in your village. "We'll just kill your father or your sister or whoever."

The Perilous Journey Through Mexico

Accounts of the journey through Mexico, either from Central Mexico or from southern Mexican states like Chiapas and Oaxaca, are often harrowing.[5] Some interviewees described violence and sexual violence by Mexican border patrol agents at the Guatemalan border. In one case described by a consulate staff member a bus was boarded by border agents and a migrant woman was singled out. When "she got down off the bus to use the restroom . . . the border patrol agent saw her, thought that she was pretty, kept her, detained her, violated her, assaulted her" before she was allowed to get on the bus to rejoin her children.

Migrants often travel through large parts of Mexico by train or bus, many times hopping on freight trains illegally. Some are killed or maimed while getting on or off the trains, and some are electrocuted. The descriptions we heard of assaults on trains in Mexico were incredibly violent. These are often perpetrated by gangs such as the infamous Maras (Mara Salvatrucha). One interviewee said, "Our Honduran and Guatemalan boys, a lot of them just jump on those trains and they come on those trains, and they're kind of at the mercy of people that are willing to give 'em a piece of bread or tortilla or something." Many of the migrants must stop in major cities to earn enough money to continue the journey. Some are attacked while others resort to prostitution to earn their way. Several interviewees reported a series of drop houses throughout Mexico where *coyotes*/traffickers would bring the women and children. One attorney reported the following example of poly-victimization:

> I have a client that was taken from Guatemala to a drop house in Mexico where she was repeatedly raped by her guide and got pregnant with his child, the guide then abandoned her when he found out she was pregnant. She found somebody else to take her to the U.S. So from there she was taken to several drop houses in Mexico. . . . She was taken to several drop houses and then wasn't charged any money. And she and a couple of girls she was with were all brought the same day, were all raped both in Mexico and the U.S., and in the desert,

they were caught crossing the border. They [the migrants] were caught, the people, the guides were not caught.

Those who have been sexually assaulted rarely return to their hometown because of the shame they feel from the sexual assault or from pregnancy. "When she got pregnant she was afraid to go back, her dad is a police officer, and she's afraid that she would at this point, get in trouble with her family for being pregnant. So now she's afraid to go home."

The Borderlands: Intimidation and Impunity

As a migrant's journey nears the U.S.-Mexico border, smuggling operations appear to become more professionalized, with increasing links to other crime cartels, fueling increased violence. Within these operations, there seems to be an increase in the number of weapons used. Also, near the border are also an increasing number of *bajadores* (armed bandits).

Our interviewees described two main contexts for sexual violence in the borderlands. The first are perpetrated by the *coyotes*, who are leading the groups of immigrants through the desert or mountains, traveling mainly at night, while hiding during the day. Women traveling alone or responsible for small children are especially at risk. Sometimes the sexual violence is based on coerced "consent." One interviewee told of common situations her clients would describe, where a *coyote* might say, "here I'm gonna get you across no problem . . . you just sleep with me or whatever." Another reported: "the coyotes have all the control and are armed, they have all the control, and the sexual violence is part of that control." Consistent with increased professionalization and use of weapons, we heard reports of knives or guns held on the victims, while other assaults were perpetrated while victims were drugged and barely conscious. Often the groups are split up, with male family members separated from the women and children. At other times, the women fall behind, or one or two women are intentionally separated from the group, and then they are attacked. Sometimes the sexual assaults happen while the group is resting. A woman or girl is taken a short distance away from the group and raped while the rest of the group is powerless to stop the attack.

For example, one migrant aid worker told us about a rancher who lived near the border and often came across migrants looking for help. A woman came to his ranch seeking food and water. She was one of two women who had been traveling with a large group of migrants. At a certain point in her journey the group left her friend behind. One of the *coyotes* went back for her and instead dragged her out in the desert and repeatedly raped her. This woman heard the screams of her friend, and then heard nothing. When the *coyote* came back, he raped her as well. The group kept walking, and as soon as the woman had an opportunity to leave she ran away. She arrived at the ranch and asked for help and told the story. The woman and the rancher went out to look for the woman's friend, who had been left in the desert, but they never found her. The assaults were not reported to the police, nor did the woman receive medical attention, as she just wanted to continue on her journey.

The second situation occurs when *bajadores* attack the group. Sometimes the group is taken as a whole, while other times, the bandits rob the migrants and then sexually assault the women and girls. In a situation such as this, being with family members is of little help: "whether you have two or ten relatives there is nothing you can do to overcome the bandits with weapons." The bandits are always armed, and their attacks tend to be much more violent. They will often wear ski masks and carry automatic weapons.

A law enforcement official described a case involving Central American migrants that happened near the border, most likely on the Mexican side. The group was walking in the early evening hours when a group of *bajadores* approached. They put a knife to the throat of one woman and said if she resisted they would kill her. After sexually assaulting her, the *bajadores* robbed her and other members of the group. When the group was later detained by the Border Patrol, one of the men reported that they heard screaming but could not do anything because they were being held captive.

To add to the atmosphere of intimidation, the perpetrators will often leave evidence of the sexual assaults in the form of what are generally known as "rape trees." These trees are found at various points along migrant trails and contain the underwear of girls and women who have been sexually assaulted. These trees are distressingly common. Indeed, one author of this essay has seen a number of such trees along migrant trails throughout the border region. On one tree the author came across, a pair of underwear that must have belonged to a preteen girl was left hanging. Several interviewees conjectured that the rape trees are a kind of trophy—a disquieting form of counting or a way to intimidate future migrants, to instill terror.

There have been several highly publicized cases of U.S. Border Patrol agents sexually assaulting girls and women along the border (see Falcón 2007 for an in-depth discussion of cases from the late 1980s and early 1990s), but we found little evidence of this, at least in a widespread fashion.[6] Border Patrol agents now mostly conduct patrols in teams, with backup units almost always nearby. There also seems to be a greater level of scrutiny about these issues. We did hear stories from several interviewees of Border Patrol agents using excessive force and humiliation during the apprehension of migrants. This included kicking, pulling, pushing, yelling, and using racial or ethnic epithets. We were told about one shocking case of a migrant girl who was forced by Border Patrol agents to strip naked and do push-ups. The migrant aid workers and others who closely monitor the actions of the Border Patrol expressed dismay that even when these incidents were reported, very little was ever done to investigate. One consul told the story of a woman who, along with the rest of her group, tried to flee from the Border Patrol. When she was caught, "I guess [they] let out their aggressions, and beat her up really badly, they [the consul's office] wanted to file charges but the woman didn't want to, she wanted to just go back, she was like 'just let me out of here.'"

Drop Houses in Phoenix and Tucson

If the migrants make it through the gauntlet of the border, including law enforcement officials, bruising terrain, and the *coyotes* and *bajadores*, they are usually picked up along roadsides at night and taken by trucks, vans, or cars to either Tucson or Phoenix. Tucson is something of a temporary way station, while the vast Phoenix metropolitan area is the main distribution point of migrants to elsewhere in the United States, as well as a stopping point for many of the migrants. Migrants are often kept in drop houses before continuing on their journeys (Simmons, Menjívar, and Téllez, Forthcoming). Many of these houses are gathering places where migrants are reunited with their families or friends.

However, as the cartels and other organized crime groups have become more involved in the lucrative business of migration it has become more militarized and corporatized, with the drop houses increasingly becoming places of involuntary detention where, in some cases, migrants are kept in (near) slave-like conditions. It appears from our data that, in general, the drop houses in Phoenix are much more violent than those in Tucson.

In Tucson, there are two major types of drop houses. The first are smaller in scale and usually run by friends or family members of the migrants. These are places for the migrants to rest and be nourished, and to wash up before continuing on their journey. The second are more systematized and run by criminal syndicates. These houses are much more secure, often with plywood screwed to the windows from the inside and doors that lock from the outside. The accommodations are sparse, and weapons are ever present. Frequently, migrants are kept in these houses against their will and are allowed to leave only once family members or friends pay an "extra fee" or ransom. Rarely, however, are migrants, even in these organized drop houses, kept for more than a night or two in Tucson. Therefore, there were only a few reports of sexual assaults in the drop houses in Tucson.

The second type of drop house is much more prevalent in Phoenix, and the number of sexual assaults is greater. It was widely reported that Phoenix became one of the world's leading cities for kidnapping (ABC News 2009), but the numbers have recently declined with the reduction in overall undocumented migration. The overwhelming majority of these incidents stem from migrants being held against their will in drop houses or attacks on drop houses by other gangs or cartels where migrants are kidnapped and taken to yet another drop house. At the peak of drop house activity, from about 2007 to 2010, ICE officials raided approximately 160 to 200 drop houses per year, with somewhere between 20 and 60 of these involving hostage situations, including a house in the affluent suburb of Scottsdale that held close to two hundred migrants.

The drop houses associated with criminal syndicates are truly a state of exception, where the smugglers have near-complete control, and the migrants have little recourse to the authorities or legal remedies. The violence reported at these drop houses is staggering, described by one law enforcement official as follows: "murder, pistol whipping, electrocution with lamp cord wires, they will put plastic bags over their heads, shooting over someone's head, shooting someone, a lot of verbal abuse, rape/sexual assault, gun to the head." One agent described what she labeled "sexual torture," including sexual assault using inanimate objects and rapes of migrant men. We also heard stories of migrant men forced to rape migrant women or perform oral sex on other migrant men. Many women were raped repeatedly, day after day, by the smugglers and any associates of the smugglers who came to the house. A law enforcement official reported the story of a girl who was kept in a hotel room and raped three times a day for a full week by the smugglers. She eventually escaped through the bathroom window to seek help. "The police went to the hotel and found 60 to 70 people."

The sexual assaults are part of the total control exercised by smugglers over the migrants. One law enforcement officer said, "Sometimes the smugglers will take a migrant in the closet and others in the house can hear them crying out and the other migrants in the house know what is coming. So it sends a message to the group." The men and women are often kept in separate rooms, with the smugglers choosing women to be assaulted in a special room set aside for that purpose.

> They pick and choose, ok, I want you today, or I want you next, I want you tomorrow. . . . And she said if I didn't do it . . . they *will* make you do it. You know they grab you and they throw you into a room and you cannot leave . . . they keep threatening you that if you don't do what they say, they *are* going to kill your family, I know where your family lives . . . so on and so on . . . so she said it's because of that reason she couldn't fight too hard. She tried to push him away, she tried to say no . . . but neither of those worked (emphases original).

The smugglers generally see the migrants as mere commodities, so they do what they can with them as they please, as long as it does not damage the value of the commodity. "The young girls, sometimes they want to keep their virginity intact so they violated her orally because they thought they could get more money for her as a virgin." Other women after being raped are told how to "clean up" to erase any incriminating evidence before they are released. In a sadly ironic nod to traditional gender roles, many of the women, in addition to being exploited sexually, are required to cook and clean and take care of the smugglers while held captive in the house.

The length of time migrants remain in the drop houses depends on how long it takes for their family members to come forward with additional payment. While waiting for the family members, "it is an opportunity for them for [smugglers] to sexual assault/rape the women." We even heard stories of the smugglers being "on their phone with the relatives in some cases while they are raping the woman . . . it is a power thing, they are not really nice people."

Several law enforcement officials expressed dismay that drop houses exist (and indeed, thrive as grotesque examples of entrepreneurship), in part because of the acquiescence of homeowners who have rented their houses to smugglers or the failure of neighbors to report them. One said, "the people in the neighborhood need to know these people are being victimized. It really is their responsibility." The prevalence of drop houses in Phoenix seems to have been reduced after the antimigrant fervor there, including the controversial migrant sweeps by Maricopa County Sheriff Arpaio. But several agents were clear that this just meant the crimes were increasingly being taken to other areas, such as New Mexico and Texas, or the demand for ransom from family members was taking place earlier in the journey, such as in Mexico.

Beyond the Drop Houses

The sexual violence these women and children face does not end when they are united with their family and friends. Several previous studies have shown that rates of intimate partner violence are much higher among immigrant women than U.S.-born women (e.g., Bauer et al. 2000), and our interviewees reported many similar incidents. Furthermore, the abuse migrants suffer from their family and friends is exacerbated by the lawlessness that they experience. Their undocumented status and distrust of law enforcement increase their vulnerability. One social worker in Phoenix said, "I have a case with a woman raped quite often by her husband (they have children together), they have established residence here. And he is using the whole situation . . . . you better not report me because I will have INS ship you back to Mexico and I'll keep the children. She doesn't want to pursue the case in such situations." Similar statements were told to us about women forced to work as prostitutes. Some migrants are told that if they do not cooperate or if they report the assaults, they will be returned to the desert to let the Border Patrol take care of them, or if they are in Maricopa County, they will be turned over to the notorious Sheriff Arpaio. Also, we heard a few stories about sexual abuse in places of work.

The women know that if they report any abuse, they risk undermining everything they did and endured in order to get to the United States. They might not be able to work anymore, they might be removed from the United States, and they might be separated from their children.

Accountability and Impunity

The sexual violence in the borderlands is a form of terror that we believe could meet the international standards of a crime against humanity; that is, widespread and systematic attacks against a civilian population with the acquiescence of governmental authorities (Falcón 2007). At minimum, the experiences of many women and children migrants would meet the international and national definitions of human trafficking. The 2000 Trafficking Protocol establishes the international legal definition of trafficking as

> the recruitment, transportation, transfer, harboring or receipt of persons, by means of the threat or use of force or other forms of coercion, of abduction, of fraud, of deception, of the abuse of power or of a position of vulnerability or of the giving or receiving of payments or benefits to achieve the consent of a person having control over another person, for the purpose of exploitation.

At a minimum, the violence they endure is a violation of local, state, and federal laws in both Mexico and the United States.

There are numerous challenges to pursuing any form of accountability for these crimes. Here we will discuss two that stood out in our interviews: underreporting and the physical, emotional, and social effects of multiple victimizations.

Reporting and Prosecution

The crimes in the borderlands are almost always done with impunity, in part because of the geographic and jurisdictional vastness of the crime scene, with migrants often not even sure in which country they were assaulted. They may be severely disoriented by the perils already encountered along the journey, including the confusing landscape, exhaustion, thirst, and hunger. There were also several reports of *coyotes* forcing migrants to take drugs, supposedly to provide them with energy but which often are similar to Rohypnol or other "date rape" drugs that cause significant disorientation. Furthermore, law enforcement officials rarely find out about these crimes, as the victims and any potential witnesses are distrustful and fearful of being removed from the country. When law enforcement officials are informed, it may often be several days after the incident, and there will be precious few leads for investigators to follow. As one officer summarized, "I have never had anyone recognize someone in the desert. The women are exhausted, tired,

disoriented and they don't know where they are. There is no frame of reference."
Also, there is little incentive for officials to pursue these crimes, as their operational priorities are with large-scale traffickers of drugs, money, and guns—
those at the top of the criminal syndicate hierarchy. "Common" migrants
who are apprehended are to be processed as quickly as possible, and removed
from the United States.

Furthermore, despite the horrendous nature of their crimes, very few
smugglers are prosecuted for more than minor smuggling charges. Many
cases described to us have clear connections to prostitution and would meet
the legal definition of human trafficking, yet very rarely are these cases seen
by law enforcement as trafficking in persons. One law enforcement official
reported that he had never seen a case of trafficking, even though he had
been part of several raids on drop houses. Even law enforcement agents with
training regarding human trafficking did not see these cases as meeting the
legal criteria. The victims are usually dehumanized and seen as 'illegal' to be
processed quickly and removed from the country. The victims and the numerous witnesses are also very reluctant to confide in U.S. law enforcement
officials. As one official said, even when "we get a report from a male that a
female in the house was being raped/sexually assaulted . . . the female will
never admit it." Agents even described something akin to what psychologists
have termed "Stockholm syndrome," in which the women fall in love with
the smugglers, or at least get closer to them for their protection. If a woman
is released by the smugglers and reunited with her family, she will rarely tell
anyone what happened, including members of her own family.

Indeed, what became clear from our interviews was that an individual
single migrant's legal status is quite fluid over time. Often they begin as migrants hiring smugglers to guide them to the United States. The journey can
last from less than a week to many months, with numerous stops along the
way. At some point on the journey, many of the migrants will experience the
"threat or use of force or other forms of coercion . . . for the purpose of exploitation" and thus would meet the international legal definition of trafficking
outlined above. It is not unusual for a migrant to be smuggled at the beginning of the journey, be held against her will at some point during the journey,
and then be released to become a migrant again (Ugarte, Zarate, and Farley
2003: 149). She then might hire another guide or smuggler, and then again
experience trafficking or even kidnapping. Since the migrants often do not
know how much freedom they have to leave their guides at any given point

in time, and the forms of coercion can be subtle, they might not know that they are being trafficked.

The Effects of Multiple Victimizations

And that's the challenge of working with girls who have, have gone through—there's, just there's *so much there*, because it's not just . . . the, the trafficking, there's so much more that started very, very early; abandonment by mothers, I mean, at very, very young ages, babies, toddlers, abandoned by moms, being bounced around from home to home, incurring abuse and physical abuse in all those homes, neglect, it's tough, it's *tough*. And so . . . you get all of that and then this happens . . . it's just, it's just a *lot* of . . . trauma. (Phoenix social worker)

Though we did not talk with the women directly, we did get a sense of how they experience sexual trauma and how this fits in a chain of victimizations they have suffered. Incidents that would make sensationalistic media headlines about sexual predators or serial rapists on the loose if the victims were white, not people of color and not immigrants, do not seem to be, at least on the surface, defining or "life-changing" events for these women. The assaults seem to be perceived as part of a larger condition of violence that these women face and endure over extended periods of time. As part of their condition, and often as part of a long-term calculus, the women do not come forward or complain about sexual assault, because it is "the least of their problems." Instead, they often find ways to cope with it in isolation when they can find the time. One interviewee said their attitudes often are "I will deal with it, I just need a job," and that "it is not a priority to report the assault or to get therapy—the priority is to get a job and their kids." The assaults can be seen as part of a well-calculated decision made intentionally, with varying levels of knowledge of the risks involved, to make the journey in the first place.

Previous studies show that when Mexican women migrate it is often after much discussion within the family and sometimes even against the wishes of their husbands (King 2007: 900). They also take steps to prepare themselves for possible risks. Some are aware of the risks from previous trips of their own, from stories from family members and friends, or from warnings in the mass media. Often indigenous migrants will shed their traditional clothing in order to better "pass" as nonindigenous. Those from Central America often know to tell law enforcement officials if they are apprehended that they are from Mexico, so that they will be deported only across the line, where they can attempt the journey again.

Knowing that sexual assault is a very real possibility, women and girls take steps to prevent assault or to ameliorate the possible consequences. For example, they sometimes take birth control pills before leaving on the journey in case they are sexually assaulted. We even heard a story about nuns at a Catholic mission in Mexico requesting birth control pills from a humanitarian mission so they could dispense them to the girls and women making the journey. Many also wear several pairs of pants and underwear to help thwart assaults. Some migrants deprive themselves of sleep or do other things to make themselves less attractive to ward off sexual assaults. The girls or women often try to pair up with other migrants to be safer. Some interviewees said that migrant women might not know about the specific risks of sexual assaults but take these preventative measures out of a general distrust of males.

Physical, Emotional, and Social Effects of Multiple Victimizations

Of course, intentional decision making about migration does not mean that migrant women and children are not affected in profound ways—physically, emotionally, and socially—by the sexual assaults. The effects are extremely varied, but it is clear that the assaults have a major impact on their lives. One social worker said: "I know they don't talk about it. . . . They completely keep it to themselves . . . they put it away; they compartmentalize it, depending on how horrific the trauma was. In general, the trauma is huge. When they talk about it they talk about it as though it just happened yesterday. The trauma is horrific and huge in their lives."

The physical effects of the sexual assaults are diverse. In the immediate aftermath of an assault, many women must seek care in hospitals for cuts, bruises, broken bones, and other physical traumas. Even so, the women's physical well-being often is not their top priority. One woman who had been assaulted by a *coyote* in the desert was described as bleeding, "having head-aches, and aching all over." When asked if her boyfriend knew what happened, she replied: "he knows that I'm not well and I fell and I have cactus thorns everywhere, but I didn't tell him about the assault." In addition to the immediate physical effects, repeated sexual violence has been shown in numerous studies to have profound long-term physical effects.

One of the major physical (and emotional and social) challenges the women and girls face is unwanted pregnancy. Rarely will the migrants be using birth control, and the women and girls who become pregnant from attacks by *coyotes*, *bajadores*, or others will rarely seek or have an abortion because of family traditions and religious values. Furthermore, the Catholic Church, through such important programs as Catholic Charities and the Kino Border Initiative in Nogales, is at the forefront of providing aid to these women, so they will often not be counseled about abortion. Most of the girls and women give birth, and most do not consider adoption. "The feelings they have toward their child are kind of mixed in with how they feel about the perpetrator," making it "very difficult to accept that baby." One social worker described a girl who basically has only minimal connection to her child: "she feeds the baby, she diapers the baby, she puts the baby to bed, and that's about it. I mean, there's no mommy and baby time; that play time, sponta-neous play." In addition, despite some counseling services, the women and girls lack basic parenting skills, the effects of which are often exacerbated by the lack of good parental role models. As several interviewees pointed out, the youth who have babies are still trying to grow up themselves: "she's 16; she wants to go out, she wants to go to the movies, she wants to go to prom . . . and she has a two year old."

Not surprisingly, many migrant women and children suffer emotionally and psychologically as well, suffering from depression, post-traumatic stress disorder, and low self-esteem (cf. Annan 2006: 168). Many of the girls are reported to have nightmares and sleep disorders, and they commonly dis-sociate. Some women and girls internalize their experience, with the case-workers reporting no overt physical manifestations: "I mean some girls will tell me about it, and they're very emotionless about it and then other girls will look through streams of tears coming down their face, and tell me about all the abuse they had at home, and they were raped, by a *coyote* here and there. . . . I'm sure they're all really traumatized, but some of them show it more than others."

Women and children who have suffered trauma from multiple victimizations also suffer socially. Not surprisingly, they experience a general level of distrust, especially of men and authority figures, as well as having numerous problems communicating in healthy ways. They have few models of healthy family relationships; instead they have witnessed "constant violence," as one social worker reported. "Not only do they see it with their parents, it was all over the village, it was all over the neighborhood, so this is common. So I have a lot of girls that just don't understand how it can be any different."

They have trouble developing healthy relationship with their peers, especially romantic relationships. One interviewee who works with unaccompanied youth said, "we struggle with boundaries, they have very poor boundaries, and we have a lot of problems in the relationships—in the romantic relationships." This same lack of boundaries finds the girls and women befriending strangers with little ability to discern healthy influences. "Some of our girls just try to find some guy, and they attach—and many times it's not the best person for them. It's someone that's—is abusive, is alcoholic, is a substance abuser. They feel like that's the only way to, you know, make it. It's sad." Many of them "don't think that a husband can be faithful or a boyfriend can be faithful."

The children who are fighting for asylum or another type of immigration relief are placed in foster homes and must be enrolled in U.S. public schools, where they face a number of additional challenges. The violence they have endured surely aggravates what must be a difficult transition experience for children from rural Mexico or Central America living with new families and taking a bus to attend a public school that is taught solely in English. Many lack motivation or have only basic learning skills. Some are physically aggressive in school. Many of the boys are targeted by gangs, often as potential recruits, and they are threatened if they spurn the gangs' advances. Many of the boys and girls have a drug and alcohol history that might go back to their days in their village or that began on the migration journey. Then, in order to cope and fit in in an American school they might resort to alcohol and drugs again.

Given all these effects of sexual abuse, exacerbated by attempting to transition into a foreign culture, the social workers had precious few success stories to relate. Even the small victories were mixed at best. As one social worker said, "You know, there's this thought that . . . once they're here and we give them all these tools and all these services that they're just going to *flourish*, well, that doesn't happen." One counselor reported, "What I tend to see in my work, is they'll make one or two steps forward and I'll think 'Okay, here we go,' and then boom! We're ten steps back."

Conclusion: Obstacles to Assisting Migrants, and Their Resilience

We do not know how many migrants experience sexual violence, but we do know that immigration policies in the United States and Mexico, along with systematic structural violence, leave them vulnerable in their home lives, throughout the journey, and beyond. We can confidently assume that thousands of migrants experience sexual violence each year. This is a massive human rights abuse that is almost completely unknown and done almost completely with impunity.

These multiple victimizations stem from multiple vulnerabilities, and the same structural violence mediates how these women experience the sexual violence and the provision of services for them. Previous studies (cf. Decker, Raj, and Silverman 2007) have shown that immigrant women and girls, in general, require distinct social services to deal with sexual violence, but those previous studies did not consider the sexual violence that migrants face on their journey to the United States. The women and children we discussed above are much more vulnerable because of their documentation status, possible continued relationships with their abusers, and language barriers. Furthermore, services and agencies that might be able to assist them must work around nativist policies (such as Proposition 200, passed in Arizona in 2004, which requires proof of citizenship to receive public services) and the various policies that allow state and local officials to check the immigration status of suspected undocumented immigrants. In addition, the enormous number of migrants, especially those who have been abused, overwhelms the system.

Even the legal remedies that have been established by federal law to assist immigrants that are victims of violence are infrequently used. The women and children described above are most likely eligible for relief from deportation in the form of U-Visas for victims of violence against women, T-Visas for victims of trafficking, or SIJS relief for those who show Special Immigrant Juvenile Status. Rarely are these pursued. First, there is a general lack of awareness of these options among the migrants and those who work with them. Law enforcement officials do not inform the migrants of these opportunities, and the officials often balk at filing the necessary certification. To be eligible for a U-Visa or T-Visa, the victims must be willing to testify against their attacker(s), and law enforcement officials must certify that they remain cooperative. Several of those interviewed expressed exasperation with law enforcement officials for refusing to certify: "We do have a client right now that we're seeking a visa for because she was raped in the drop house, and we're having trouble because in Phoenix right now the judges, the prosecutors, basically nobody will sign the visa. Even if somebody can testify and help them, but nobody will help. No one will sign the visas, and they face deportation after their testimony." More generally, law enforcement agents, including those of the Border Patrol and ICE, evince a lack of training and sensitivity on issues of sexual violence against migrant women and children. It is not their operational priority, but this is aggravated by the dearth of female agents and agents who speak Spanish. Also, the government has privatized the transportation and detainment of migrants, and private companies, such as Wackenhut, are not well prepared to work with or transport migrants.

Several other issues remain to be addressed, including how these women and children cope with multiple victimizations through private means and grassroots channels. We also intend to expand on our legal argument that this type of sexual violence meets the international definition of trafficking in persons and is widespread and systematic enough to meet the international definition of a crime against humanity.

Again, we want to reiterate that we do not know the exact number of migrant women and children (and men) who are sexually assaulted. We are also somewhat uncomfortable with the language of victimization, even though we have used it here. Many thousands of migrants make the journey without incident. Those who are sexually assaulted may be deeply traumatized, but the incident rarely defines their lives in their minds, and we are acutely aware that we should not define them merely as victims of sexual assault. They are, above all, survivors. They are navigating a very difficult transition to a new country and new culture while dealing with severe trauma, and yet to the degree possible they remain focused on their families and improving their economic situations.

We came across a number of migrant women who have created support groups for victims of sexual violence. These group sessions are often coordinated by counselors or social workers, almost all of whom are doing so on their own time, and some of whom have only tangential training in this area. They see a need and move to fill it. One described herself this way: "I am creating ideas for the needs that I saw first with my family and for the needs that I am seeing in this society, in this community."

Clearly, the immigration system is broken, and the consequences of this failure are not abstract. They are concrete, embodied in the daily lives of migrant women and children. The failure of immigration policies, alongside extant structural inequalities that disadvantage women and children, directly leads to their exploitation. Further enforcement strategies by themselves will not stem the tide of migration but lead to increased militarization, further control by organized criminal syndicates, and vulnerable migrants, especially women and girls, being treated like commodities. Failure to change immigration policies, or changing them in ways that are injurious to immigrants themselves, will expand the state of exception—paradoxically, the more law, the more lawlessness. And, in the perception of law enforcement officials and the public, migrant men, women, and children will be seen first and foremost as lawbreakers and not as the human beings they are.

CHAPTER 3

Immigration Enforcement at the U.S.-Mexico Border: Where Human Rights and National Sovereignty Collide

Timothy J. Dunn

In recent years there has been a tremendous expansion of U.S. immigration enforcement activities in the U.S.-Mexico border region, most notably by the U.S. Border Patrol, with the growing involvement of the military. This has been spurred by the strong anti-immigrant political sentiment in the United States directed largely at Hispanic (or Latino) immigrants and unauthorized immigration. The heightened border enforcement has resulted in hundreds of deaths of border crossers each year, more than 6,600 bodies recovered from 1994 to 2012, a doubling of the death rate from approximately two hundred to four hundred per year, and a sevenfold increase in the death rate for Border Patrol apprehensions (U.S. GAO 2006: 16; Cornelius 2006: 5–6; Dunn 2009: 2; Jimenez 2009; Rosenblum 2012: 30; Isacson and Meyer 2012: 40; Anderson 2013: 1, 3). The American Public Health Association in 2009 designated these mounting border crossing deaths as a "public health crisis" and stated that the "Border Patrol should comply with international standards of health and human rights by adopting policies and strategies that do not endanger the lives and health of migrants" (APHA 2009). In addition, there have long been less severe, but more direct rights abuses such as denial of due process, beatings, inhuman detention conditions, verbal and psychological abuse, and so on by U.S. authorities along the U.S.-Mexico border in the name of immigration and border enforcement (e.g., see Human Rights Watch 1995; U.S. Commission on Civil Rights 1997; Amnesty International 1998; American Friends Service Committee 1998). However, it is important to point out that migrant rights abuses by Mexican authorities are much worse overall (see, e.g., Amnesty International 2010).

This tragic situation can be seen as a clash between citizenship and national sovereignty on the one hand and human rights on the other. The upholding and reinforcing of borders, as well as determining whom and what to let enter, is a fundamental element of the sovereignty of any nation (Agamben 1995: 19), while the safety, well-being, and human dignity of all people, regardless of national origin, are an essential part of human rights listed in the 1948 Universal Declaration of Human Rights. In other words, in the citizenship/national sovereignty framework, rights are granted to, or won by, citizens of the nation-state, which is assumed to have full sovereign control over the nation, including determining who is a member and who is allowed to enter the nation; rights are essentially conditional on following duties and state mandates. The human rights perspective, in contrast, assumes that all people have rights because they are human beings, and that those rights are transnational, not determined by any nation-state, or one's national origin, citizenship, or immigration status; rights are unconditional, existing beyond any state's control, while duties are secondary.

This chapter first provides an overview of U.S. immigration enforcement efforts in the U.S.-Mexico border region over the past two decades and some key human rights consequences of these enforcement efforts as they relate to the protection of immigrants from Mexico to the United States. I use this example to clarify and contrast the uses of the citizenship/national sovereignty and human rights frameworks. The data are drawn from my own extensive interviews and fieldwork in the El Paso, Texas, and southern New Mexico area (see Dunn 2009), as well as from government documents, news media, and human rights reports. In the conclusion I propose some new ideas about national sovereignty based on this case study of immigration enforcement and human rights.

Competing Rights Frameworks: Citizenship and National Sovereignty Versus Human Rights

Before proceeding to the data, a fuller elaboration of the national sovereignty and human rights frameworks is in order, particularly as they relate to immigration. National sovereignty in the modern era is fundamentally based on the relationship between nation-state and citizen—the prototype being the French Declaration of the Rights of Man and of the Citizen, which declares that all sovereignty rests with the state (Agamben 1995: 127–28; 2000: 21). Consequently noncitizens, notably refugees and immigrants who will not or are not allowed to become citizens, pose a threat to national sovereignty (1995: 131). Therefore, the rights of immigrants are suspect at best in this framework, and many are typically excluded because of their lack of citizenship status. Thus, denationalized persons are stripped of their rights and can be "legally" subjected to great persecution (2000: 22).

A further threat to traditional citizenship and national sovereignty is the emergence of what Sassen (2006: 305–9, 413–14; 2007) terms "denationalized citizenship"—the delinking of citizenship and rights from nation-states, even if within national institutional settings in cases where a government recognizes that certain basic rights are not exclusive to formal, native-born citizens. She sees this especially in the growth of human rights discourse, the granting of rights by states for undocumented immigrants, as well as dual nationality and EU citizenship. She claims that these trends and practices "explode the boundaries of citizenship" (2006: 307) and for some mark a "devaluation of citizenship" (306), though she allows that this denationalization of citizenship remains thus far incipient and partial. However, she sees the denationalization of citizenship as an inexorable trend and argues that the current anti-immigrant backlash of "renationalizing of membership politics" of citizenship and rights in many developed nations is a just "a last gasp" of a dying system (414). A host of other scholars have proposed that immigrants, especially unauthorized ones, are a threat to national borders, national sovereignty, and citizenship (e.g., Soysal 1994; Jacobson 1996; Castles and Davidson 2000; Huntington 2004; Somers 2008). Regardless of the political sentiments of the scholars, this view fits quite well with the anti-immigrant sentiment that seems to be a constant feature of the U.S. political scene (and that of many other advanced nations) over the past three or four decades.

This preoccupation with national sovereignty (and citizenship), and the near sacred status accorded to borders is highly selective, however, and applied mainly to immigration (e.g., Koulish 2010). In contrast, cross-border movements of goods and capital by transnational corporations are ever more free and unfettered, as governments have willingly dealt away national sovereignty in international trade agreements such as the North American and Central American Free Trade Agreements, and to global trade organizations such as the World Trade Organization. Indeed Sassen (2006: 417; 2007), among many others, notes that transnational corporations are detached from geographic borders and nation-state authority and are granted new international protections, far more than is the case for people, either citizens or immigrants. For example, the international human rights regime is far weaker than the provisions of the World Trade Organization, as the latter are highly enforceable and regularly applied in specific cases, while human rights have no such global enforcement body and are rarely enforced (though many nation-states voluntarily abide by them at least selectively). Yet such global free movement of capital and goods has a much more profound impact, and by no means always positive, on those countries and their citizens. In developing countries, the economic downsides of globalization are key factors in creating the "push conditions" that spur international migration (Sassen 1998, 2007). For example, in Mexico in the two decades after NAFTA began in 1994, two million peasants lost their land, wages stagnated or fell for industrial workers, and the country experienced very weak job and overall economic growth (Faux 2006; Zepeda, Wise, and Gallagher 2009). Yet this decline of sovereignty in economic matters is taken as a near given in the era of globalization (Sassen 1996, 2006, 2007). Thus we are in a borderless world for multinational corporations and the movement of commodities and capital, but a heavily reinforced-border world for the movement of ordinary people.[1] Unauthorized international migration by Mexican peasants and members of the working class can be seen as resistance to the vagaries of international capital and globalization (Rodríguez 1996), and heightened U.S. border enforcement against them a part of a "global apartheid" system of racialized labor control and subordination (Nevins 2008, 2010; Spener 2009).

The international human rights perspective (especially in my field of sociology) is less developed, especially in relation to immigration, than are frameworks on national sovereignty and citizenship. And even those who use human rights as central concepts often reframe them in terms of some variant of citizenship—denationalized (Sassen 2006) or global (Cabrera 2010. The most prominent U.S. sociological writer explicitly addressing human rights, Judith Blau (Blau and Moncada 2005, 2006, 2007, 2009; Blau and Frezzo 2012), bases her approach on a rather face-value reading of the list of rights in the main UN human rights treaties. However, some sociologists take a more conceptual perspective, such as Turner (1993: 178; 2009: 187–88), who proposes that human rights are an especially important basis to challenge abuses of power by nation-states. Sjoberg et al. (2001: 25) define human rights more broadly as "claims made by persons in diverse social and cultural systems upon 'organized power relationships' in order to advance the dignity of (or, more concretely, equal respect and concern for) human beings." While acknowledging that enforcement is infrequent and generally lacking, Sjoberg (2009; Sjoberg, Gill, and Williams 2001) maintains that human rights constitute an important, independent standard by which to at least evaluate and hold morally accountable powerful complex organizations/bureaucracies (both governmental and corporate) that undermine human dignity. Nonetheless, Sjoberg (1996: 285–89; 1999: 55–56) also proposes that powerful bureaucracies tend to undermine the human rights of the "truly disadvantaged" (or most subordinated groups) through a process of "social triage," in which consideration of their well-being is "sacrificed" (written off or even repressed), because meeting their needs would be "inefficient" for the powerful. In this light we might view the dignity and well-being of unauthorized immigrants as being sacrificed for the enhancement of national sovereignty, citizenship, and powerful organizations. Bustamante (2002: 345–46) goes farther and maintains that when nation-states refuse to grant at least basic, minimal human rights to unauthorized immigrants, they grant impunity to those who would abuse this vulnerable group.

As noted previously, however, Sassen and others hold that the international human rights discourse is a vital element in the overall trend toward increasing rights for noncitizens, even for unauthorized immigrants, in highly developed nations. This more optimistic view is debatable for the United States in recent years, and it is almost entirely missing in immigration enforcement on the U.S.-Mexico border since the early 1990s. Here, the critical views of bureaucratic power and nation-state power as undermining the human rights of unauthorized immigrants are more applicable.

Overview of Border Immigration Enforcement

Since 1994, official U.S. policy along the U.S.-Mexico border has been to promote "prevention through deterrence," in which the U.S. Border Patrol has sought to deter unauthorized border crossing/immigration through highly visible deployments of enforcement resources in or near key urban areas on the border where the vast majority of such crossings had long taken place (U.S. Office of Border Patrol 1994: 7, 8–12; 2004; Dunn 2009: 1–2). This strategy was pioneered in the El Paso, Texas, Border Patrol sector in September 1993, and subsequently became the border-wide strategy.[2] It had the predictable effect of diverting would-be unauthorized immigrant border crossers from urban areas to remote, less fortified desert and mountainous portions of the border that are rife with other dangers, such as extremely high temperatures. Immigration officials initially expected the harsh natural environment of the desert and mountains to deter unauthorized crossers, but in 2000 the head of the U.S. Immigration Naturalization Service, which oversaw the Border Patrol, admitted the strategy had failed in that regard (INS 2000). Border Patrol apprehensions/arrests along the border remained very high, typically above 1 million per year, until 2007 and the beginning of the economic recession (Nuñez-Neto 2008: 14; Rosenblum 2012: 20), although there was a spatial shift away from urban areas to rural zones, especially in Arizona (Nuñez-Neto 2008: 16, 17). Nonetheless, the strategy has remained in place and has expanded significantly since 1994, while deaths of unauthorized border crossers have risen sharply.

This border enforcement escalation is reflected in the enormous increase in resources devoted to the U.S. Border Patrol since the mid-1990s. From 1993 to 2012 Border Patrol funding jumped 873 percent (to $3.5 billion per year) and staffing 431 percent (to 21,394 agents, with 87 percent posted along the U.S.-Mexico border) (Nuñez-Neto 2008: 6, 13, 35; Dunn 2009: 205–6; U.S. Department of Homeland Security 2013a, b). A number of other types of enforcement have been put into place along the U.S.-Mexico border. One of the most visible is the construction of over 900 miles of new fencing or walls along the 1,900-mile border—a combination of lower fencing to prevent vehicle crossing and two layers of pedestrian fencing/wall (over 3 meters high) to keep people out—nearly all built since the passage of the "Secure Fence Act" in 2006 (U.S. Customs and Border Protection 2009; Nuñez-Neto and Garcia 2007; Dunn 2009: 222–23). This new "Berlin wall" was constructed mainly to prevent unauthorized immigration; it appears to be the longest modern border barrier in the world. In addition to the new physical barriers, the U.S. DHS has also tried in vain since 2006 to create an $8 billion "virtual fence," termed SBInet (Secure Border Initiative network, contract with the Boeing Corporation), of pervasive electronic surveillance along the U.S.-Mexico border. However, there appears to be no technological solution to reinforcing national sovereignty at the border, as the "virtual fence" has been a failure beyond two small (each approximately 30 miles long), poorly functioning pilot projects (U.S. GAO 2009), and DHS halted the project indefinitely in March 2010 after spending $1.1 billion (Hsu 2010b; Archibold 2010a).

A more drastic escalation of border enforcement, and thus by definition an upholding of national sovereignty, has been the expanded, more overt militarization of the border for immigration enforcement purposes in recent years (for background, see Dunn 1996, 2001) despite the fact that unauthorized immigrants pose little to no physical threat to the country. From mid-2006 through mid-2008, the Bush administration sent 6,000 National Guard troops to the U.S.-Mexico border to assist the Border Patrol, expressly for immigration enforcement purposes at a time when the issue was growing in political prominence. The Obama administration resumed this mobilization on a smaller scale in summer 2010, with some 1,200 National Guard troops deployed through early 2012 (Isacson and Meyer 2012: 25–26). Their main activities were to provide help with border surveillance (ground and aerial) as well as support roles behind the scenes, such as maintenance and intelligence analysis. They were prevented from making arrests, searches, or seizures (Dunn 2009: 218–19, 225–27; McConahay 2006). This was the largest deployment of military troops on the border by the United States since the Mexican Revolution ninety years earlier, and resonated with the growing anti-immigration sentiment nationally, especially against unauthorized immigrants. In addition to National Guard troops, since 2004 active duty and reserve unit U.S. military troops have been used on a smaller scale periodically to explicitly assist the Border Patrol in immigration enforcement, again often conducting surveillance missions with high-tech military gear, and on several occasions even using tank-like Stryker armored personnel carriers (Dunn 2009: 180–81), including a February 2012 large-scale deployment in New Mexico and Arizona for the Border Patrol (Isacson and Meyer 2012: 24–25). This has been coordinated by Joint Task Force—North based at the U.S. army base Fort Bliss in El Paso, Texas, begun in 1989 as JTF-6 with an anti-drug mission and subsequently expanded in 2004 to the interdiction of "*suspected transnational threats*" consisting of "*international terrorism, narcotrafficking, [and] alien smuggling*," as well as to "disrupt transnational criminal organizations" (U.S. Northern Command, n.d., emphasis added).

In addition, armed vigilante "volunteer militia" groups have emerged along the border since 2005, mainly in Arizona, expressly to uphold U.S. national sovereignty against unauthorized immigrants by monitoring the border, reporting observed unauthorized border crossers to the Border Patrol, and sometimes even making "citizen's arrests" (see Doty 2009; Cabrera 2010). Much of this military and vigilante militia activity has been motivated by heightened "national security" concerns in the post-September 11 world of antiterrorism (see Barry 2011).

The Unintended Consequences of Increased Border Enforcement

While national sovereignty concerns loom large in border enforcement efforts, results in limiting unauthorized immigration have been mixed at best, yet border crossing deaths have mushroomed into a major human rights tragedy. The key question for policymakers and the public is whether this drastically increased immigration enforcement along the U.S.-Mexico border since the mid-1990s has lowered unauthorized immigration. The short answer is that it appears to have had little effect in reducing unauthorized immigration—at least not until 2007, after which it is debatable. Highly regarded immigration scholars, led by Douglas Massey and Wayne Cornelius and colleagues, found in separate studies of migrant-sending communities in Mexico that the expanded border enforcement has had no effect on the likelihood that migrants would attempt to cross illegally and succeed, at least through the middle of the first decade of the new century (Massey, Durand, and Malone 2002; Massey 2005, 2007; Cornelius 2006; Cornelius and Salehyan 2007; Reyes 2004; Orrenius 2004; Fuentes et al. 2007). However, they found it had increased the costs and dangers of such a journey, and unauthorized Mexican immigrants were staying longer once they entered the United States, a shift away from traditional short-term circular migration between the two countries, effectively keeping unauthorized immigrants in rather than out (see Massey 2006). The costly services of immigrant smugglers have become more important in helping unauthorized immigrants evade the increased border enforcement to enter and remain in the United States (see Spener 2009). Thus, ironically, increased border enforcement was a key factor in the near tripling of the total undocumented immigrant population in the United States since the early 1990s to 2007, to an estimated 11–12 million people by the mid- to late part of the first decade of the twenty-first century, 60 percent from Mexico and 15 percent from Central American nations (Passel 2005; Passel and Cohn 2009). Paradoxically, increased border enforcement has had exactly the opposite of the intended effect, at least through 2007.

Nonetheless, proponents of greater border enforcement have been heartened in recent years by a significant drop in Border Patrol apprehensions, which have declined 69 percent from 2006 to 2011, to some 327,000 (Rosenblum 2012: 20–21; Nuñez-Neto 2008: 14; Rytina and Simanski 2009), and remained similarly low, at some 356,000, in 2012 (Anderson 2013: 3). This is typically presented as evidence of the success of the expanded enforcement. Independent sources also estimate a drastic slowdown in unauthorized immigration to the United States (see, e.g., Passel and Cohn 2009). However, this drop in apprehensions and immigration also coincides with the most severe economic recession and highest unemployment rates in the United States in more than three decades, all of which began in 2007 for the immigrant-worker-laden construction sector. Thus, it is unclear whether greater border enforcement or economic decline is responsible for fewer apprehensions. It is likely some of each, but we will not know how much until the economy recovers and labor demand grows again.

While the impact of sharply escalated immigration enforcement along the U.S.-Mexico border in lessening unauthorized immigration is quite debatable, the deaths of unauthorized immigrants in the region have increased notably since the mid-1990s. This heightened loss of life has become the most glaring human rights problem in U.S. border enforcement, constituting a sort of structural, (mostly) indirect form of violence. As noted above, more than 6,600 bodies were recovered from 1994 through 2011 (U.S. GAO 2006), but Cornelius (2006: 5–6) estimates that the actual number of dead may be twice the number of bodies recovered, which would mean approximately 13,000 unauthorized immigrants have died from 1994 to 2012 trying to cross the border. The U.S. General Accountability Office (2006: 16), relying largely on Border Patrol data, reports a doubling of the number of annual unauthorized border crosser deaths from 1999 to 2005, and a remarkably tragic tenfold increase (900 percent) in such deaths per year in Arizona from 1998 to 2005 (see also Rubio-Goldsmith et al. 2006), where approximately half of all such deaths have been recorded in recent years. Meanwhile, Massey (2007: 2) found a tripling of the border-crossing death rate of Mexican unauthorized immigrants from 1992 to 2002. Especially notable is that the annual number of deaths from 2006 to 2011 remained quite high, despite the 69 percent decline in Border Patrol apprehensions (Rosenblum 2012: 20) with border crossing deaths recorded (recovered bodies) dropping only 21 percent from 2006 through 2011 (Dunn 2009: 2, 226; U.S. Customs and Border Protection 2009; Rosenblum 2012: 33). Border crossing deaths jumped to 477 in 2012 (the second highest total on record, after 492 in 2005), despite only a slight increase in Border Patrol apprehensions (Anderson 2013: 3). To take a longer view, from 1999 through 2012, recorded border crossing deaths rose more than 90 percent (from 249 to 477), while during the same time Border Patrol apprehensions fell 77 percent (1, 3). The result is that unauthorized border crossers are apparently seven times more likely to die, as deaths per 10,000 apprehensions jumped from approximately two to fourteen (2).

The deaths of unauthorized border crossers have taken place largely out of sight, in remote rural areas, and attracted little attention outside the border region. These are the victims of the bureaucratic "social triage" process conceptualized by Sjoberg (1996, 285–289; 1999, 55–56), as caused by U.S. border immigration policy implemented by the U.S. Border Patrol—the lives of this drastically subordinated group have in effect been written off as an unfortunate (though typically seen as justifiable) tragedy in the name of upholding national sovereignty. The Border Patrol does mount some rescue efforts to save lost, stranded crossers in danger, but this does nothing to alter the enforcement strategies and tactics that drove crossers to such dangerous routes in the first place (and pushed them into such by grave economic hardships in their home country). Addressing such deeper concerns is apparently "inefficient" for elites.

Beyond the issue of border crossing deaths, a number of reports have shown other significant human rights abuses that have taken place as a part of immigration enforcement along the U.S.-Mexico border (Human Rights Watch 1995; U.S. Commission on Civil Rights 1997; Amnesty International 1998; American Friends Service Committee 1998; Border Network for Human Rights 2003; Frey 2012; No More Deaths 2011; Stack et al. 2013). These abuses include unjustified shootings, sexual assault, beatings and physical abuse, inhumane detention conditions, denial of due process, verbal and psychological abuse, and destruction of property by law enforcement officials, the Border Patrol most notably. A key feature of these problems is lack of oversight to remedy and prevent such abuses of authority by border enforcement authorities, as many of their victims are mainly noncitizens, especially those who are unauthorized immigrants, and have little access to any reporting system or the courts.

Local Challenges to Increased Border Enforcement

In the face of such abuses, there have been significant protests and challenges to U.S. immigration policy. In general, these actions are consistent with the broader definition of human rights posited by Sjoberg and colleagues (Sjoberg, Gill, and Williams 2001: 25) as "claims made by persons in diverse social and cultural systems upon 'organized power relationships' in order to advance the dignity of (or, more concretely, equal respect and concern for) human beings." The massive protests of millions of immigrants and their supporters during spring 2006 and 2007 in key cities across the country were a response to the draconian Sensenbrenner-King bill passed by the House of Representatives in late 2005. This measure would have made criminal felons of unauthorized immigrants and any persons who assisted them in nearly any way, including religious workers, and called for a 700-mile border wall; the latter was subsequently passed into law separately (see Dunn 2009: 222–23; Portes and Rumbaut 2006: 152–53; Balz and Fears 2006; Gonzales 2009). "Comprehensive immigration reform" was offered as a solution by the Bush administration and the U.S. Senate in 2006 and 2007, with three main elements: a large-scale legalization program for the millions of undocumented immigrants already here, much expanded work visas for future immigrants, and heightened border enforcement. To show its resolve on the latter and secure more support for reform legislation, the Bush administration deployed 6,000 National Guard troops for two years in May 2006, as previously noted. However, the reform legislation never passed the Senate, and in spring 2010 the Obama administration and Congress again took up the same general plan with no substantive progress. However, in 2013, in the wake of the Republican Party's abysmal showing with Latino voters in the 2012 elections, the Senate did finally pass a comprehensive immigration bill that included legalization for undocumented immigrants as well as a lengthy process to eventual citizenship, and expanded visas for future migrant workers. The bill also included a massive $46 billion "border surge' of enforcement to double (yet again) the border patrol to some 40,000 agents and deploy the repeated failed high-tech "virtual fence" of electronic surveillance over some 700 miles of border, and much more in what is essentially a huge give away to military-security contractors (Tanfani and Bennett 2013). The House or Representatives has yet to take up the bill and is unlikely to do so, balking at the legalization and citizenship elements.

At the more local level along the U.S.-Mexico border, the early part of the first decade of the twenty-first century saw increased immigration enforcement, especially in outlying, less urban U.S. border communities, targeting those of Hispanic appearance (suspected as unauthorized Mexican immigrants). This is a shift from the post-1993 tactic of relying on massive deployments of enforcement resources in key urban areas as part of the "prevention through deterrence" strategy pioneered by "Operation Blockade" in El Paso, Texas (see Dunn 2009). This border blockade approach was increasingly supplemented with increased immigration enforcement—such as checkpoints, stops and questioning, roving patrols—away from the immediate border in poor, rural, Hispanic border communities, by both Border Patrol agents and, increasingly, local police (Dunn 2009: 169–72, 215–17; Nuñez and Heyman 2007). The 2010 Arizona state law, SB 1070, partly upheld by the Supreme Court in 2012, mandated that local and state police engage in precisely this sort of activity, checking the immigration status of anyone they stop and who they have a "reasonable suspicion" may be in the country illegally. Some critics, including Arizona police officials, maintain this will result in ethnic and racial profiling of Latinos or Hispanics (Portillo 2010; Hsu 2010a). The Arizona law is just one of dozens of such state and local anti-unauthorized immigrant measures passed around the country in recent years, many of which amount to usurping national control of immigration policy (see Koulish 2010). One of the more drastic examples of this type of local police-Border Patrol collaboration is found in New Mexico, near El Paso. It involved an immigration raid in the fall of 2007 led by a southern New Mexico county sheriff's department in a very poor small town some twenty miles from the border. The deputies went house to house and even to a local school, arresting twenty-eight people, who were turned over to the Border Patrol for deportation (Gilot 2007). This raid was ostensibly part of a larger federally funded anticrime and border security measure, even tied to antiterrorism (Operation Stonegarden), though no suspects of such serious crime were arrested or charged in this raid (Dunn 2009: 217, 258). In addition, during the early years of the first decade of the new century the Border Patrol also began to selectively take up more aggressive immigration enforcement within the city of El Paso for the first time since 1993, targeting several key immigrant social service providers. In the process an agent killed an unauthorized immigrant outside a shelter run by Catholic Church volunteers in a tragic misunderstanding and unjustified escalation (Dunn 2009: 172–76).

Such measures provoked protest and mobilization by immigrant and human rights activists and organizations in the area. For example, the El Paso-based Border Network for Human Rights (BNHR) recruited hundreds of new volunteers, mainly in poor outlying communities. Many were trained as *promotores de derechos* (rights promoters) not only in U.S. civil and constitutional rights but also in international human rights (Dunn 2009: 170–72, 216–17). The BNHR and other activist organizations documented hundreds of rights abuses by Border Patrol and other law enforcement authorities which sought to rein in abusive practices and led to some legal challenges. Most notably, a broad-based mobilization was mounted against the much expanded immigration enforcement efforts by the El Paso County Sheriff's office and successfully convinced the county council to prohibit such efforts (Staudt 2008). Shortly afterward, a new county sheriff was elected who promised to stay away from immigration enforcement. The BNHR joined with immigrant rights activists in New Mexico and Arizona to form the Border Community Alliance for Human Rights to advocate for immigration reforms at the national level, enlisting the support of many local border-area political officials in this cause.

There have been numerous other examples of local and regional protests against increased immigration enforcement along the U.S.-Mexico border. One of the most remarkable was the host of local pro-immigrant street demonstrations of up to 6,000 people in the spring of 2006. For the first time in fourteen years in El Paso, a very large political gathering took up the cause of undocumented immigrants residing in the community and called for their legalization and recognition as contributing members of the community rather than castigation as criminals (Dunn 2009: 217). This was especially remarkable because since the inception of Operation Blockade by the Border Patrol in fall 1993, border enforcement against undocumented Mexican immigrants was very popular locally across ethnic lines, including among Mexican Americans (see Vila 2000; Dunn 2009). Thus, at least briefly, the national political movement led to a change in local political sentiment about unauthorized immigrants and an opening up of the broader human rights agenda. This change in sentiment seems in part rooted in the fact that the focus shifted from unauthorized border crossers temporarily present to unauthorized immigrant residents of the community, who were more widely recognized as making many positive contributions.

Beyond the street protests, local officials have played a contradictory role. On one hand, the city councils of both El Paso and nearby Sunland Park, New Mexico, passed resolutions protesting the initial deployment of thousands of National Guard troops on the border in 2006. The El Paso city council in 2006 and 2007 joined several other Texas border cities in passing a resolution against the hundreds of miles of new border wall/fence and even joined a lawsuit against it, which ultimately failed (Dunn 2009: 218–19, 223). On the other hand, El Paso officials and institutions, and those in other border communities, are anxious to capitalize economically on the ever-increasing "Border Security Industrial Complex" or "Homeland Security Complex" (Barry 2009). The border enforcement-related projects and forces provide jobs and lucrative contracts.

There have also been important and growing efforts by humanitarian groups in recent years to assist unauthorized immigrants in danger of dying while trying to cross the border. This has been perhaps the starkest challenge to the national sovereignty view of border immigration enforcement and the strongest measure in promoting the human rights perspective. Most of these efforts have been centered in southern Arizona, the epicenter of the border crossing death crisis. Such groups as No More Deaths/No Mas Muertes (see their report, No More Deaths 2011) and Samaritans/Samaritanos, inspired at least in part by religious principles, place water at key locations along migrant trails in the desert and rescue migrants unable to continue (Menjívar 2007; Hagan and Rymond-Richmond 2008; Hondagneu-Sotelo 2008; Caminero-Santangelo 2009; Cabrera 2010; Rose 2012). They have gained publicity for their cause and helped broaden the immigration debate to include more humanitarian concerns, at least at the local level in Tucson, though they have manifestly failed to get the issue on the agenda in Phoenix. They have also faced hostility from anti-immigrant forces and the constant prospect of prosecution by federal authorities for breaking the law (e.g., by transporting distressed unauthorized immigrants to the hospital instead of turning them over to the Border Patrol). Two young volunteers were even prosecuted for a time, but charges were eventually dropped. In El Paso, Texas, Hermanos al Rescate (Brothers to the Rescue) was formed in 2005 to fly over the desert in search of unauthorized immigrants in danger. Members of this group drop water and supplies to immigrants and radio for rescue help should they need it (Dunn 2009: 178–79).

While humanitarian groups risk possible federal prosecution, armed vigilante groups are mostly tolerated by authorities. They are quite free to monitor the border for unauthorized immigrants and sometimes even detain them for the Border Patrol to pick up, though with some limits. Thus, the national sovereignty framework reigns supreme, even when enforced by nongovernmental actors.

One final development has further heightened the imperative for border enforcement and strengthened the national sovereignty framework: the escalating drug-cartel and other violence in the neighboring city of Ciudad Juárez, Chihuahua, Mexico (see Campbell 2009), and throughout key parts of Mexico's northern border region. Since 2008, Juárez has been reported to have the highest murder rate of any city in the world, as more than 5,000 people have been killed from 2008 through spring 2010 (Borunda 2010; Molly Molloy, personal communication). Much of the violence is tied to conflicts between rival drug cartels for control of this lucrative border drug smuggling zone, though additional violence has spilled into the political and social vacuum caused by the drug war. This crisis has shown that the Mexican state is often incapable of maintaining basic social order. In contrast, El Paso has had very few murders per year and has among the lowest crime rates of any large city in the United States. The violence in neighboring Juárez has not spilled over—despite numerous claims that it has.

Such violence and societal breakdown in Juárez have illustrated a need for border protection from violent criminals. However, increasing law enforcement or even use of the military is not the sole or best answer to the spiraling violence. In the spring of 2008 the Mexican federal government deployed 2,000 military troops to Juárez and later expanded that to upward of 10,000 troops. While troop levels were ultimately scaled back, they were replaced by a similar number of federal police, ostensibly to try to stop the crisis. Yet the violence and murders have continued to increase, as have reports of human rights violations by authorities (Beaubien 2009). The drug problem needs to be addressed as a much broader social and public health issue, rooted in reducing drug demand and addiction as well as increasing social and economic opportunities for many (especially youth) on both sides of the border (Campbell 2009). However, such a broader, more humanitarian view of the drug problem has not been promoted by either government, and instead the use of force to reinforce nation-state authority and sovereignty has been the preferred option, at the expense of many lives.

Toward a New Understanding of National Sovereignty

Many anti-unauthorized immigrant political actors propose heightened border enforcement as a means to protect the nation and its people from economic drain, crime, and even terrorism. And immigration enforcement along the U.S.-Mexico border by U.S. authorities has sharply escalated since the mid-1990s, as part of the broader process of upholding national sovereignty and citizenship, concepts widely viewed as fundamentally important. However, the pursuit of these notions in border immigration enforcement has caused great hardships, significant human rights abuses, and even humanitarian crises, most notably more than 6,100 deaths of unauthorized border crossers. Specifically, immigration enforcement along the U.S.-Mexico border puts at risk the following rights enshrined in the Universal Declaration of Human Rights: Article 1: All people are born equal in dignity and rights; Article 2: All are entitled to rights without distinctions of national or social origin or language; Article 3: The right to life, liberty, and security of person; Article 5: The right to freedom from torture, or cruel, inhuman, or degrading treatment; Article 13: The right to freedom of movement, including the right to leave one's country; and Articles 23 and 25: Everyone has the right to a standard of living adequate for the health and well-being of himself and of his family. Clearly, border immigration enforcement by U.S. authorities has undermined the dignity and rights of people (Article 1), largely on the grounds of suspected national origin and language as an indicator of such (Article 2). The right to life and security of person (Article 3) has been much infringed upon by enforcement strategies and tactics that drive migrants into ever more dangerous crossing zones, in the absence of expanded legal entry visas. Likewise, this process has sometimes entailed cruel, inhuman, and degrading treatment (Article 5) of migrants, especially those detained. Freedom to leave one's country (Article 13) is obviously blocked by U.S. border enforcement efforts, though there is no recognized human right to enter another country (rendering it difficult practically to leave one's country). Finally, most migrants are coming to seek work precisely because of their inability to provide an adequate living and health for their families in their home countries

(Articles 23 and 25), which is stymied by uneven economic development in their home regions and then by border enforcement (and lack of visas) blocking access to U.S. jobs. However, there is no real enforcement mechanism for these universal, unconditional human rights, especially for migrants (Turner 2009), as evidenced by a 2005 decision by the Inter-American Commission of Human Rights to dismiss a complaint against the U.S. government for deaths caused by its border enforcement policies (Feldmann and Durand 2008).

The national sovereignty/citizenship framework fills the vacuum with its clear means for enforcement, with courts and executive branch policing agencies. Hence, this more enforceable route, with existing civil rights falling under the citizenship and national sovereignty framework, has been the traditional avenue taken by social movements seeking greater rights and inclusion such as proposed by Mexican American rights advocates and even those opposing border enforcement rights abuses (see, e.g., Dunn 2009: chap. 2). However, this convenience comes at some cost, as civil rights are determined by the nation-state and are generally conditional (Turner 2009)—one has to perform duties and fulfill obligations to earn most civil rights (e.g., follow the law). Unauthorized immigrants are readily excluded by definition, as their mere presence is a legal violation and infringement of national sovereignty, which is one of the most popular points made by anti-unauthorized-immigrant activists. Immigration scholars, including those quite supportive of unauthorized immigrants, also frequently rely on some variation of the citizenship framework (see, e.g., Sassen 2006, 2007; Oboler 2006; Chavez 2008; Buff 2008).

Thus, at the U.S.-Mexico border, Sassen's (2006, 2007) contention that citizenship has been "denationalized" is not borne out. Instead U.S. immigration enforcement measures have been greatly expanded and are entirely legal under U.S. law, despite the deaths of thousands of unauthorized immigrants (the ultimate "denationalized citizens"). Moreover, the growth of local and state police collaboration in immigration enforcement, crystallized in Arizona's SB 1070, and the likely resulting ethnic profiling also suggest that a "renationalization" of citizenship is unfortunately not experiencing its "last gasp," as Sassen maintains. Nonetheless, Sassen is correct in that there have also been a number of important episodes of resistance by local groups and governmental bodies to the heightened border enforcement, suggestive of some movement toward human rights and "denationalized citizenship." However, this is a very asymmetrical struggle with national sovereignty and traditional notions of citizenship backed by vastly more powerful cultural and political forces.

Thus far, human rights concepts have been relatively overlooked in immigration debates, but the international human rights view provides an alternative perspective for evaluating policies and practices of powerful organizations (Sjoberg, Gill, and Williams 2001; Sjoberg 2009) that are legal under national law but violate international human rights standards. This human rights view provides a framework for challenging and critiquing excesses committed by nation-state authorities and policymakers that heighten a targeted group's vulnerability and human frailty (Turner 1993: 2006), painfully evident in the case of immigration. Moreover, the loss of life and less severe rights infringements that occur in border immigration enforcement may best be seen as instances of the larger process of "social triage" (Sjoberg 1996: 285–89) that is endemic to large, powerful organizations in the modern world, where the well-being and dignity of the "truly disadvantaged" groups are "written off" because to adequately address them would be "inefficient" for those organizations and societal elites. And in failing to grant basic human rights to unauthorized immigrants, the nation-state does effectively grant impunity for those committing abuses (Bustamante 2002: 345–46), including its own agents and policymakers.

Meanwhile, economic globalization (via free trade agreements, the World Trade Organization, etc.) has expanded with comparatively little public or political outcry. Thus, concern over national sovereignty is quite selective—with immigrants targeted as a threat to it, but the international movement of capital and goods by transnational corporations treated as "natural" and hardly thought of in terms of national sovereignty, despite its far greater impact. It is apparently easier to blame unauthorized immigrants for eroding national sovereignty, as they are the visible and relatively powerless human face of globalization, than it is to recognize and challenge the faceless power of transnational corporations and their allies at the highest levels of nearly all governments. Yet the latter much more profoundly undermine national sovereignty and economies than do immigrants—particularly as many of the popular negative stereotypes about immigrants are debatable at best.[3]

Rethinking National Sovereignty

While international human rights have certainly become more prominent globally, national sovereignty also clearly has a role to play in the modern world and is not about to disappear. Thus, we need a less hypocritical consideration of national sovereignty, and to consider it in broader terms. I propose then that the larger issue is national sovereignty for what end? Rather than seeing it as an end in and of itself or for national security, we would do well to consider it as a means to a variety of ends. We might view national sovereignty in an expanded sense as a means to promote the well-being of the people residing in a nation, just as the U.S. Constitution refers to "the people" and "persons," interpreted legally to mean all residents, not just citizens (which some find quite troubling; see Jacobson 1996: 101–3). Based on this definition, we can then reconsider both unauthorized immigration and economic globalization in terms of national sovereignty as well-being.

National sovereignty in economic terms (often ridiculed as "protectionism") has been readily surrendered by nations in the form of free trade agreements for the free movement of goods and capital, constructed largely to the profitable benefit of powerful transnational corporations and financial institutions (Sassen 2006: chap. 5; 2007; Sjoberg 2009). Meanwhile, the well-being of the majority of the Mexican population under NAFTA has hardly been enhanced since its inception, particularly in the case of the Mexican peasantry and working class (the vast majority of the population), many of whom have lost land and faced weak job growth and falling wages. This has increased the "push conditions" driving unauthorized immigration to the United States, just as the proliferation of low-wage jobs in the United States (as well as an aging population) has created stronger "pull conditions" luring workers—an expression of the greater inequality in the United States (Harvey 2007; Sassen 1998, 2007). Without some sort of massive investment in the social infrastructure and development for the poorer classes in those countries (à la the EU model), corporate-led free trade agreements with less-developed neighboring nations will inevitably lead to more immigration from them.

International trade and economic globalization more generally could be crafted to benefit broader sectors of the population (e.g., through enhanced labor rights, living wage minimum standards, support for sustainable agricultural practices by small farmers, etc.), but neither country has chosen to challenge transnational "corporate sovereignty" with such expressions of national sovereignty based on well-being. And indeed, U.S. residents (immigrant and citizen alike) could benefit as well from greater labor law (not immigration) enforcement regarding safety and wages, to reduce incentives for employers to engage in extreme exploitation of workers (Massey et al. 2002: 162). Upholding U.S. labor law is also a form of upholding national sovereignty. However, we have seen instead national sovereignty concerns overwhelmingly targeted at a vulnerable group, unauthorized immigrants, that has a less significant impact on society (and by no means an entirely negative one), rather than toward badly needed regulation of vastly more powerful transnational corporations and financial institutions, whose impact on societies is deep and profoundly troubling (see Johnson 2010). To address unauthorized immigration, governments must address the underlying push-pull structural conditions in which they and transnational corporations are deeply involved. Residents on both sides of the border would do well to reevaluate their country's economic policies regarding free cross-border movement of goods and capital by transnational corporations and financial institutions. Some balance in the direction of promoting the well-being of each country's residents is in order to resolve the adverse effects of neoliberal economic globalization. In turn, this more human rights-oriented approach to economic policy, broadly speaking, may lessen the pressures for immigration. Meanwhile, offering some legal status to the millions of unauthorized immigrants already living in and contributing to the United States, as well as making more visas available for future migrant workers, would regulate and make more humane the century-old cross-border migration of workers and families that both countries have come to rely on. Thus, the publics of both countries may be best served by some easing of national sovereignty in immigration while heightening it in economic policy regarding transnational corporations and the movement of capital and goods—the near opposite of current policy.

PART II

The Mexican Drug War in
Binational Contexts

CHAPTER 4

Politics of Death in the Drug War: The Right to Kill and Suspensions of Human Rights in Mexico, 2000–2012

Julie A. Murphy Erfani

[T]he ultimate expression of sovereignty resides, to a large degree, in the power and capacity to dictate who may live and who must die. Hence, to kill or to allow to live constitute the limits of sovereignty. . . . To exercise sovereignty is to exercise control over mortality and to define life as the deployment and manifestation of power. . . . *War, after all, is as much a means of achieving sovereignty as a way of exercising the right the kill.*
—Mbembe 2003: 11–12; emphasis added

Sovereignty as the Right to Kill: Accusations of Drug War Crimes

In November 2011, Mexican president Felipe Calderón stood accused of war crimes by a group of his own country's citizens.[1] Prominent Mexican lawyers, journalists, academics, and 23,000 petitioners filed a criminal complaint against him with the International Criminal Court (ICC) in The Hague. Spearheaded by leading figures, including UNAM legal scholar John Ackerman and organized crime expert Edgardo Buscaglia of the United Nations, the war crimes complaint alleged that Calderón and several of his cabinet members had committed crimes against humanity in Mexico's drug war (LAND Blog 2011). More specifically, the Mexican complainants alleged that beginning in 2006 the Calderón government had waged a drug war that permitted the torture, kidnapping, disappearances, and extrajudicial killings of civilians. Also charged with war crimes were the secretaries of the army, navy, and public safety—some of Mexico's top security officials—and Mexico's top drug kingpin, Joaquin "El Chapo" Guzman of the Sinaloa gang. In late 2011, ICC chief prosecutor Luis Moreno Ocampo refused to take up the case, stating that "we [at the ICC] don't judge political decisions or political responsibility" (*Latin American Herald Tribune* 2011). Contrary to this statement, however, in June 2012, the ICC's newly appointed chief prosecutor Fatou Bensouda responded cryptically to a question about U.S.-Mexico drug war crimes suggesting that unlike her predecessor, she is focused on the Mexico human rights situation. Arguably, the Calderón government's potential implication in war crimes remains an open question.

The issue whether outgoing Mexican officials and Sinaloa kingpin El Chapo Guzman could theoretically be tried for war crimes is in and of itself an important legal question. Mounting evidence indicates that public officials, armed forces, and gangsters have all made extralegal decisions about who would live and die in the "drug war" in Mexico (Human Rights Watch 2009c; cf. Gibler 2011). Heinous murders, deaths by mutilation, and the fatal severing of body parts have proliferated as drug war combatants have denied people the "right to have rights" (Arendt 1951: 296–97), especially in drug hot spots.

In this chapter I explore how various government and nongovernment actors could be found culpable for the atrocities committed during the drug war. In particular, I examine (a) how the Mexican government and drug gangs altered codes of conduct about who has the right to kill during the drug war, and (b) how the U.S. government fueled the carnage through legal and illegal arms shipments to Mexico and through repeated refusal to demilitarize and decriminalize immigrants and marijuana, the largest volume traded drug.

I argue that drug war atrocities have occurred not just because civilians were caught in the crossfire between the Sinaloa, the Juárez, the Gulf, or other drug gangs. Atrocities have also occurred because the United States has transferred massive quantities of weapons to Mexico; because some Mexican officials are complicit with drug gangsters; and because military and police officers in Mexico have tortured, raped, and murdered people with impunity in the name of fighting the drug war. In Mexico, decisions resulting in extrajudicial killings have spread across a multiplicity of actors, both private and public. Although both the Mexican and U.S. governments claim to fight the "drug war" legally, the Mexican military has acted as a police force that has repeatedly committed crimes against civilians while using weapons often supplied by U.S. gun manufacturers and the U.S. government (Cook, Cukier, and Krause 2009: 276–77; cf. Gibler 2011: 29). Drug gangsters using U.S. weapons have committed atrocities as well (Williams 2009b: 329; Gibler 2011: 35–40). These mounting atrocities have led to an estimated 55,000 plus deaths by a scattered array of sovereign actors making decisions about life and death.[2] Finally, U.S. government policies like the deadly border crackdown on migrants, and the Mexican military's impunity in "fighting" the "drug war," exacerbate the preexisting narco-culture and its human rights abuses.

In effect, the U.S. and Mexican governments have normalized disregard for civil and human rights under the guise of various "national emergencies." Both governments have employed languages of emergency and war to justify human rights abuses as necessary to the protection of national security. Clearly, such abuses violate international human rights law and national constitutional guarantees to citizens. To clarify that the culpability for these crimes is binational and involves governments as well as gangsters, I employ the theoretical lens of necropolitics that holds that the right to kill is the ultimate form of sovereignty. Necropolitics posits that multiple actors—governments and gangsters—have practiced the sovereign right to kill. This analysis moves past previous scholarly works that viewed the drug war as a simple binary between criminal gangsters and innocent governments. Fueled by the importation of weapons, the number of actors who have the right to kill has expanded exponentially, and therefore numerous groups, both governmental and nongovernmental, can claim sovereignty. While Weber defined the state as that entity which can legitimately use force, it is clear that in Mexico today the state no longer has a monopoly over force.

In the next section, I show that both the Mexican and U.S. governments, acting within frameworks of states of emergency, have contributed to the military clout of drug lords by directly and indirectly arming gangs and thus have expanded the number of individuals who have the capacity to use force. In what follows, I also provide evidence of a close relationship between the Calderón government and the Sinaloa drug trafficking organization.

Gangs with Military-Grade Weapons from the United States: Binational Policies Contributing to Multiple Deployers of Violence

> The necropolitical order, as "contemporary forms of the subjugation of life to the power of death" thus results from . . . overlapping forces, a heterogeneous network of deployers of violence: the confluence of state armies, paramilitary groups, private armies, private security firms and armies of drug lords and ruling elite—all claiming the right to exercise sovereignty [Mbembe 2003: 31]. . . . In this emerging necropolitical order, multiple forms of sovereignty are intertwined with the suspension of human rights. (Fregoso 2006: 114)

This section documents a growing influx of illicit arms to Mexico (complementing the chapter by Mueller in this volume)—a story that cannot be divorced from the various states of emergency that have been declared by the U.S. and Mexican governments. A deadly arms race in military-grade weapons developed among drug gangs in Mexico, especially after President Calderón's declaration of a drug war in 2006. The U.S. Clinton and George W. Bush administrations fueled the arms race by expanding a militarized state of emergency at the U.S. border with Mexico. By stepping up the numbers of armed U.S. Border Patrol agents and National Guard troops, the Clinton and Bush administrations made it more difficult, more militarily dangerous, and also more lucrative to smuggle drugs, people, and money across the border. In the face of such militarization and growing intergang competition for border-crossing zones, organized smuggling gangs acquired larger and more deadly weapons arsenals, increasing their firepower and overall destructive capacity.

The Mexican government also contributed significantly to the state of emergency and the arms race between drug gangs. In particular, when the Fox administration arrested several drug kingpins in the early and mid-2000s, the arrests triggered intense turf wars and power struggles as gangs fought to acquire the vulnerable turf and trade routes (*plazas*) of the arrested kingpins (Gibler 2011: 26–27). Williams (2009b) refers to this growing violence as part of a fragmentation of drug gangs in a process of "transitional violence" in which state domination of the drug trade breaks down and new codes of conduct of state-gang relations are yet to emerge (327). The most contested drug trade routes in Mexico have been through the northern border states of Baja California, Chihuahua, and Tamaulipas.

Two of the most important arrests were the 2003 apprehension of top Gulf leader Osiel Cardenas Guillen, based in Tamaulipas, and the 2006 arrest of top Tijuana gang leader Francisco Javier Arrellano Felix, from Baja California. In a struggle to replace Gulf chief Cardenas Guillen, the Sinaloa drug gang fought a series of ongoing battles to seize control of Gulf "cartel" trade routes leading through southwest Texas. Ongoing battles between the Sinaloa and Gulf drug gangs to control routes from Mexico through southwest Texas transformed Ciudad Juárez into one of Mexico's most violent drug hot spots (Meyer 2010).

In December 2006, President Calderón deployed soldiers and federal police across the country and thus declared a de facto state of emergency in Mexico. In response to the president's declaration of a military "war on drugs," organized drug gangs bolstered their military arsenals. In other words, by launching a militarized war within Mexico, the government prompted drug gangs to stockpile and employ higher-grade weaponry against competing gangs, to battle corrupt police loyal to opposing gangs, and, if necessary, to battle government troops (Small Arms Survey 2012). The Small Arms Survey confirms that "cartel violence [in Mexico] has only grown in intensity, lethality, and brazenness since the crackdown [of 2006], with attacks by cartels on army troops at an all-time high." Confronted with thousands of armed Mexican soldiers across the country, various gangs found themselves fighting each other for police to bribe in order to gain or maintain transit routes (Williams 2009b: 327, 330; cf. Gibler 2011: 36–38). As competition intensified, drug smugglers and dealers employed greater firepower to defend and expand turf where drugs are sold domestically and to protect rural territories where farmers grow marijuana and opium poppies. Both marijuana and poppy producers must protect their fields both from competing drug dealers and from the government (Booth and Fainaru 2009). Between 2006 and 2011, as drug gangs fragmented and multiplied in number, drug-related homicides and drug gang attacks on Mexican armed forces grew markedly.

The stakes in the "drug war" are high because profits from illicit drugs sold in the United States are large. The National Drug Intelligence Center estimates that "Mexican and Colombian DTOs generate, remove, and launder

$18–39 billion in wholesale illicit drug proceeds in the U.S. annually" (National Drug Intelligence Center 2008: III). With the monetary stakes so high, drug gangs in Mexico have the monetary resources to acquire assault rifles of increasing firepower and use military-grade weapons to battle each other, the Mexican military, and, sometimes the U.S. Border Patrol. Seized weapons from traffickers' arsenals include grenades, grenade launchers, shoulder-fired anti-tank rocket launchers, .50-caliber rifles, armor-piercing munitions, body armor, and Kevlar.

The United States as Chief Arms Supplier to Multiple Deployers of Violence

According to Castillo and Roberts (2009), among the *traceable* handguns, rifles, and ammunition seized in Mexico in 2007, about one-third were sold by licensed U.S. firearms dealers. Mexican officials seize many more guns that are not traced for a variety of reasons, so the actual percentage of 2007 guns seized that were sold by gun dealers in the United States is unclear and may be significantly higher than one-third (Castillo and Roberts 2009). Even more unclear are the sources of seized military-grade weapons, such as 9-mm grenade launchers, anti-tank rocket launchers, and .50-caliber Barrett sniper rifles capable of penetrating armored vehicles. These military-grade weapons have been used to attack Mexican police, the Mexican military, and rival gangs. Over about six months between October 2008 and March 2009, military-grade weapons were used in ten Mexican states (Ellingwood and Wilkinson 2009). In less than one month in February and March 2009, criminal gangs in the state of Michoacán launched five grenade attacks on police vehicles, police stations, and a police commander's residence. Clearly, drug gangs' military-grade weapons enabled gang leaders to wield weapons superior to those of local police and thereby exercise the sovereign right to kill across wide tracts of territory.

The U.S. public and private sectors play significant roles in the transfer of military-grade weapons to Mexican drug gangs and to the Mexican military. In terms of illegal weapons transfers, some licensed U.S. firearms dealers, particularly in the three border states of Texas, California, and Arizona have sold weapons to drug gangs (Gonzalez 2010; Cook et al. 2009; cf. Goddard 2009; see also McKinley 2009). For instance, weapons sold by a particular licensed firearms dealer in metropolitan Phoenix were seized at multiple shoot-out sites around Mexico. In January 2008, Mexican Special Forces recovered a .38-caliber Super pistol sold by this dealer when ex-Sinaloa kingpin Alfredo Beltran Leyva, "El Mochomo," was captured (Associated Press 2008a). In late May 2008, Mexican officials recovered seven AK-47 assault rifles after a shoot-out at an alleged Sinaloa safe house; the seven weapons were traced back to the same Phoenix dealer (Associated Press 2009). On November 2, 2008, another .38-caliber Super pistol also sold by that particular dealer was recovered in Nogales, Sonora, at the site where the chief of police of Sonora was gunned down (Associated Press 2008b).

In these arms transfer cases, U.S. firearms dealers sell to straw buyers working for drug gangs; the buyers then transfer the guns to gang operatives who smuggle them into Mexico for use by gang members. Analysts, such as Lumpe (1997) and Cook (2009), refer to this type of weapons trafficking as *tráfico hormiga*, or "trail of ants," and note that drug gangs usually organize such gunrunning. These microlevel arms transfers typically involve pistols and semiautomatic assault rifles (Osorno 2012). In other cases, weapons transfers to gun runners and drug gangs occur at gun shows in U.S. border states such as Arizona, where loopholes in state and federal laws allow private parties who are not licensed firearms dealers to sell guns without performing background checks on purchasers. In all of these cases, private gun sellers and firearms dealers in the United States as well as U.S. weapons manufacturers profit from what ultimately results in weapons transferred to organized criminals in Mexico.

Beyond pistols and rifles, however, many military-grade weapons often turn up in gangs' weapons stashes in Mexico. These military-grade weapons, including anti-tank rockets and armor-piercing munitions, are generally not available for sale to U.S. civilians, and individual straw buyers could not easily purchase such weapons. Nevertheless, they have flowed into Mexico, and an arms race among drug gangs has ensued. A *Los Angeles Times* report in March 2009 argued that the use of rocket-propelled grenades, in particular, reflected a new military-grade phase of the drug war (Ellingwood and Wilkinson 2009). It speculated that such weapons had been sold in the global black market in arms and then smuggled across Mexico's southern border. The drug cartels appear to be taking advantage of the robust global black market and porous borders, especially between Mexico and Guatemala. Some of the weapons also appear to be left over from the wars the United States helped fight in Central America, according to U.S. officials (Ellingwood and Wilkinson 2009).

Other news analysts documented how U.S.-based weapons manufacturers were selling military-grade weapons to Mexican armed forces and police, and theorized that some of those legally sold weapons were likely being funneled to drug gangs. Conroy (2009), in particular, analyzed data on U.S. government-approved private arms sales to Mexico and theorized that some U.S. State Department-approved private arms sold to the Mexican military and police were ending up in the hands of drug gangsters. Conroy's central thesis was that corrupt military and police officials resell such military-grade weapons to drug dealers. In this way, some of the most lethal weapons in the hands of drug gangs may have derived from legal, U.S. private-sector sales licensed for export by the State Department. Conroy cited State Department data specifying the types, volume, and dollar amounts of defense hardware and services authorized for "Direct Commercial Sales" (DCS) to Mexico from 2004 to 2007. He concluded that "although it is possible that some of the deals authorized under the DCS program were altered or even canceled after the export licenses were issued, the data compiled by U.S. State does provide a broad snapshot of the extensive volume of U.S. private-sector arms shipments to both Mexico and Latin America in general" (Conroy 2009). Conroy noted that the State Department officially approved more than $1 billion of private-sector weapons exports to Mexico over the years 2004 to 2007, not including any provided through the Mérida Initiative consisting of direct U.S. government weapons transfers.

With Mexico's military averaging 1,200 desertions per month in 2006 (Conroy 2009), it appears that national stockpiles of weapons intended for use by the Mexican military and police are frequently diverted to illicit use (Conroy 2009; Cook et al. 2009: 277). Legal U.S. arms exports often become black market arms deals to drug gangs after arriving in Mexico. A former U.S. Customs inspector concurs that legal U.S. arms sales likely become illicit weapons transfers once inside Mexico: "I would agree entirely [that] DCS (and DoD gifted, as opposed to DCS sold) weapons are obviously the simplest explanation for the massive rise in the number of fully automatic weapons, grenades, rockets, etc. obtained by the narcotics gangs. . . . That is to say, they are obtaining their weapons from their own, Mexican government, by various illegal means" (Conroy 2009). A former DEA agent was even more emphatic, saying that State Department-authorized shipment of military hardware to the Mexican government is equivalent to "shipping weapons to a crime syndicate" (Conroy 2009).

In terms of the changing field of power in Mexico, U.S. arms transfers of military-grade weapons clearly enabled some drug lords to act as warlords militarily capable of carving out territorial "zones of impunity" where narco-forces wield greater firepower than local police (Osorno 2012).[3] During the 2000s, a patchwork of zones of impunity emerged that fragmented sovereignty across various gangs exercising authority in specific locales across Mexico (Fregoso 2006; Wright 2011). Across this patchwork of fragmented sovereignty, gang leaders employed private armies to patrol their own private drug *plazas*. In the midst of this multiplicity of actors exercising the sovereign right to kill, the Mexican state internalized some of the criminal fragmentation as various public officials cultivated ties with various rival gangs. Corrupt state officials linked to the Sinaloa gang have partly harnessed state authority to the emerging predominance of the Sinaloa drug gang. By the same token, other corrupt officials, such as the army generals accused in 2012 of ties to the rival Beltran Leyva gang, have fragmented state authority by cultivating the Beltran Leyva and Zetas gangs, which compete with the Sinaloa gang (Associated Press 2012). As explained in the next section, the rest of Mexico's drug gangs, particularly the Zetas, have been fighting the dual forces of the Sinaloa gang and the Mexican state in a battle to maintain a hold over key turf and routes important to transnational drug smuggling. In some respects, the Mexican state and the Sinaloa gang have generally prevailed in the "drug war," but they still face rivalry and violence from the Zetas, a gang with major profit incentives to keep fighting to preserve trade routes and turf.

Politics of Death in Mexico: Blurred Lines Between Criminals and the State

The lucrative cross-border trade in drugs has multiplied the number of participants in the politics of death in Mexico. Drug traders have usually been connected in some fashion to crimes producing death: murders for hire, mutilations, executions, forced disappearances, and shoot-outs. President Calderón's declaration of a militarized war on drug gangs ignited an already volatile criminal landscape in which private drug dealers and some public officials participated in and benefited from drug commerce. As drug corruption spread in the public and private sectors, the lines between private criminals and public officials blurred as elected officials, political appointees, armed forces and law enforcement officers accepted bribes in exchange for cooperating with, protecting, or otherwise facilitating drug gang activities (Gibler 2011: 33–37). The military forces deployed by the president in various regions of the country began to replace and disarm local police forces. This replacement process left the practice of law enforcement in occupied areas in the hands of the armed forces and ultimately the presidency rather than the local police.

Roots of the Mexican State of Emergency
and "Legal Civil War"

According to leading Mexican analysts Ruben Aguilar and Jorge Castaneda, Calderón's sudden drug war declaration was quintessentially politically motivated to consolidate presidential power during the postelection transition. A number of commentators (Aguilar and Castaneda 2009; Gibler 2011; Osorno 2012) have argued that Calderón suddenly declared the war on assuming office in December 2006 to deflect the political fallout of a 2006 teachers' strike and popular insurgency in Oaxaca and deflect protests of his own razor-thin electoral victory in July. The mass protests accusing Calderón of electoral fraud from July through December 2006 in Mexico City alleged that the PAN had stolen the election, but these massive protests were rather quickly overshadowed by the new president's show of military force and his popularity for getting tough on crime. The first show of force occurred in the interim between the election in July and the inauguration in December. In October 2006, a new federal police force, the Federal Preventative Police (PFP), composed of ex-military members entered Oaxaca and effectively broke the Oaxaca teachers' strike by November. The second show of force commenced with Calderón's declaration of a drug war on his inauguration. He quickly began sending soldiers into the streets and along highways to replace the police in drug hot spots around the country and rapidly militarized governance. This militarized governance became the modus operandi of his entire six-year term (Aguilar and Castaneda 2009: 13; Osorno 2012). Thus, he redirected mass political attention away from popular *political insurgency* mounted against his own alleged electoral fraud to the government's battle against a *criminal drug gang insurgency* cultivated in part by the government itself.

At his inauguration, the president himself initiated a politics of death by launching the idea that an insurgency of drug criminals threatened the nation-state. He insisted that a drug war be fought against drug gangs to protect the nation: "all we Mexicans of our generation have a responsibility to declare war against the enemies of Mexico. . . . [T]herefore, in this war against delinquency, against the enemies of Mexico, there will be neither truce nor barracks" (Calderón 2006, my translation). Constitutionally, President Calderón failed to obtain first the obligatory permission of the Mexican Congress as required by the Constitution (Article 29) before instituting his de facto state of emergency. The newly invented "emergency" situation set the stage for a massive expansion of military spending and executive authority to fight the war.

Under de facto emergency conditions, some armed forces proceeded to violate the civil and human rights of civilians on a major scale. Civilian human rights complaints against armed forces mounted into the thousands (Bricker 2011: 2). Criminal cases brought by civilians against soldiers consistently ended up in military tribunals, where guilty verdicts and punishment seldom, if ever, occurred. According to Human Rights Watch (2009a), the judicial system repeatedly failed to transfer cases alleging soldiers' abuses of civilians' human rights from military to civilian courts. In the wake of growing evidence of military involvement in extrajudicial killings, forced disappearances, and torture, the Inter-American Court of Human Rights (IACHR) issued several binding rulings in 2009 requiring Mexico to reform its justice system to ensure that *all* human rights abuse cases be tried in civilian courts (Bricker 2011). In October 2010, after the U.S. State Department sanctioned Mexico by withholding some U.S. funds for Mexico's drug war, Calderón sent draft legislation to Mexico's Congress proposing civilian trials for armed forces personnel only for three types of cases: rape, torture, and forced disappearances (Archibold 2010b). In July 2011, the Mexican Supreme Court complied with IACHR rulings to strip the military of its right to try soldiers accused of violating civilians' human rights. The court directed Mexico's Congress to reform the Code of Military Justice in favor of civilian jurisdiction. However, by 2011 the only IACHR-compliant reform proposal in Mexico's Congress was the Arce Initiative (Bricker 2011). Bricker urged that "the UN and Inter-American Commission on Human Rights should maintain their pressure on the Mexican government to reform the Code of Military Justice to ensure all human rights violations are tried in civilian courts." In other words, the legislation requiring that all human rights cases be remanded to civilian courts was still tenuous as of 2011.

Insufficient judicial reform to protect human rights can be better understood through the critical lens of philosopher Giorgio Agamben, who theorizes that so-called democratic governments often normalize human rights violations by implementing de facto states of emergency. He argues that modern governments are actually totalitarian in orientation in using so-called national emergencies to establish *legal civil wars*:

> modern totalitarianism can be defined as the establishment, by means of the state of exception, of a legal civil war that allows for the physical elimination not only of political adversaries but of entire categories of citizens who for some reason cannot be integrated into the political system. Since . . . [the Third Reich], the voluntary creation of a permanent state of emergency (though perhaps not declared in the technical sense) has become one of the essential practices of contemporary states, including so-called democratic ones. (Agamben 2005: 2)

President Calderón established a quasi-legal civil war from the beginning of his presidency when he, Mexico's chief executive, donned a military uniform and declared a military war on drug gangs. As a political phenomenon, the precedent of a sitting Mexican president wearing military garb has been essentially nonexistent since the Mexican Revolution of the early twentieth century. Calderón, nevertheless, consolidated his otherwise tenuous presidential power through a drug gang "emergency" and described his presidential duties in a language of war: at his command, the military was to chase, capture, and kill anyone assumed to threaten public order. In such a civil war, any one identified by the president and armed forces as threatening public order could be eradicated without such killing being considered unlawful. A state of emergency enables the national executive to expand its authority to deploy troops, issue decrees, and institute other extraordinary measures that would otherwise be construed as violations of people's constitutional rights and civil liberties (Agamben 2005). In Mexico's drug war, Calderón unleashed the Mexican army and navy to target whomever the military and the government unilaterally deemed worthy of attack (Gibler 2011: 38; Osorno 2012).

A Selective War on Drugs

In addition to allowing the government freedom to target people almost at will, Mexico's state of emergency allowed the government to wage a selective war against some but not all gangs. Significant evidence (presented below) suggests that the Calderón government vigorously targeted virtually all drug gangs except one, the Sinaloa gang. Evidence of the government's exemption of the Sinaloa organization is substantial and has exacerbated violence precisely because all other gangs except Sinaloa became government targets (Gibler 2011: 28; Osorno 2012).

Scholarly and news investigations of the Calderón government's record of detentions point to selective detentions, with a much higher percentage of arrests of operatives of all other drug gangs, compared to Sinaloa gangsters. UN crime expert Edgardo Buscaglia and prestigious news organizations, such as *Proceso* and National Public Radio (NPR) in the United States, analyzed detention data and found that since 2006 the Mexican government and armed forces targeted and arrested all other major drug gangs with significantly higher frequency than they did the Sinaloa gang (Delgado 2010). All three sources found the Sinaloa gang to be relatively exempt from government attack (Burnett, Peñalosa, and Benincasa 2010). Buscaglia studied arrest records and found that only 941 people arrested for organized crime in Mexico over the past six years were affiliated with the Sinaloa gang, out of a total of 53,174 arrests (*The Economist* 2010). These widely disparate arrest figures are despite the fact that the Sinaloa gang is probably the largest cartel in the country and is generally considered the most powerful of all the cartels (Marosi 2011). All other major trafficking organizations—the Tijuana, Gulf, Juárez, and Beltran Leyva gangs—have suffered serious setbacks and losses of leadership and/or *plazas* (territorial drug routes) since 2006.

NPR found that of the 2,600 drug gang members arrested or subject to enforcement action between December 2006 and mid-May 2010, the greatest number of arrests—1,144 people, or 44 percent—were members of the Gulf-Zeta gang. Arrests of Sinaloa gang members accounted for only 12 percent of all arrests, only 312 Sinaloa gang members of a total of 2,600. NPR also analyzed cases that involved charges of cartel bribes of public officials.

Municipal officials were involved in most of these cases. The data suggest that bribes by the Sinaloa cartel focused on federal and military officials. Of 19 cases, 14 involved federal and military officials. The Juárez cartel, in contrast, was charged with bribing 10 officials, 9 of them municipal (Burnett. Peñalosa, and Benincasa 2010).

Moreover, anecdotal evidence of Mexican military cooperation with the Sinaloa gang is substantial. One example of cooperation involves a local military commander in Durango who reportedly provided security for the July 2007 wedding of Sinaloa kingpin Joaquin "El Chapo" Guzman and his third wife, Emma Coronel, in Canelas, Durango (Wilkinson 2008). Speculation about PAN ties to the Sinaloa gang is substantial as well. In particular, there is wide speculation in Mexico that Calderón's predecessor, PAN president Vicente Fox, allowed El Chapo Guzman to escape from prison just before the kingpin was to be extradited to the United States. In the second month of the Fox presidency in January 2001, El Chapo "escaped" while incarcerated in Puente Grande, a maximum-security prison in Jalisco. The Mexican government's official story is that El Chapo allegedly escaped in a laundry cart with the assistance of seventy-eight federal prison authorities, including the head of the prison (Beith 2010: 368).[4]

The Zetas Versus the Sinaloa Gang and the Government

The Zetas gang remains a holdout as of 2012—that is, the Zetas still vigorously contest Sinaloa gang dominance and government conduct of the drug war. Originally, the Zetas served as the enforcement arm of the Gulf gang. The Zetas became an autonomous criminal organization in early 2010 following the conviction of Gulf kingpin Cardenas Guillen in the United States. In the ensuing rupture, the Zetas repositioned and allied with the Beltran Leyva gang, the former enforcement arm of the Sinaloa gang. The allied forces of the Zetas and Beltran Leyva gangs began to battle the Sinaloa and Gulf gangs in struggles for smuggling routes and market share. The original split of the Zetas from the Gulf derived from an internal battle over who would manage the Gulf's lucrative commercial operations known as "The Company." The Company consisted of all of the Gulf gang's illicit commercial activities beyond narcotics, such as human trafficking, product piracy, extortion, kidnapping for ransom, and oil siphoning theft (Frontera NorteSur 2010; Roebuck 2010a; Logan and Sullivan 2010). Gulf operatives refused to hand over

The Company to the Zetas in January 2010. Instead of complying with the Zetas demands, the Gulf organization killed Zetas lieutenant Victor "Concord 3" Peña Mendoza, in Reynosa, Tamaulipas. The Zetas, notorious for brutality and mutilation-murders, prepared to retaliate by gathering troops along the Tamaulipas border.

To confront the new concentration of Zetas troops, the Gulf gang allied temporarily with its old rival, the Sinaloa gang, and with La Famila Michoacana to battle the Zetas in the states of Tamaulipas and Nuevo León. A tentative truce averted major war between the two opposing camps (Roebuck 2010b). The alliance of the Gulf and Sinaloa gangs—however temporary—apparently altered the balance of power long enough for the Zetas to withdraw to Nuevo Laredo, making a truce operable (Roebuck 2010a). Nevertheless, the Zetas continue to battle government forces and the Sinaloa and Gulf gangs and remain serious combatants in the drug war up to the present in late 2012.

In the end, the Calderón government's conduct of the war bolstered the Sinaloa organization, which emerged from the drug war as the hegemonic gang. The symbiotic links between the Sinaloa gang and the Mexican state and drug trafficking are multifaceted. Drug profits are one of Mexico's top three sources of foreign exchange, ranking up at the top along with oil exports and migrant remittances (Haddick 2010). If the state were to eliminate virtually all illicit drug trade, Mexico would lose billions of dollars of foreign exchange each year. One study estimates that the drug trade brings in $39 billion a year to the Mexican economy; equivalent to 4.5 percent of Mexico's economic output in 2009.[5]

Zones of Impunity and Human Rights Abuse: Politics of Life and Death in a Transnational Drug War

As the war crimes complaint to the ICC suggests, there has been wide speculation alleging that the Calderón administration was criminally complicit with the Sinaloa gang. As yet, it is unclear how Calderón's presidential successor, Enrique Peña Nieto, will address such allegations. Similar to the Calderón government, the Bush and Obama administrations' military support in Mexico's drug war leaves the U.S. government open to charges of aiding foreign armed forces that engage in extrajudicial executions, kidnapping, and disappearances. Although human rights activists have pressured both governments to stop Mexican armed forces from torturing, raping, disappearing, and executing people, nevertheless, Mexican judicial reforms have fallen short of IACHR judicial reform mandates (Meyer 2011), and U.S. weapons shipments through the Mérida Initiative have, for the most part, continued as of July 2012.

As numerous analysts indicate, during the Fox and Calderón administrations, a variety of drug gangs came to control areas of subnational territory (Aguilar and Castaneda 2009: 51–52) essentially acting as multiple sovereigns (Fregoso 2006: 113–44) and controlling mortality with impunity in the drug war (Wright 2011: 723–27). Coexisting with Mexican state authority, drug gangs have bribed police officers and public officials to gain effective control of a considerable number of municipalities across the country. Mexico had as many as 2,437 "zones of impunity" in 2008–9, per official figures estimated two years into the Calderón term (*Milenio* 2009).[6] By June 2009, this estimated number of gang-dominated "zones of impunity" had dropped substantially to 980 zones controlled by gangs. It would be a mistake, however, to conclude that this drop in gang-controlled territory necessarily reflects a Mexican state more committed to protecting human rights or a state less corrupted by drug commerce. Instead, numerous experts conclude that the Calderón government's pattern of arrests reflects a targeting of all drug gangs, except Sinaloa (Hernandez 2010; Gibler 2011: 24–29; Buscaglia 2009; *The Economist* 2010 [quoting Buscaglia]).

The criminal impunity enjoyed by Mexican armed forces adds to the abuses perpetrated with near impunity by the drug gangs. In drug hot spots, nearly all soldiers and police were, until 2011–12, virtually exempt from civilian criminal prosecution for human rights abuses (Human Rights Watch 2009a: 37–56). The Inter-American Court of Human Rights has periodically attempted to remedy key aspects of military impunity with some limited success. In November 2010, the court sanctioned Mexico by ruling in favor of the plaintiffs in a case brought by two indigenous women raped by Mexican soldiers in Guerrero. The court found that Mexico had violated three different inter-American conventions on human rights and had denied two victims access to justice by remanding the cases to a military tribunal (Osberg 2010: 1–6). The court then ordered Mexico to pay reparations to each of the two victims. As previously discussed, in 2009 the Inter-American Court ruled that Mexico had to pass legislation to ensure that all human rights abuse cases be tried in civilian courts rather than in military tribunals. In spite of such Inter-American juridical oversight, however, analyst Maureen

Meyer and journalist Kristin Bricker present evidence that the Mexican state still had not promulgated sufficient legislation to meet the requirements for judicial reform imposed by the court (Meyer 2010; Bricker 2011). Overall, the Mexican state and judiciary still offer human rights abuse victims little effective police protection or legal recourse. Instead, crime victims still face considerable fear of criminal retaliation when they report gang or armed forces abuses of human rights (Human Rights Watch 2009). Some residents of Ciudad Juárez in particular report that they fear military and police forces as much as drug gangs and find little difference between the two sets of actors (Wright 2011: 722–23).

Impunity and Necropolitics

> M]ilitary operations and the exercise of the right to kill are no longer the sole monopoly of states, and the "regular army" is no longer the unique modality of carrying out these functions. . . . [A] patchwork of overlapping and incomplete rights to rule emerges, inextricably superimposed and tangled . . . and plural allegiances, asymmetrical suzerainties, and enclaves abound. (Mbembe 2003: 31)

The history of the politics of death in Juárez, as Wright (2011) points out, clearly illustrates Mexican governments' tendency to criminalize murder victims rather than pursue justice. Wright documents how local and national government minimized crimes of femicide by insinuating that women murder victims, in particular prostitutes, were themselves criminals. This practice of blaming the victims has persisted to this day. Along the same lines, the Mexican state at various levels has insinuated that murder victims in the drug war were drug criminals themselves (Wright 2011: 721). This strategy of criminalizing murder victims, including mutilation-murder victims, reflects, as postcolonial theorist Achille Mbembe (2003: 16–17) argues, a politics of killing, a necropolitics, as a methodology of governing people.

Necropolitics as a theoretical concept incorporates Agamben's idea of government controlling peoples' lives via the sovereign state's extrajudicial power to maintain or end life. However, Mbembe's necropolitics goes beyond state authority over life; he posits a necropolitics whereby multiple actors exercise extrajudicial power over death practices as a means of governing. In effect, multiple actors, including the state and gangsters, exercise the right to kill with impunity, often using heinous methods defying all reasonable concepts of human rights.

The public officials and private gangsters who make decisions about who dies and how people are killed govern people through death threats and publicizing heinous killings. Decapitation of victims, the display of severed heads in public spaces, bodily dismemberment, the charring of bodies with fire, and the dissolving of bodies in acid have been common murder practices. The goal is to govern by employing the spectacle of horrific death to instill fear and compliance (Carlin 2012: 506, 512). Mexico's mutilation-murderers, professional assassins-for-hire (*sicarios*), and hit men are often revealed to be active-duty Mexican soldiers, military deserters, or police officers from the municipal, state, or federal level (Bowden 2010: 177–88). Given that law enforcement officers are often criminals themselves, Mexican residents of drug hot spots live under state of emergency conditions that normalize a status of rightlessness for all those caught in the crossfire. Thus, the Calderón government, the Mexican armed forces, and drug gangsters have exercised the sovereign right to kill with virtual impunity. Human rights protections clearly have not been at the forefront of Mexican (or U.S.) national policy concerns.

Thinking Past Criminality and Killing:
Toward Decriminalizing U.S.-Mexico Relations

Drug smugglers have operated for decades in Mexico, but transnational crime and human rights abuses rarely overwhelmed U.S.-Mexico relations as they have from 2006 to 2012.[7] Several alternative futures are possible, including more peaceful ones based on decriminalization.

Transnational drug gangs operated throughout the administrations of Ernesto Zedillo (1994–2000) and Vicente Fox (2000–2006) without provoking binational crime emergencies in Mexico and the United States or steady bloodbaths in Mexico. In the wake of escalating violent crime since 2006, an array of presidents in the Americas have advocated a policy shift from narcotics prohibition toward legalization of marijuana across the hemisphere. The presidents contend that such legalization would reduce violent crime and human rights abuses across the Americas (Cave 2012b). For instance, former presidents Fernando Henrique Cardoso of Brazil and Ernesto Zedillo and Vicente Fox of Mexico argue that narco-violence could be substantially reduced if the U.S. and Mexican governments would shift away from national prohibition of drugs toward a national policy of regulating drug sales and treating addicts. Moving marijuana into the legal trade category, they argue, would drastically reduce the profits from the highest volume narcotic sales and generate tax revenues from drug sales. The U.S. government has thus far refused to shift drug policy from prohibition and criminalization to regulation and drug addiction treatment. This refusal helps perpetuate the flow of criminalized narcotics demanded by U.S. consumers and exported from Mexico.

The Mexican government in turn has waged a "drug war" in lock step with U.S. drug prohibition policy. The U.S.-Mexico border, already militarized and criminalized by U.S. prohibitions on immigration, has been further militarized during the "war on terror." In compliance with the U.S. government's criminalization of narcotics, the Calderón administration waged a war of drug prohibition that failed to stop cross-border drug smuggling. UN drug crime expert Edgardo Buscaglia (2009) publicly declared that this war on drugs is a "sham."

There are several indicators that the Mexican drug war will not continue indefinitely. National states typically contain rival agencies, personalities, and factions with conflicting and shifting agendas. First, ties between portions of the Mexican military and the Sinaloa gang do not simply make the entire Mexican state a "narco-state" run by Sinaloa leader El Chapo Guzman. Second, the Mexican government's excessive reliance on the military for authority is potentially short-lived, as President Peña Nieto has indicated that he may not continue to send armed forces to occupy cities or to replace the police. Indeed, Peña Nieto employed his first six months in office to shift the country's public discourse and practice away from armed assault on drug gangs toward economic development and compensation for drug war victims (Shear and Archibold 2013). Third, as the Sinaloa gang appears to have emerged as the hegemonic drug gang in Mexico, El Chapo is emerging as a potential ally of Peña Nieto, according to Sylvia Longmire, a leading U.S. consultant on Mexican drug gangs (Carrasco Araizaga 2012). Longmire points out that the continued government targeting of the Zetas gang resonates with El Chapo's interest in weakening the Sinaloa gang's fiercest enemy. Clearly, the Mexican state is not simply a puppet state run by drug lords who pull all the strings. At the same time, billions of dollars in foreign exchange earnings from illicit drug sales will remain important to the Mexican state and economy for the foreseeable future. If the U.S. government were to legalize, regulate, and cooperate with Mexico to tax marijuana, those tax revenues might help reduce current U.S.-Mexico fixations on drug gangs and criminality.

On a larger, binational scale, demilitarization by both the U.S. and Mexican governments would perhaps do the most to broaden and change the focus of U.S.-Mexico relations. In the United States, demilitarization of the southern border would obligate the U.S. government to shift away from criminalizing migrants to regulating an immigrant workforce. That would involve the U.S. Congress passing effective immigration reform, including the implementation of a viable guest worker policy regulating Mexican migrants wishing to work in the United States. By decriminalizing and regulating migrant workers, the United States could shift paradigms away from ineffective and costly southern border enforcement. The U.S. Border Patrol and Department of Homeland Security in general could be retooled to focus on the complexities of preventing actual terrorist and other security threats to the United States rather than intercepting Mexican migrant workers who cross the southern border looking for work. Decriminalization of border crossing would help shift the focus of U.S.-Mexico relations away from criminal emergencies, military enforcement, and death toward economic collaboration.

In Mexico, demilitarization would require, first, that the government roll back the state of emergency by scaling back the use of soldiers for policing and law enforcement. Soldiers are not trained to do police work and have little familiarity with laws protecting citizens' civil liberties. A better policy would be to expedite the replacement of corrupt local police forces with newly hired, well-trained, and better-paid police officers trained to respect civil rights laws. Second, the Mexican Congress should pass legislation that fulfills the requirements of the Inter-American Court, terminating completely the practice of military tribunals trying any cases of human rights abuse regardless of type of allegation. All cases of soldiers torturing, raping, robbing, or otherwise abusing human rights should be remanded to civilian judges and tried in civilian courts with no exceptions. Third, the government should shift spending priorities away from military armaments and deployments of soldiers to emphasize instead training and competitive salaries for newly recruited police forces. Finally, per the recommendations of Jorge Castaneda (2010), former secretary of foreign relations under Vicente Fox, the Mexican government should shift its national priorities away from military enforcers chasing after rival drug dealers and toward Mexico-U.S. bilateral development processes to encourage the development of a middle-class society in

Mexico. Decriminalization, demilitarization, and rolling back states of emergency in Mexico and at the U.S. southern border would all help reduce binational emphasis on the sovereign right to kill as a means to control territory and people. A decline in the politics of death in U.S.-Mexico relations could open up the possibility of a new North American integration process. That integration process would grow a regional economy that is not only legal but also increasingly equitable, thereby shrinking illicit trade and extrajudicial killing across the continent.

CHAPTER 5

Migration, Violence, and "Security Primacy" at the Guatemala-Mexico Border

Luis Alfredo Arriola Vega

Most international state borders are loci entangled in power disputes. This interplay may involve adjoining polities or may be about localized tensions among inhabitants of the border. External actors who are neither state-related nor resident frequently also play a role in such contested arenas. This chapter focuses on the glocal[1] dynamics happening at one particular area of the porous border between Guatemala and Mexico (see Figures 1 and 2) with an emphasis on the connections between migration and violence, the result of crime, most notably the illicit drug trade. Transit migration to the United States via Mexico is a phenomenon of regional and international scope that plays a role in the geopolitics of the North American subcontinent (Mexico, the United States, and Canada). While simultaneously keeping sight of agendas that may situate local communities at odds with the Mexican and Guatemalan state apparatuses, respectively, I focus on the growing influence that drug trade organizations (DTOs) exert on the migrant stream.[2] The rise of the organization known as Zetas, in particular, and its involvement in the victimization of migrants passing through Mexico, have raised important concerns at high-level spheres in the U.S. and Mexican governments. The Zetas and competing DTOs are destabilizing stakeholders because they erode a perimeter set as part of current U.S. interests, one that increasingly "borders out" its securitization framework, as I will argue. To the extent possible, this work integrates a binational approach regarding cross-border issues, that is to say, a perspective informed by on-the-ground condi-

Figure 1. The Guatemala-Mexico border. Figure by author.

tions and unfolding processes at the borderlands that Mexico and Guatemala share.

Methodology

Qualitative methods informed this investigation, which started out as a study on outmigration and transit migration.[3] Initial exploratory trips took place at border Mexican communities in two Tabasco townships (*municipios*): Balancán and Tenosique. Formal and informal, structured and semistructured interviews produced the bulk of the data. Depending on the setting, the level of rapport established, and the topic under discussion, interviews could be concise or far-reaching. Interviewing migrants proved challenging, typically involving brief, informal encounters, when the situation permitted, as subjects

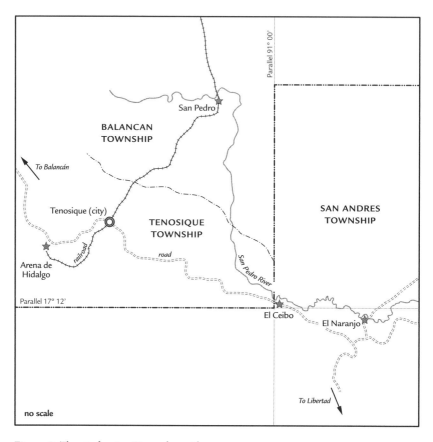

Figure 2. The study site. Figure by author.

frequently behaved evasively. By contrast, two key interviewees provided first-hand information regarding delicate topics without hesitation. One of them lived in a community near the border, and thus was a firsthand witness of local events. The other knew how the drug trade organizations operated in the city of Tenosique and its surroundings. Most field data collection took place in 2009–10. As relations and contacts grew locally, so did the chances of interaction with Guatemalan nationals inhabiting border hamlets (*aldeas*). People crossed over to buy goods and sell their agricultural products at Mexican corner stores, a setting that provided an opportunity for intermingling. Conjugal couples made up of a Guatemalan and a Mexican partner living on Mexican territory offered yet another source of information.

Through direct observation I gained a fair sense of in-transit, non-Mexican migrants. They entered Mexico unauthorized and traveled in groups that ranged from two to twenty individuals. Males made up the majority of groups, usually young adults (seventeen to thirty). Over time I witnessed a progressive increase in the number of minors attempting to reach "el norte." The majority of migrants traversing the Petén-Tabasco border are Hondurans or Guatemalans, and to a lesser extent Salvadorans and Nicaraguans. On occasion one encounters Cubans, Ecuadoreans, Brazilians, and even Chinese, among other nationals.

The Setting

Because of a dearth of specialized literature about this part of the Mexico-Guatemala border, I start with a detailed description of the area with a focus on irregular migration routes. This investigation concentrates on the adjoining border strip zone between Tenosique and Balancán and the township of San Andrés, on the Guatemalan side. The study region is part of the lowland plains that characterize the Yucatán Peninsula; Petén, Guatemala, constitutes the southernmost part of the peninsula. Southeastern Tabasco can be considered, to some extent, an outlying extension of this geographical landscape. The common border zone features rivers, wetlands, some natural grassland, and extensive man-made pastures. Livestock production is a dominant, yet declining, economic activity in Tabasco. Agriculture prevails in Petén's countryside, centered mainly on corn, beans, and dried pumpkin seed.

As will be explained shortly, the area remained scarcely populated until recently, something that accounts for the relative isolation of the border zone. Isolation is less pronounced on the Mexican side as second-class roads connect practically all rural communities with their respective township seats; settlements are stable and well established. Public transportation, though unreliable, is available between major populated centers and outlying areas. Old-growth forest vegetation and swaths of cut-down primary forest characterize the Guatemalan scenery, dotted with recently founded, unsteady frontier hamlets.

Porosity at the border is an essential element to the thriving of irregular activities. The 111 km Tabasco-Petén borderline is open country, not much different from what one finds at certain points along the U.S.-Mexico border. Most significantly, the presence of law enforcement authorities is limited.

Mexican police officers get called in from the township seats whenever serious offenses occur (i.e., robberies, assassinations), but no force remains on a permanent basis in distant rural communities. Controls of any other type are random and sporadic. Agents from Mexico's National Migration Institute (Instituto Nacional de Migración; INM), which has a permanent post in Tenosique, conduct rounds from time to time, but a shortage of personnel, underfunding, and the vast territory they are to cover undermine their efforts at checking unauthorized migration flows. There is an army garrison on the outskirts of Tenosique from which patrols and convoys are deployed to scout local roads, mainly in search of contraband, guns, and drugs. A smaller outpost is located in San Pedro, Balancán, but its operations are limited in scope. The army keeps two or three permanent roadblocks at strategic intersections and, from time to time, establishes checkpoints along main roads.

Interviewees reported that the Guatemalan armed forces carry out routine on-foot reconnaissance trips once or sometimes twice a year along the borderline strip. These expeditions, however, have few if any lasting, tangible results; they are fleeting forays into the faraway, hard-to-reach confines of frontier territory, accessible only by mud trails that become impassable during the rainy season (June through November in a normal year). Without a permanent presence, army units rarely ever achieve a major score in terms of busting a drug cargo or seizing guns, for example. Thus, border porosity remains a critical issue for the two countries' governments.

The two main "urban" centers in Tabasco (Mexico) and Petén (Guatemala) are, respectively, Tenosique, seat of the namesake township, and El Naranjo, a village in the municipality of La Libertad. The former (pop. 32,579 according to official sources in 2010) is the main business center for Balancán and Tenosique. The city of Tenosique is the center for services, commerce, industry, and amenities. Tenosique is the urban location closest to the only formal border crossing between the two countries, known as El Ceibo a distance of 56 km, which enhances the city's strategic significance. For transit migrant flows Tenosique also plays a key role as a convenient stopover on the journey north. Because the cargo railroad line bound to central Mexico passes through Tenosique, migrants board the train in the city and at nearby points.

El Naranjo is located some 30 km from El Ceibo. With 6,000, perhaps 7,000 inhabitants, it is a major hub of financial and agricultural activity in the wide territory north and east of the San Pedro River. Stores supply all sorts of basic goods and manufactured items to dozens of *aldeas* in the vicinity. El

Naranjo is the departure point and terminus for boats from eastern locations on the San Pedro and buses to and from central Petén and beyond. Buses make direct trips from the Guatemala-Honduras border to El Naranjo loaded with migrants. For these and other migrants the village serves as an entrepôt of sorts before entering Mexico. Lodging, transportation, and *coyotes* are readily available to cater to migrants' needs. From this point on, travelers can choose to enter Mexico through different locations. The more complex plan involves heading north or northwest to the frontier settlements described in the next section. This is a costlier, harsher choice because migrants have to walk long distances through livestock paddocks and secondary and old growth forest. The advantage of this option is the absence of major controls along the route. However, it may not be the best choice for inexperienced migrants because guides who take advantage of first-time crossers can make the journey much longer than it need be. A knowledgeable migrant (someone who has traversed the area before) can get on a pick-up truck at El Naranjo and reach the border in about four hours during the dry season; and from that point he or she can opt to catch the train inside Mexico at one of several locations. The faster and (sometimes) cheaper way to approach the border is to get on a minibus and head to El Ceibo. The ride takes no more than thirty minutes, but the presence of migration authorities at El Ceibo makes the process of entering Mexico more complicated.

Since 2000, when a paved road connected Tenosique with the border, El Ceibo has experienced an astonishing transformation. An informal market comprised of makeshift vendor stands has turned into a prosperous commercial village. Ever since, Mexicans from afar have traveled to El Ceibo to buy diverse merchandise. Items sold in El Ceibo are cheap for two reasons. First, a fair number of goods available in El Ceibo may be contraband items, and second, custom offices are not fully operational and rather relaxed at the border. The swift rise of El Ceibo as a border market is challenging El Naranjo's historical primary role as *the* border town on the migrant trail. The paving of the road leading to the border on the Guatemalan side in 2008 delivered the final blow to this process. Economic activities connected to the in-transit flows are increasingly shifting to El Ceibo, where there is an active exchange of goods and humans, both legal and illegal (Arriola 2010, 2012).

In the context of drug trafficking, the Petén-Tabasco borderlands have functioned as a transshipment location since at least the early 1990s (Dudley 2011). History and geography explain, in part (see Arriola 2012), why this area has become a strategic setting for contemporary, transnational "shadow networks" (Nordstrom 2001). In the recent past, two developments further complicated conditions at the border: the ongoing confrontations among DTOs (most prominently the dispute among the Zetas, the Sinaloa, and the Gulf organizations)[4] in their efforts to gain sway over transit routes, and up to 2012 the Mexican government's frontal attack on all drug-trafficking activity. As a result, DTOs had been compelled to rearrange their logistics, seek new territories of operation, and recruit new manpower. Thus, the Zetas have moved to Guatemala, where conditions have facilitated the expansion of drug business operations; reportedly, their organization is active in Honduras, too (Arnson and Olson 2011). In this light, the Mexico-Guatemala border gains added strategic significance with regard to the transnational movement of drugs. The geopolitical implications of this development directly relate to current U.S. security policy thinking, as I argue shortly.

Contrasting Realities at the International Border

On the Mexican side of the border, communities have achieved basic economic, social, and political stability while maintaining an active relationship with the Mexican central state. They turn to the state for better infrastructure and to attain material and financial support (agriculture subsidies and aid to the elderly, among other things). Simultaneously, they try to sidestep the state through noncompliance with certain state directives. Otherwise, the rule of law prevails. Even though economic circumstances are tough, people make ends meet. Middle-aged and elderly Mexicans compare current conditions in neighboring Guatemala hamlets to the situation their own communities endured some forty or fifty years ago.

On the Guatemalan side of the border, conditions differ but are directly influenced by events in Mexico. Frontier settlements, established during the last three decades, have flourished in a milieu where active state presence is sporadic at best and people take matters into their own hands (from exerting the law to deciding who can purchase land and so on). The most fundamental services and infrastructure, including health care, education, drinking water, electricity, and roads, are lacking. Hence, Guatemalans depend on Mexico for their livelihood. The fact that it is easier for Guatemalans to enter and exit their communities by traveling on Mexican border roads to reach

El Ceibo underscores the degree of isolation they face. Life is rough in these twenty-first-century borderlands, a place where peasants, cattle ranchers, outlaws of various sorts, and organized crime members converge. To complicate matters, Guatemalan hamlets are located inside the Maya Biosphere Reserve, an area designated for conservation purposes, and hence people lack official sanction to settle permanently, which compromises their "legal" status. Such a precarious state of affairs creates favorable conditions for illegal practices and tenuous relationships vis-à-vis adjacent Mexican communities. Not surprisingly, members of these outlying villages participate, sometimes in collusion with Mexicans, sometimes on their own, in malfeasances.

The Dark Side of Globalization and the Externalization of U.S. Policy

The existence of extrastate economies and illegal practices (Heyman 1999) characterizes life on this international border. The illicit buying and selling of contraband, such as forest products, wildlife, and archaeological artifacts, has enjoyed social legitimacy among members of the border population for decades. Cattle and timber smuggling also has a long history and, to some extent, continues to the present. Livestock is usually stolen in Mexico and taken into Guatemala, while illicit lumber travels in the opposite direction.

Some border residents participate in the most lucrative businesses, namely the transportation of migrants on their way to the United States, and, on occasion, the trafficking of drugs and arms. Of utmost concern are the scale and nature of illegal practices in which the Zetas have become involved, including trafficking of migrants. With the Zetas' range of operation stretching from Mexico to several Central American countries, the fragile situation of this border has become a matter of "national security" in a wider geopolitical context, with far-reaching consequences. What takes place at the Guatemala-Mexico border is no different from what goes on at other remote international borders, except that it directly and indirectly affects a powerful country. Mounting concern in the United States about security and defense of the "homeland" affects the outer limit of its southern neighbor: perceived threats at a distance from the U.S. border are progressively embedded in a security rationale in which the idea of homeland is ironically situated away from home. This particular viewpoint advances what Demetrios Papademetriou, president of the Migration Policy Institute, a Washington, D.C.-based think tank, has referred to as "pushing out of the border" (Papademetriou and Collet 2011), an idea that also resonates with an externalization of migration policies in first-world destination countries (Lavenex and Ucarer 2002, quoted in Collyer 2010). Correspondingly, the United States progressively approaches this border zone from a "security primacy" lens (Konrad 2011).[5] In this light, one may argue that Mexico will increasingly play a filter role in relation to an externalized U.S. migration policy, and in the interim it may figure as a security gate.[6]

Historically a repertoire of strategies was in place and more or less worked, so that underground economies' business-as-usual between border residents and authorities went on without major disruptions. For local inhabitants these stratagems included hiding, evading, bribing, or looking the other way. These arrangements were shattered as a result of external driving forces that are part of the clandestine side of globalization acting locally (Andreas 2003). Two sets of related conditions explain this recent shift. First, the aforementioned turf war among Mexican drug organizations in places like the Tabasco-Petén border zone brought violent confrontation in a battle for hegemony.[7] Second, the continued ascendance of the Zetas as an autonomous force changed the modus operandi and logic that underlie shadow practices. Power disputes among drug organizations turned extreme and terrifying. Violence no longer was limited to shootings between rivals; it also included kidnappings for ransom (among both civilians and migrants), beheadings, and other terrorizing tactics. This part of the Mexico-Guatemala border became quite dangerous, however not at the scale reached in northern Mexico.

Migrant Flows and the Rise of the Zetas

To further illustrate the mounting violence, and its repercussions, I discuss international migration flows through the area in connection to the rise of the Zetas. The migrant stream has a history of about three decades, but it peaked after the late 1990s; currently, this route ranks third among the Mexico-Guatemala border crossing areas used by unauthorized migrants. Until recently a *coyote* accompanied many of these migrants, usually in groups, taking them to an intermediate destination or all the way to the U.S.-Mexico border. In 2008, approximately, the Zetas began charging fees to coyotes that escorted migrants at the starting point of their journey through Mexican territory.[8] The hired hands of the Zetas now run the whole operation, including surveillance, extortions, kidnappings, and executions. If *coyotes* try to get through the area without paying dues to the Zetas they get purged, or worse, killed. Unaccompanied migrants have become easy prey to the Zetas' rapacious tactics, too. To entice (or deceive) potential victims, the Zetas recruit compatriots of the migrants. For example, Hondurans passing as *coyotes* (deliberately hired by Zetas) are in charge of convincing fellow countrymen that they will help and facilitate their journey. A point of clarification is in order here. Many specialists, and the general public at large, take for granted the existence of a close nexus between Maras and Zetas.[9] It is feasible that they may enter into occasional alliances; for example, Maras may be playing the same role the Zetas fulfilled before for the Gulf DTO, namely as operatives (hit men and kidnappers).[10] However, and to the best of my knowledge, before 2012 there were no direct, permanent, much less organic links between these groups in the Tabasco-Petén zone; such a relationship, if any, was tenuous at best.

When migrants fall prey to the Zetas they face collective ransom demands and will be killed if they do not comply. In this way, mass killings have taken place.[11] The much-publicized tragedy that occurred at the San Fernando Ranch, in the state of Tamaulipas, in mid-2010 is one among many events of this type (BBC News 2010b; *La Jornada* 2010). The initial count of the San Fernando carnage put the total number of bodies at 72, with most of the victims Central Americans. As of mid-April 2011 the number had increased to 145 (BBC News 2011a; *La Jornada* 2011b). By the end of July it had risen to more than 200 (*La Jornada* 2011c). I had heard of mass kidnappings taking place at least two years earlier, in southeastern Tabasco. For instance, the earliest media reporting inside Mexico concerning such a mass killing appeared in a well-known weekly magazine, *Proceso*.[12] The massacre took place at a ranch near the border between the municipalities of Tenosique and Emiliano Zapata in early July 2009 (Martínez 2009a); however, the story of this massacre never made it to the mainstream, national media. While such atrocities have certainly dissuaded many migrants from attempting to cross Mexico, the flow of Central American migrants coming through the Tabasco-Petén border area continues unabated.[13]

Prior to 2013 the Zetas were trying to gain full control of the drug trade as well. This thesis is supported by the Zetas' expansion into Guatemala and Honduras. For instance, journalists' reports frequently discuss the operation of Zetas cells in various locations around Guatemala, particularly in the north.[14] Even though the violence subsided for most of 2012, previous research (Espach et al. 2011; InSight Crime 2011a)[15] painted a bleak outlook for Petén. The province has become a vital corridor of the south-north drug trail, especially for warehousing and transporting narcotics. Local Guatemalan DTOs (sometimes in alliance with their Mexican counterparts, sometimes on their own) have an active presence in Petén. Influential *Petenero* politicians have set up powerful local networks to gain economic and social power, sometimes through differing degrees of involvement or ties with drug organizations. The wave of violence experienced in Petén during 2011 involved disputes among criminal organizations over territories and routes, a phenomenon that may have begun in 2008 because of the arrival of the Zetas, according to one source (Espach et al. 2011: 11–12).

The massacre that took place on May 2011 at a ranch some 30 km southeast of El Naranjo, in which innocent people died at the hands of hired gunmen, illustrates the escalation of drug trafficking-related violence that has recently befallen Petén. The news of the carnage made headlines all over the world (CNN News 2011; *New York Daily News* 2011). In what originally seemed to be a scheme to kill the owner of the ranch, who had purported ties to the local drug underworld and happened to be absent at the time, at least twenty-seven ranch laborers were brutally killed. A longtime acquaintance from El Naranjo told me that there was much more to the event than the published sources revealed. The body count may have been as high as twenty-nine. Most accounts identified the ranch as Los Cocos, but its real name is San Juan. The motive for vengeance arose from the rancher's seizure of a drug cargo from another local group, yet there is no certainty that he stole it from the Zetas. Most intriguing is the fact that it is extremely difficult to know who actually carried out this slaughter. In other words, groups outside the law are using the Zeta "trademark," as my interviewee keenly pointed out, to carry out all sorts of barbarities.[16]

While Mexico's federal government under then-president Felipe Calderón followed a large-scale military strategy against drug trade organizations as a matter of state policy,[17] no similar approach, or policy of such magnitude, has been implemented in Guatemala. The national government has limited resources to fight drug trade organizations; its state institutions are weak; and, allegedly, drug-related money has infiltrated several sectors of society. So far, DTOs pose little threat to the Guatemalan state, although this may well change. To complicate matters, Guatemalan society is beleaguered by internal tribulations inherited from recent civil warfare (Manz 2008; Pearce 1998).

Toward a Human Security Perspective

The radius of influence of U.S. security policy extends beyond the Rio Grande, in what I referred to above as an externalization of a security schema. To some extent, Mexico's policies respond to U.S. directives through the hardening of its own measures to stop the flow of migrants and drugs passing through its territory. For migrants such a strategy has led to the multiplication of life-threatening scenarios. Policies have failed because migrants continue to be the main victims of a business that operates at the micro (local), meso (regional), and macro (national and international) levels, and at the hands of all kinds of groups, on both sides of the law. Such critical conditions call for an alternate paradigm to dominant policy models: human security.

Two premises inform my conceptualizing of human security. First, it is a multidimensional way of looking at security, something that concerns and relates to populations, not only regimes, territories, or elites (Nef 1999). Second, threats to security are no longer individual, regional, or national; their scope is international and global. Today pandemics, socionatural disasters, and drugs compromise human security on a global scale. Hence this paradigm calls for a holistic approach to understanding and addressing security issues, in direct opposition to doctrines that advocate a state-centered, militaristic, unilateral, hegemonic perspective.[18] Concern for human security is seriously lacking in policy thinking, particularly when it comes to migration, drugs, and arms.

Migration is a prime example. Progressive immigration reform in the United States was, until recently, unlikely because of strong, irreconcilable viewpoints, both political and economic. Even though some steps have been taken in the right direction in Mexico, the country still has a long way to go. The national legislature has recently approved a new migration policy, yet the latest law continues to espouse, overall, a restrictive migration policy, one within a securitization framework. As of this writing a renewed National Security Act was under discussion, too. In its current form, the spirit of the proposal embraced a centralized, pro-military doctrine. For instance, the proposed statute grants increased discretionary powers to the president and armed forces to act in situations that, from their viewpoint, threaten internal and national security.

Policies informed by a human security perspective can set the course to alleviate grievances and violations committed against migrants whether at the hands of corrupt state officials or by groups outside the law. The same applies to potential solutions to drug trafficking. Human security could provide the guiding principles to start thinking outside the box. For example, changes are needed regarding narcotics policies in the United States, including but not restricted to the decriminalizing of certain drugs as a way to lower consumer demand. The handling of such urgent problems, as they occur in the Guatemala-Mexico border zone, demands a comprehensive solution that settles historical binational differences, tends to cultural idiosyncrasies, and is sensitive to populations on the move.

Final Remarks

The Petén-Tabasco area at the Guatemala-Mexico border is a backdrop to power struggles of a diverse caliber, skirmishes between the state and criminal organizations, and infighting among these groups. In the midst of all this conflict are local residents and transient populations. The flow of people and goods intersects at local and global levels, making this a glocal setting. In light of the dynamics of violence taking place at the border and beyond, a particularly interesting issue is the way certain actors undermine and weaken state authority without seeking to overthrow the establishment or replace the state. The sheer force and violence of these organizations challenge the capacity of weak states to react accordingly. These circumstances make it extremely difficult to closely study criminal organizations and the consequences of their actions.

The glocal character of the Tabasco-Petén border zone is not only economic but also political. Mexico's southern border has taken center stage as part of a scheme aimed at deterring the flow of people and drugs bound for the United States. The violent flux in these borderlands will endure as long as drug trade organizations continue to expand their areas of influence, their routes, and their connections at the local, regional, and international levels (in Mexico, Guatemala, and to some extent other countries, such as El Salvador and Honduras). Disputes between groups operating on the dark side of globalization at porous, frail borders are economic in nature, yet their reper-

cussions are political. For better or for worse, and in line with a policy of pushing its borders out for the sake of a narrow, one-sided conceptualization of
security, the U.S. government will continue to play a significant role in the
area. In June 2011, at an International Security Conference, held in Guatemala
City, the World Bank launched a well-funded initiative to deal with security
issues in Central America (Central American Regional Security Initiative,
or CARSI). Following suit, U.S. Secretary of State Clinton announced that
the United States pledged $300 million toward a "regional security partner-
ship."[19] CARSI follows in the footsteps of the Mérida and Beyond Mérida
Initiatives, both of which included U.S. funding for Calderón's drug war
(Silkee and Finklea 2011).

Despite this increased attention to the region, the causal factors behind
massive migration and the rise of the drug trade go largely unaddressed. For
instance, we must bear witness to a rise of what I tentatively call extrastate
violence in connection with the motivations for migration. Extrastate violence emanates from the private sphere (as in gender-oriented violence and
family-generated violent behavior) as well as from the public domain (i.e.,
"common delinquency," via gang wrongdoing, robberies, kidnappings, extortions, etc.), ripping through the fabric of entire communities, urban and
rural alike. Structural violence (institutionalized social exclusion, extreme
deprivation, and chronic poverty) feeds extrastate violence and hence contributes to further outmigration; the augmented power of DTOs exacerbates
violence against migrants en route to the United States. To halt this impending human rights crisis a different paradigm is urgently needed, one that pri-
oritizes human security instead of shortsighted policies that focus on narrow
interests, instead of the greater good.

PART III

Structural Violence and Civil
Society in Ciudad Juárez

CHAPTER 6

The Binational Roots of the Femicides in Ciudad Juárez

Carol Mueller

In approximately 1993, a series of grisly murders began to target poor, young women in the Mexican border town of Ciudad Juárez. Esther Cano Chávez, who ran the only shelter for battered women in Ciudad Juárez before her death, noted the treatment of victims as worthless, disposable women and characterized these deaths as *feminicidos*, or feminicides. Cano Chávez and others pointed to a combination of sexual violation with signs of torture and mutilation on the bodies of victims (Monárrez Fragoso 2001, 2000; Wright 2004, 2001). Many of the women's bodies were disposed of like worthless objects in shallow graves. One of the definitive reports on the murders, published by Amnesty International in 2003, characterized them as follows:

> A common factor in many of these cases is that the young women were kidnapped, held captive and subjected to brutal sexual violence before being killed. The types of violence include rape, biting, beatings, stab wounds and mutilation. The cause of death in over 70 percent of the murders was either asphyxia resulting from strangulation or injuries caused by blows. (AI 2003c: 18)

The broad term *femicidio*, or "femicide," could leave the impression that all the murders of women during this period were more or less the same, but then the tragic circumstances of individuals would be lost. To avoid this danger Monárrez Fragoso(2000) used local newspapers as well as data from official records to distinguish each of 162 feminicides between 1993 and 1999 based

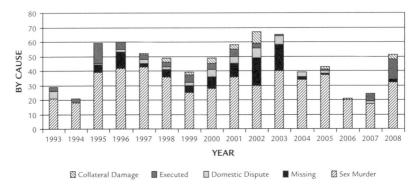

Figure 3. Femicide victims in Ciudad Juárez, 1993–2008. Terry Collins and Carol Mueller, "The Measurement of Femicide," paper at Annual Meeting of the Association of Borderland Studies, Albuquerque, 2009.

on manner of death, location where the body was found, poverty of the neighborhood and its level of turnover, and personal characteristics like the age and occupation of the victim. While recognizing the diversity of circumstances, her study nevertheless underscored a dominant pattern of victims who were very young (only 26 of the 162 were over thirty, and 6 were younger than eleven), from poor neighborhoods, and either in school or working in the maquiladoras (foreign-owned manufacturing plants), in bars, or as prostitutes. Details of the means of death were as gruesome as those reported by the media and activists. Further examination of murders after the turn of the century (Collins and Mueller 2009) corroborates this picture.

In addition to brutal and insolent treatment by perpetrators of the murders, the response of law enforcement and other public officials disparaged the moral worth of the victims (Ensalaco 2006). They often dismissed the women as prostitutes who led double lives or as immoral women who frequented bars and nightclubs, deserving no better than what they got. Such attitudes and resulting impunity for the crimes has led to ongoing mobilizations by activists in the state of Chihuahua and throughout Mexico as well as garnering the attention of transnational activists in the international human rights community (Staudt 2008; Aikin Araluce 2009; Anaya Munóz 2009a). The response to the femicide by human rights activists locally in Juárez and Mexico as well as internationally has been amply documented, but it has also been noted that international attention waned sharply after mass marches and demonstrations in 2003 and 2004 (Mueller, Hansen, and Qualtire, 2009; Staudt 2008) without a corresponding decline in the killings.[1]

Indeed, the femicide was a premonition of what was to come as a result of the recent drug cartel war, on a much larger scale throughout the country, targeting men as well as women, the middle-aged as well as the young, but almost always the poor. By 2010, Juárez had become the most dangerous city in the world, and it was increasingly difficult to distinguish the continuing femicide from the mass murders occurring on a daily basis in the city.

Most feminists, however, would argue that such violence against women is hardly unique (Russell and Harmes 2001; Caputi 1987; Brownmiller 1975). Large-scale violence against women, such as rape, has been a defining symbol of warfare and peacetime since the beginning of human history.[2] Thus, we begin with the assumption that the Juárez femicide is a natural extension of a misogyny that takes specifically brutal forms when configurations of time and place are conducive.[3] As sociologists, we attempt to explain this long-running femicide in the sense that theorists like Charles Tilly (2008) refer to as "historicization" or exploring time and place as the major determinants of an outcome. This is not a way of saying that these young women were "in the wrong place at the wrong time." Rather, we refer to a confluence of forces that came together in this particular city at this particular time to create a pattern of victimization that then spread to the larger society. To state this more modestly, I seek to construct a binational narrative in which the causal links to the localization of the femicide in Ciudad Juárez at this particular time and place are clarified—if not totally explained.[4]

Since hundreds of young women have disappeared or have been mutilated and murdered in and around Ciudad Juárez, the first question is, what historical circumstances made so many young women so vulnerable? What brought so many young women to the border? And why the city of Juárez? To locate the Juárez femicide historically, we also have to ask why now, even if "now" reaches back almost twenty years. And, finally, how could such barbarous events go on for so long? What has prevented law enforcement, at the local, state, and federal levels, from intervening? How is it that these murders eventually came to define not just a city, but the border itself?

Economic Forces Gather the Victims in One Location

For this scale of femicide to occur, large numbers of vulnerable women, young and poor, had to be drawn to the large, sprawling city. In the mid- to late 1980s, macrolevel economic forces created one of the necessary conditions for an unprecedented femicide at the U.S.-Mexico border. While there is no evidence of intent to create the conditions for femicide, there was every intention of bringing poor, young women to the U.S.-Mexican border towns, particularly, to Ciudad Juárez.

As for the poor throughout the world, the opportunities for a young Mexican woman living in poverty are constrained by her country's economic struggles at any given time. The main factor that molded a peculiar susceptibility in the early 1990s was an accelerating flow of trade, legally and illegally, from a developing country into the world's leading economy. The rise of neoliberal strategies for economic development in the 1980s accelerated this interdependence, as did programs enacted by the United States and the International Monetary Fund (IMF) to address repeated debt crises in Mexico.[5] In addition, in the face of repeated economic crises, direct foreign investment grew in importance. As we will show, these changes in macroeconomic conditions became the impetus for a large number of young women to migrate from Mexico's increasingly impoverished hinterlands into the marginal territory of the U.S.-Mexican border towns, some of which, like Ciudad Juárez, became enormous cities overnight.

The Rise of Maquiladoras

The first maquiladoras were opened in 1965 as a result of the end of the Bracero Program, and the implementation of the National Border Development Program or PRONAF.[6] The Bracero Program involved cooperation between the United States and Mexico in bringing migrant workers north to work in the U.S. agricultural sector. It officially ended in 1964, but it had the long-term impact of increasing the influx of Mexican immigrants to the border towns, especially Ciudad Juárez. Even after the program ended, the population of Juárez continued to grow from laborers expecting to find work. In order to provide jobs for the rising population of Mexican laborers accumulating in the border towns, Mexico enacted PRONAF, allowing foreign corporations (mostly U.S.-based) to bring raw materials into Mexico, assemble the product, and then export merchandise with prices made competitive by Mexico's low wages and tariffs, based only on the value added by Mexican labor. The value of the program for foreign manufacturers was enormous (Kagan 2005). In addition, with the increased importance of foreign investments and implementation of the structural adjustment programs in the

1980s and 1990s, the maquila sector became even more important. In response to the peso crisis of 1982 the Mexican government allowed maquiladora goods to be sold inside the country and permitted the licenses of maquiladoras to stand indefinitely.[7] The laws that governed maquiladora investment within Mexico reflected the new level of cooperative effort between the United States, Mexico, and Canada culminating in the implementation of NAFTA in 1994 (Scott, Salas, and Campbell 2006).

At the same time, owing to the devaluation of the peso and the adoption of NAFTA in 1994 and the newly imposed "structural adjustment programs," the agricultural situation of the rural population became precarious (White 2004). Not only did farmers have to compete with giant agricultural corporations exporting wheat and corn from the United States to Mexico, but they were unable to establish or increase credit lines. An increasing number of small and medium-sized farmers were forced to sell their land and find other means of employment. As a result, employment in maquiladoras rose from 40,000 to 800,000 between 1991 and 2000 (Scott, Faux, and Salas 2006), and "tens of millions of Mexicans . . . moved from the impoverished countryside to the overcrowded cities where they could find work in and around the mostly foreign-owned maquilas" (Landau 2005)

Jobs from foreign direct investment were eventually created throughout Mexico, but originally they grew primarily along the border, especially in Tijuana and Ciudad Juárez, where transportation costs were lower. While there has been much debate on the effectiveness of NAFTA in improving Mexico's financial situation, there is little doubt that such initiatives expanded foreign investment in the border region.

Young Women and the Maquilas

As indicated in the work of Monárrez Fragoso (2000), not all the victims she was able to identify worked in the maquilas. Many were in school or worked in bars or as prostitutes. Nevertheless, it was the maquilas that brought most of these young women to the border, and it was the maquilas that offered the greatest opportunities. Although the macroeconomic policies were initially designed to address male unemployment in the 1960s, economic crises and neoliberal remedies created a different destiny for the border as millions of young women migrated there. Although Mexican policymakers were surprised by the feminization of the border labor force, they should not have been

(Torres Ruiz 2011), as the development of Export Processing Zones (EPZs) around the globe, based on liberalization policies, has been consistently associated with increased employment of a young female labor force due primarily to the lower wages they receive (Sing 2000; Pearson 1991). And as subsistence agriculture was simultaneously under pressure from foreign imports enjoying lower tariffs, rural communities were the most likely source for the young women attracted to the expanding maquiladoras—women and girls who were not only young, but also unaccustomed to living in large cities.

Since the early 1990s, 85 percent of the maquila jobs have been taken by women (Fernandez-Kelly 2008). This gender shift in the workforce is attributed to the fact that women were willing to work for cheaper wages, to endure unhealthy work environments, and to accept discrimination concerned with pregnancy. Because of the assumption that they were secondary wage earners in their families, women were also expected to be less likely to organize and form unions (White 2004). Despite the youth of many women workers, it was assumed that their primary role remained that of caregiver to their families. Women were more easily controlled in the labor market, and because of the Mexican government's decreased support for social services, they also had much more to lose. Many maquila employment practices were designed to minimize the possibility of having to pay for maternity leaves for pregnant women. Employers required women to take pregnancy tests before employment, encouraged women workers to use birth control, and tested for menstrual cycles (Kagan 2005).

Maquiladoras in the border regions focused initially on labor-intensive industries where women's unskilled labor was most likely to be required. This includes clothing and footwear, shifting gradually to electrical products, both requiring low-skilled, labor-intensive work. Although women were hired because they were paid less than men, the maquilas still offered the highest pay rate for unskilled labor in the country—and the best opportunities for young women, without education, leaving the rural areas (Torres Ruiz 2011). In the early years of developing the border as an EPZ, these young, unmarried women were considered the ideal employees. However, as most EPZs mature, they are likely to shift to more capital-intensive labor requiring a higher level of technological investment and providing more openings for jobs associated with male workers such as engineers and technicians.[8] By 2000, women's overall maquila employment in Mexico was down to 48 percent; even in textiles, it was reduced to 65 percent (Brown and Cunningham 2002). The process of defeminization was accelerated by increased competition from China after it gained admission to the World Trade Organization in 2001. As China became a leading exporter to the United States, women in the maquilas were more likely to be laid off than men. Border industries had to increase productivity to become more competitive, accelerating the shift to a more capital-intensive workforce. Under these pressures, the ratio of men's to women's maquila employment continued to grow as did the wage differential (Torres Ruiz 2011).

Impunity of Law Enforcement

While economic crises, neoliberal policies, and the growth of maquiladoras on the U.S.-Mexico border are contributing factors that brought an increasing number of young women to the border in the 1980s and 1990s, a more proximate cause of the femicide in Ciudad Juárez has been the impunity for criminal activities due to corrupt, inept, and overwhelmed local and state law enforcement.[9] Impunity is commonly found in areas where the rule of law is weak because of the special protection of security forces, a weak judiciary, and systems of patronage or other forms of corruption. That such conditions are endemic to borderlands between countries and/or administrative jurisdictions is hardly new. What is new is the systematic and blatant abuse of the human rights of poor, young women recently drawn to the U.S.-Mexico border in support of a globalizing economy (Mexico Solidarity Network 2005).

From the beginning of the femicide in the early 1990s, the mothers and families of the victims as well as human rights activists who sought justice were repeatedly frustrated and humiliated by law enforcement and other public officials. If even a few of these early murders had resulted in arrests and fair trials, followed by just verdicts and appropriate punishment, a femicide of this scale could never have happened. But no credible system of law enforcement ever addressed the femicide in the past. Nor has it yet.

Impunity and the Drug Cartels

The major source of impunity on the U.S.-Mexico border, as in many border regions, is the remarkable potency of organized crime, particularly the drug cartels that supply the U.S. market (Andreas 2000).[10] The globalizing conditions that have contributed to the growing role of nonstate actors are not limited to transnational corporations or advocacy networks but also include transnational organized crime. Shelley (1999), for instance, argues that organized crime represents a new form of authoritarianism that involves the infiltration of government, the assumption of governmental functions, and the neutralization of law enforcement. She finds these new forms of authoritarianism in former socialist states, failed or failing third world states and other states, such as Mexico, in the process of transitioning to democracy. In most of these, it is the relatively unincorporated territories that are particularly vulnerable. Many regional leaders are obligated to, or complicit with, organized crime. As we have seen in Ciudad Juárez, the reach of the central state was not sufficient to protect its citizens, long before the drug war initiated by President Calderón. After taking office in December 1994, for instance, president Ernesto Zedillo received an official report stating that "The power of the drug-trafficking organizations could lead to situations of ungovernability . . . .The advance of drug-trafficking promotes impunity and uncertainty in public institutions, justifies violence, and increases intimidation of the authorities" (quoted in P. H. Smith 1999: 193).

Until the 1980s, Mexico's role in regional drug trafficking was as the major supplier of marijuana for the United States and as one of its major suppliers of heroin, largely organized through local, Mexican organizations (Toro 1995). With the success of the U.S. campaign to drive cocaine trafficking out of the Caribbean in the 1980s, the Columbian cartels turned to overland routes through Mexico while developing new and far more lucrative alliances for Mexican drug smugglers. Not only was the route for cocaine trafficking redirected, but the means of transportation changed as well, from aircraft to trucking (Andreas 2000; Payan 2006; Cook 2008). These changes occurred at a particularly propitious moment for the traffickers, as the Mexican economic crises led to the government's fervent embrace of neoliberalism's emphasis on foreign exports, and more open transit through key cities on the U.S.-Mexican border. Indeed, the growth in the power and influence of the drug cartels operating through Mexico has been part of the "collateral damage" of free market reforms responding to financial crises and globalization (Nordstrom 2006; Naím 2005).[11] As Andreas (1999) points out, trade liberalization, privatization, deregulation of trucking, the pressure of foreign debt payments in poor countries, the decline in public sector salaries, enhanced opportunities for money laundering, and the opportunities for rural survival through cultivation of illegal substances have all contributed to the increased power and influence of drug cartels in Mexico. The growing influence of the cartels, coupled with the importance of Ciudad Juárez as a critical point on the drug trafficking routes into the United States, made that city particularly vulnerable to corruption of its law enforcement when the femicide began.

The Cartel Wars: Escalating Violence Along the Border

At the beginning of President Calderón's war on the cartels, the Congressional Research Service (CRS) reported that there were seven known drug cartels in Mexico (Cook 2008). Many of the smaller cartels had formed an alliance called the "Federation," which was headed by the Sinaloa Cartel and controlled much of the Pacific coast of Mexico as well as the border region. The Juárez Cartel controlled traffic through the city from which it took its name. Although the Sinaloa and Juárez cartels each retained some independence, the Gulf and Tijuana cartels formed an alliance in response to formation of the Federation. Drug trafficking in the border region was dominated by the Gulf, Juárez, and Tijuana cartels. However, these alliances shifted dramatically once the Calderón-initiated drug war began in December 2006.

Violence and assassination along the border stem from the ongoing pressure from drug enforcement agencies, the Mexican military, and the U.S. Border Patrol as well as the continuous struggle for power between competing drug organizations. These cartels have been locked in a continuous battle for control of transit routes along the border since the 1980s, but since Calderón's drug war began, the competition has grown more intense. The government strategy of taking out or arresting the cartel leaders led to bloody fights of succession. In addition, enforcers such as Las Zetas, who had once worked for the Gulf Cartel, became independent contractors working for the Juárez Cartel and the Beltran Leyva Cartel, which split off from the Sinaloa Cartel. The notorious Zetas raised the brutality of the violence to a new level. Formed in 1998 by fourteen former Mexican soldiers, they have grown to command more than 10,000 gunmen from the Rio Grande deep into Central America. Decapitation, dismemberment, the use of acids, burning, and hanging as well as direct attacks on security forces are all part of their repertoire (Grillo 2012). The ongoing history of the Mexican cartels is one of bloodshed and violence driven by the enormous payoffs for the production and trafficking of drugs.

As a result, violence in the border region of Mexico and the United States has grown dramatically, particularly in Ciudad Juárez. The city became a battleground between the Juárez and Sinaloa cartels as they tried to monopolize the major transit route from the central corridor through the United States. Following the ninth assassination of a state police officer in December 2006, newly elected President Calderón sent 36,000 troops to work with the federal police in nine states, including Michoacán, Guerrero, and the "golden triangle" of Sinaloa, Durango, and Chihuahua (Emmot 2008). Instead of pacifying the border town of Juárez, citizens say the influx of troops made the town a battleground between the military and drug cartel enforcers. Although there have been successes, such as finding corruption and freeing kidnapped civilians, the violence and death in the city of Juárez continues.

This region has seen a marked increase in drug-related killings, with 2,221 in 2006 and 2,561 in 2007 (Williams 2009a). In the eighty-one days between January 1 and March 21 2008, organized crime had exceeded all records for killings in the state of Chihuahua: 175 people murdered, including 40 corpses found in a mass grave. Part of the increase in violence was the result of fragmentation among the trafficking organizations, with the Beltran Levya organization defecting from Guzman. As well, the remnants of the Arellano Felix organization engaged in an internecine succession struggle, with Guzman reportedly involved. By the end of 2010, the annual report for Ciudad Juárez was 3,111 murders, including 304 women and 149 from various branches of law enforcement (Del Carman Sosa 2010).[12]

The current tally of drug-related killings throughout Mexico attributed to the drug war is also subject to dispute. Repeated demands by media and human rights groups for an authoritative count finally led the government to release figures in January 2012, reporting 47,515 people killed since December 2006 (Cave 2012a). However, Molly Molloy, a librarian at New Mexico State University, who closely tracks deaths in Ciudad Juárez and other parts of the country, says that the Mexican census agency offers more reliable information. It identified 67,050 homicides in Mexico from 2007 to 2010, nearly double the government count for the same period (cited in Cave 2012a). Most media seem to have compromised on a current drug war death toll of 55,000 (Grillo 2012).

The number of women murdered is climbing again. Amnesty International's (2012) briefing paper to the UN Committee on the Elimination of Discrimination against Women (CEDAW) reports that the number of women murdered in the state of Chihuahua increased from 180 in 2008 to 218 in

2009, and then sharply increased to 584 in 2010. This was also the year with the largest number of murders in the state, at 16,421. Of these, 320 were the murders of women in Ciudad Juárez. In the first six months of 2012, Chihuahua had registered 130 women murdered, more than were ever killed during a single year in the first wave of the femicide. The impunity of law enforcement that permitted young women to be disappeared, tortured, and murdered in the 1990s eventually led an entire city to fall prey to lawlessness.

Thus, the impunity that characterized the failure of law enforcement to respond to the earliest murders of young women in Ciudad Juárez was just the tip of the iceberg and a premonition of what was to come. President Calderón's militarization of the conflict with the drug cartels reflected this breakdown in state and local law enforcement. In searching for a solution to the pervasive impunity on the border, he selected an unlikely tool, the military (see the chapter by Murphy Erfani in this volume for one possible explanation for this choice). Whether this was a good decision can be debated, but it drastically escalated the scale and brutality of violence that had already been revealed in the 1990s by the Cuidad Juárez femicide.

When "Local" Includes the Northern Neighbor

The drug war, like the femicide, has never been entirely a Mexican affair. Although U.S. law enforcement has long played a role in trying to stop the flow of drugs across its southern border, it is seldom recognized that Mexico's northern neighbor is as implicated in the state of impunity as it was in creating an export processing zone on the border. This is most readily seen in the combination of high demand for illegal drugs rafficked north across the border and provision of the guns that are trafficked south to empower the drug cartels.

The Market for Illegal Drugs

Although European drug consumers are not negligible, the driving force behind illegal drug trafficking throughout the world is consumption in the United States.[13] According to the UN *World Drug Report* (2008), in 2006 U.S. drug users consumed $39 billion worth of cocaine, $16 billion of heroin, $25.2 billion of methamphetamine, $23 billion of marijuana, and $2.3 billion of other illegal drugs. Indeed, Mexico is the main supplier of three of the most profitable drugs (cocaine, heroin, and marijuana) and a growing supplier of methamphetamine, and thus, much of the profit from the $105.5 billion spent on drugs in the United States each year goes to the Mexican cartels (UN 2008).

According to the same UN report, 46 percent of all cocaine produced around the world is destined for North America. It is estimated that 530 to 710 metric tons of cocaine entered the United States in 2006, with 90 percent transported through the Mexican-Central American corridor (UN 2008). The U.S. border between Texas and Mexico is the main port of entry for cocaine, with Nuevo Laredo and Ciudad Juárez the two major cities involved in the trafficking. This border region accounts for 33 percent of all cocaine seizures in the United States; the Southern California-Mexico border is next with 18 percent. Thus, these two areas alone account for over half of all cocaine seized in the United States, all coming through Mexico.[14]

The growing importance of the Mexican cartels now includes the production as well as the trafficking of drugs in the United States. The U.S. Department of Justice has found increased links between marijuana producers in the United States and Mexican cartels. At the same time, the traditional production of marijuana in California is now spreading to the Pacific Northwest and the East Coast.[15]

But there is growing unease with the current war on drugs, and not just in Mexico. Dissatisfied with what is widely perceived as the failure of fifty years of UN law enforcement approaches to drug control, two different international groups released reports criticizing this strategy on the same day the UN released its 2012 *World Drug Report*. The first of these, *The Alternative World Drug Report*, is published by the multinational anti-drug war organization Count the Costs, which documents the heavy costs of the law enforcement approach. The second report, from the Global Commission on Drug Policy, also condemns the law enforcement approach, in particular its impact on the HIV-AIDS pandemic. While the Count the Costs group is made up largely of NGOs, the Global Commission includes former government officials like Paul Volcker (former chair of the U.S. Federal Reserve) and George P. Schultz (former U.S. secretary of state), who serves as honorary chair of the Commission. Both groups point to a concession in the 2008 UN *World Drug Report* that the law enforcement approach has brought a range of negative "unanticipated consequences" in addition to failing on its own terms. That is, the UN data show that the quality of illegal drugs continues to improve and the supply grows (and prices decline), even though more and more arrests are made, shipments are apprehended, and supply routes are discovered. Among the unintended consequences noted in the 2008 *Report* are (1) the creation of a criminal black market, (2) the disproportionate diversion of resources into law enforcement, (3) geographic displacement of trafficking routes and markets from one place to another, (4) substance displacement when new drugs are invented to replace those that have come under stringent control, and (5) stigmatization of drug users. While appreciating that this recognition by the UN might lead to more enlightened policies, the report by the Count the Costs group adds eight more consequences of the law enforcement approach, in particular the corruption of law enforcement, which we have seen is a major factor in perpetuating femicides in Ciudad Juárez.

The U.S. as a Major Source of Firepower for the Cartels

U.S. complicity in legal impunity and femicide at the border is not limited to domestic demand for illegal drugs, which fuels enormous profits for the Mexican cartels. The United States has also contributed an arsenal of weapons to the cartels directly through illegal smuggling across the U.S.-Mexican border and indirectly through the redirection of arms originally intended for use by the Mexican military or Central American forces.[16]

Weapons are used at all levels of the drug trafficking process and are necessary to conduct such a lucrative, but illegal business. Without weapons the cartels would not be able to effectively protect their product during storage or transport from police, government officials, or other cartels. It is the possession and threat from the use of weapons that enable the cartels to produce fear in others. From the perspective of the cartels, gun procurement is arguably an even more vital operating expense than the well-documented corruption and extortion of Mexico's political, governmental, and police agencies, as weapons permit the cartels to operate without as much outside protection and assistance.[17]

Guns are common throughout Mexico, and the country's gun culture dates back before revolutionary times. The Mexican Constitution, as adopted in 1917, recognized Mexican citizens' right to possess arms: "The inhabitants of the United Mexican States have the right to possess arms in their homes for their security and legitimate defense with the exception of those prohibited by federal law and of those reserved for the exclusive use of the Army, Navy, Air Force, and National Guard" (Kopel 2009). Despite this legal right, Mexico has implemented some of the toughest firearms regulations in the world, particularly since the late 1960s. Between 1968 and 1995, registration of all weapons was required, and, although compliance was low, all but one gun store was closed (Kopel 2009). The store, the Directorate for Arms and Munitions Sales, is located in Mexico City and is run by the Mexican army in a "heavily guarded building near the army's headquarters" (Hawley 2009).[18]

Because the demand is high and the legal supply is low, the illicit market is crucial for the cartels: "demand for guns has created an illicit market that not only is intimately related to the U.S. market for illegal narcotics but also, in many ways, mirrors the dynamics of that market. Drugs flow north and guns flow south—resulting in handsome profits for those willing to run the risks" (Burton and Stewart 2007). In other words, the trafficking of arms from the United States to Mexico has the potential of closely matching the value of the drugs moving in the opposite direction. Since access to firearms is so strictly controlled in Mexico, drug traffickers require a dependable source of weapons from outside the country.[19] These sources consist largely of the United States and supply networks south of Mexico.

Criminal sources from the United States range from an individual who obtains guns through family members living in the United States to large, complex organizations capable of buying hundreds of weapons at a time. Other options for illegally attaining weapons include document fraud and "straw buyers." In other cases, gun dealers, government officials, or police officers are corrupt and will knowingly sell weapons to individuals who are not authorized to possess them. Guns are also purchased on the Mexican black market after being stolen, such as those taken from gun stores along the border by Gulf cartel-related groups (Burton and Stewart 2007).[20]

The United States has also been the primary supplier of these weapons legally imported into Mexico, such as those used by the Mexican military and police. Over the past seven years, it is estimated that over 100,000 soldiers have deserted the Mexican army, many of whom "took their weapons with them and joined the cartels. . . . Thousands of advanced weapons and tons of military equipment [have been] stolen from its own military and state police" (Tancredo 2009). In addition, weapons are available "from contacts along their supply networks in South and Central America, where substantial quantities of military and ordnance have been shipped over decades to supply insurgencies and counterinsurgencies" (Burton and Stewart 2007).

In 2005, the United States legally exported almost $50 million worth of weapons to Latin America. In addition, "small arms flooded Latin America during the Cold War, most significantly during the Central American civil wars of the 1980s" (Stohl and Tuttle 2009). These weapons last longer than their original purposes require and can still be traced as having origins in the United States.

High-powered weapons are a different story, as they are not available through U.S. "straw buyers" or legally provided to Mexico. The majority of fully automatic weapons cannot be found in the United States, but they are not uncommon in developing countries. It is argued that "weapons are smuggled across [Mexico's] southern borders from Guatemala and by boats landing on its 8,000 miles of coastline, weapons that often originate in Venezuela, Colombia, and Nicaragua, or from purchases in Eastern Europe" (Tancredo 2009). For instance, the 2,239 grenades and the rocket-propelled grenades (RPGs) seized in the last two years are not available in U.S. gun shops.

While the trafficking in guns may seem a long way from the femicide in Ciudad Juárez, it has roughly the same importance as the drug trade, but in reverse. Drugs go north; guns go south. Both commodities bring an unusually high price due to a limited supply and an enormous demand. As the supply is reduced, the price goes up, and the willingness of illegal traffickers to take risks increases (Burton and Stewart 2007). In a border characterized by high risk behavior, the murders of young women that began in 1993 marked the beginning of what was to become a national crisis.

Conclusion

Ciudad Juárez was thought to be a city built on an ideal of possibility and opportunity, a city built by the Mexican government to represent economic progress and international cooperation. Thousands of women migrated to this area in hopes of contributing financially to the stability and sustainability of their families. Yet, the gap between the rich and poor grew markedly over time through the disparities in economic gains from NAFTA followed by the economic losses from recessions. Poverty continues among the tin sheds and cardboard houses on the hills of Juárez that are occupied by potential laborers hoping for possible employment opportunities. Now, in this time of greatest violence, jobs are being shipped to China, and corporate managers can bargain down already cheap labor rates. The women who live in poverty become poorer and more vulnerable to violence, without the means to escape.

Modern Juárez was built on neoliberal policies. Before NAFTA, much like Nogales and Tijuana, Juárez was a hot spot for the young and the uninhibited, a place to let down your hair. The income gained from tourists supported restaurants, bars, and gentlemen's clubs. Drug cartels existed before NAFTA and profited from the uninhibited. When NAFTA came into effect the ability of drug cartels and business owners to make an enormous profit created a dramatic increase in population, particularly of young women in the early days of the maquiladoras. Because of its location with access to a major transportation route into the world's leading drug market, Juárez became a coveted prize when the Caribbean drug routes were disrupted. It was a prize worth seemingly any level of violence to the drug cartel bosses, corrupt politicians, and law enforcement officials who have fought over it.

Women who sought economic opportunity working in the maquilas became collateral damage in the violence that followed. The population of Juárez doubled again and again. With an already uninhibited city culture, the population grew, risks increased, and violence became pervasive. Although the violence was also inflicted on men, women were among the most vulnerable and, originally, most subject to its more brutal forms. With the success of Las Zetas and the increased brutality of the cartels, now everyone is vulnerable.

Several research reports have found that globalization of both legal and illegal trade, in general, has had a profound impact on communities (or countries), creating cultural shifts and inflicting enormous costs on the weak. Women have become victims of these consequences of globalization. Indeed globalization has led to a variety of threatening possibilities for women.[21]

Radford and Tsutsumi (2004) explain that women on the "periphery" are often the ones forced into abuse and exploitation. In this case the "periphery" means not only the women who are cast out into poverty, but also those on the geographic periphery of Mexico and the United States. These are women who are not always seen and are not given much worth or value, women who have been brutally murdered or women who have gone missing and are never found.

The femicide in Juárez results from the historical convergence of multiple factors in time and place: economic crises, international trade, government policy, demand for drugs, demand for guns, corruption, impunity, economic disadvantage, and poverty. Reducing the violence in Juárez, currently caused by the drug cartels, has taken priority; however, the issue of femicide and the violence against women still continues. According to Amnesty International (2012), the murders of women in Ciudad Juárez have continued to increase as the murders of men have declined. The women of Juárez continue to live in peril, their plight overshadowed by the staggering toll of the drug war. And yet, their murders go on. The current drug war in Juárez is serving as a smokescreen for more women to be kidnapped, tortured, sexually enslaved, and/or murdered.

As Hausmann (2001) points out, you do not have to be a geographic determinist to recognize that political boundaries are critical in defining the economic and political life of a nation.[22] Ciudad Juárez's location as a major entry point for both legal and illegal trade into the United States has simultaneously made it the maquila center of Mexico, the murder capital of the world.

Explanation is only complete when we stop asking why. However, with femicide, as with other atrocities, there can never be a completely adequate explanation. What we can argue is that there was no inevitability about this outcome. Neoliberalism is beginning to run its course as the only paradigm for economic development; alternative solutions to a militarized war on drugs are emerging throughout Latin America; and political opinion in the United States is increasingly willing to consider the possibility of legalizing drugs such as marijuana for medical purposes. But, in the Western Hemisphere, we have witnessed how seemingly independent processes converged at a particular time and place to create "the perfect place to kill a woman."

CHAPTER 7

Reflections on Antiviolence Civil Society Organizations in Ciudad Juárez

Clara Jusidman

The human rights situation in Ciudad Juárez, Mexico, is staggering. In 2008, 1,656 murders were recorded, and these rose sharply to over 3,000 in 2010; 2011 saw a significant drop, but the murder rate remained frighteningly high, with over 1,900 dead. Parents are afraid to send their children to school because students and teachers are being extorted by delinquents in exchange for protection against kidnapping. Businesses operate in secret so that they will not be subject to extortion for protection or face being burned down. Families and ambulances cannot pick up the wounded and take them to hospitals for fear that they will be finished off, and that those who helped them will also die (Gibler 2011). The general rule is that one should not pick up someone who is wounded until they are dead. Not surprisingly, poor migrant workers from other states are returning to their places of origin, and businessmen and local politicians are moving to El Paso, Texas.

This chapter is told from the perspective of an outside witness. It reports on the experiences and work achieved through the civil organization Citizen Initiative and Social Development (Iniciativa Ciudadana y Desorrollo Social, INCIDE Social A.C.), especially the social agenda developed in partnership with the umbrella group City Council for Social Development (Consejo Ciudadano para el Desarrollo Social). I also collected information about the dangerous and risky work that was carried out by civil society organizations (CSOs) in the last few decades to confront the growing structural violence that has converted Ciudad Juárez into the most violent city in Mexico.

This chapter also serves as a history of a city's well-publicized destruction, which has been accomplished by the most powerful gangs of organized crime in the country; municipal governments; incompetent, corrupt, irresponsible politicians and federal employees; an ambitious business class blinded by desire for profit; a Catholic church that abandoned the fight for the poor and placed itself on the side of the powerful; and political parties converted by the mechanisms that give access to power and enrich the few. The presence of all these actors in Juárez has been disastrous. Juárez now hosts the headquarters of one of the most powerful and violent cartels in the country. For six years, Patricio Martinez, an authoritarian and violent governor, limited the public budget flow to the city and hid the bodies and twisted the investigations of assassinated women in Juárez.

Speculation in land has been one of the great businesses of Juárez and one of the major causes of injustices. It is said that historically the PRI governments caused invasions of lands and that the PAN governments tried to regularize the situation of the invaded lands. This is the reason why many neighborhoods of the maquila workers have been developed in high risk areas not conducive to human settlements. Businessmen involved in land speculation control the principal political positions. One of them, Jaime Bermúdez Cuaró, developed industrial parks for the maquila industry by using public resources from the Programa Nacional de Solidaridad. Héctor Murguía while mayor built the Camino Real to increase the value of his own properties and backed the massive new development called San Jerónimo.[1] This new development will double the urban territory of Ciudad Juárez, increase the profits of a selected group of investors who speculate in land, and serve as a major source of wealth for the local elite. Another example of a perverse relation between politicians and wealthy people is the powerful Zaragoza family, which controls, or rather exploits, the distribution of natural gas and has attempted to take over land from the people who live in Lomas de Poleo, one of the poorest sectors of the city.[2] Even the heads of the Catholic Church in Juárez have abandoned the extraordinary work of Bishop Manuel Talamás to mingle with the powerful people of the city. Abused by the maquila model and by endemic corruption of the powerful political and economic sectors, the city of Juárez is a tragic example of inhumane globalization.

Nonetheless, in this context of abuse, violence, simulation, deceit, greed, and crime, there are a great number of people and civil society organizations that undertake a daily fight in order to rescue the city and its inhabitants from disaster; abandonment, poverty, discrimination, violence, crime, addictions, and disappearances. They are men and women who were born and raised in the city, many receiving their formation in Basic Ecclesial Communities and in the church committed to the poor. Others have come as university teachers or workers in cultural development; some are even businessmen who support and participate in collective community actions. They have established a fund, Fundación del Empresario Chihuahuense (FECHAC), in order to strengthen and support the work of the civil society organizations in all of Chihuahua State.

Whether it is from the adversity suffered for so many years, or for the love of Ciudad Juárez, there is great civic activism and a large number of organizations that concentrate on different problems or "social pains" (*dolores sociales*), as they are called by Teresa Almada, one of the civic leaders of the city. Many of these organizations started their activities decades ago, supporting the growing number of families who arrived to work in the maquiladoras and who had to live in uninhabitable lands with no public or social services. The defense of workers' rights and the demand for urban services such as water, drainage, and electricity were the first causes promoted by organizations like the Independent Popular Organization (Organización Popular Independiente, OPI), which eventually had a powerful presence in the area. After some years, CSOs started working with vulnerable groups such as youth, small children, women, the elderly, the indigenous, migrants, and the disabled. They developed shelters, nurseries, and centers for the prevention of and attention to domestic violence and, addictions, and defense of human rights. They offered education and special attention to people with disabilities, education for youth, and attention and support to families of the "dead women of Juárez." They reported the assassinations and disappearances of young women and followed up the investigations.

FECHAC, a social responsibility project created by local businesses, has provided important financial support, as have the Ford Foundation and the Fundación Paso del Norte, among others. This support has contributed to the development of CSO infrastructure and expertise, especially important since up to the present there have been neither policies nor significant public funds to support CSO activities in the state of Chihuahua. This lack of support contributes to the high level of tension between the CSOs and state and municipal governments.

Actions by CSOs to Deal with Violence and Human Rights Violations

Basically, five types of actions are carried out by the CSOs in Ciudad Juárez to confront violence, defend human rights, and build citizenship. I will discuss the following in some detail:

1. Publicizing and reporting violence
2. Case follow-up and claims for justice and victim compensation
3. Defending labor rights
4. Developing services to address and prevent violence
5. Social assessment and proposing public policies

Publicizing and Reporting Violence

The first femicides were registered in 1993 and 1994, totaling 133. The number increased 30 percent in 1995, and continued to increase until 1998. Women from different organizations in Juárez—including Esther Chavez Cano from el 8 de Marzo (March 8), Partricia Monreal from the OPI, Marielena Ramos from Compañeros, Yudit Galarza from CETLAC, Vicky Caraveo from Mujeres por Mujeres por Mexico, and Luz Maria Villalva from Centro de Orientacion para la Mujer Obrera—established the Coordinadora en Pro de los Derechos de la Mujer, which succeeded in placing gender violence and the homicides of women in Ciudad Juárez on the public agenda locally, nationally, and internationally.

With their voices and through the construction of networks and alliances with the national women's movement, these women pressured the authorities to establish a unit specializing in female victims of violence and also a special prosecutor's office to investigate the femicides. Since then, other people and organizations such as Nuestras Hijas de Regreso a Casa with Marisela Ortiz and María Luisa García Andrade, as well as Red de Mujeres, Red de la No Violencia, and la Mesa de Mujeres del Consejo Ciudadano, have joined forces to demand justice for the victims. Important support for the civil movement came from El Colegio de la Frontera Norte led by Guillermina Valdez de Villalba, as director, and researchers Socorro Tabuenca and Julia Monárrez.

The negligence, incompetence in investigations, corruption, consent of state governments, and absence of actions by municipal governments to deal with these crimes triggered a national movement. The local organizations' insistence that these were gender crimes, many of them with characteristics of serial murders, made it possible to place the issue on national and international agendas, and it received a great amount of attention, solidarity, and interest from around the globe.

The organizations solicited the intervention of the federal government, which established the Commission to Prevent and Eradicate Violence Against Women in the City of Juárez (Comisionada para Prevenir y Erradicar la Violencia Contra las Mujeres en Ciudad Juárez), but it lacked a clear mandate, a budget, and the power to impose sanctions. If its purpose was to improve the investigative capabilities of the state institutions and accompany and support the families of various victims, it produced very poor results. Later on, the Federal Prosecutor's Office appointed a special prosecutor to address the femicides. The organizations also called on the National Commission of Human Rights (Comisión Nacional de Derechos Humanos) and various international human rights organizations, such as Amnesty International and Human Rights Watch, as well as the Inter-American Commission on Human Rights (IACHR) and the UN Committee on the Elimination of All Forms of Discrimination against Women (CEDAW).

These actions by the CSOs led to a number of reports and evaluations by different agencies, including the drafting of recommendations from the IACHR and CEDAW, and various compensation plans and schemes offered by the Mexican government for the families of the victims. They also generated an increase in public resources, better investigative skills on the part of the state authorities, and incorporation of the femicides on the national legislative agenda. In addition, a classification of crimes for reasons of gender has been introduced into the criminal code through the 2007 Ley General de Acceso a las Mujeres a una Vida Libre de Violencia and similar state regulations. It also generated the Observatorio Ciudadano para Monitorear la Impartición de Justicia for the femicides in Ciudad Juárez and Chihuahua State. Also, documentary producers, filmmakers, and artists are constantly arriving in the city to collect stories to tell the world about the tragedy that Juárez is facing and the bravery of its people in coping with the situation.

The main question of course is whether all this has stopped or even reduced the crimes against women for gender reasons in Chihuahua and whether the perpetrators have been punished. No, the killing has not stopped, and the perpetrators have not been punished. Given the number of murders now committed daily in the city, the prevailing idea has become that all the murders have to do with revenge killings between gangs of hired killers of the drug dealers. Along with the clumsiness of local authorities to cope with so many crimes, the fear is that the killings of women are lost in this cloudy category of "getting even," that they are not being investigated, and that the perpetrators of gender crimes are going unpunished, thereby further encouraging the crimes. So, it appears that all this publicity and reporting have not reduced the crimes, and the crimes against women are becoming invisible once again.

Case Follow-Up and Claims for Justice
and Compensation of Victims

A legal team made up of the Asociación Nacional de Abogados Democráticos (ANAD) and the CSO Nuestras Hijas de Regreso a Casa (NHRC), in conjunction with the Comisión Mexicana para la Promoción y Defensa de los Derechos Humanos, has been working for many years in Juárez searching for justice for the victims of the femicides. During the first three years they were able to work on only four cases because of little or no funding. In the last few years, they have worked on more cases and widened the scope of legal actions and follow-up. Also, they have been able to make trips to Juárez every four to five weeks thanks to increased financial support.

The efforts of these CSOs demonstrate the arduous, long, and painstaking work that needs to be undertaken to seek justice. Because of their efforts much concrete progress has been made on cases that were stagnant. For instance, a case based on the femicides was heard by the IACHR—the first such gender homicide case at the transnational level. The case was eventually heard by the Inter-American Court of Human Rights and set a precedent for dealing with this phenomenon throughout the country. At the national level, the CSOs have been able to establish the identity of two of the victims who were previously unidentified. And, on these cases, they developed new lines of investigation and are now regularly reviewing the cases for progress. In another case, they managed to close four open lines of investigation that had distracted the authorities' attention. They are planning a final strategy to close an investigation because they have obtained relevant information that has determined who is responsible for the murder. This information will be presented to the authorities so that the perpetrators can be sentenced. In another case, a file was located after being "lost" for more than three years. Legal actions have been initiated against the government employees responsible for this "loss," and two expert reports are being provided to determine the cause of death of the victim, who, even though she was found with sufficient evidence, was not classified as a murder victim. Finally, three criminal complaints have been filed against different government employees of the Attorney General's Office of Chihuahua for incompetence and negligence in putting files together and for other deficiencies in carrying out investigations.

It is important to remember that the CSOs have had to litigate not *with* the authorities, but *against* them, as the authorities have developed new ways to impede the adequate development of the investigations, creating obstacles including intimidation and threats to the work of the organizations. The legal monitoring of each of the cases has been a great challenge because of their complexity and dependence on the actions of the authorities.

The work of these organizations has allowed the families to follow up and demand that those responsible for the investigations act diligently. As a result of all the work carried out, in cooperation with other civil society organizations, these CSOs were able to force the change to the Criminal Code and the Criminal Procedure Code and improve the tracking of victims by modifying the criteria for searching and locating missing women and children. They have also completely changed the area of expert services in the state Attorney General's Office, and some government employees were removed from office for their negligence in the previous inquiries and for hiding information from the families of the victims.

This work has resulted in numerous threats and intimidating acts, including insults and attacks in the media and death threats. Since June 2008, the IACHR granted the members of the NHRC and their lawyers precautionary measures that must be carried out by the Mexican state to guarantee their safety, and that of their families, and to protect their work in defending and promoting the human rights of women in the city of Juárez (Inter-American Court of Human Rights 2008). Nonetheless, the recent presence of the military and the large number of federal security forces in the city are making the work of such human rights defenders even more risky. Among other things, these forces hinder the activities of human rights defenders and accuse them of being involved in organized crime, which has generated great fear about reporting and demanding respect for human rights.

Defense of Labor Rights

Although eight of every ten people draw salaries in Juárez, there are no effective unions to defend labor rights. In a recent study, INCIDE Social A.C. conducted interviews with several different types of workers and found only two persons who had attempted to organize unions in the plants or, at the least, defend the rights of their coworkers. As a result of their actions, both workers were fired and blacklisted so that they could not be hired in any other factories.

The violation of labor rights is systemic and reflects a type of structural violence in the relationship between employers and employees. The result is absolute subordination of the workers, lack of job security, and conditioning of personal and family life to management's definitions of the length of the workday, overtime, and compensation. An agreement between factories allows blacklists to further subordinate workers. Considering the magnitude of labor issues, there are really very few organizations that defend labor rights, and they do their work in precarious conditions with generally poor results. For state and local authorities, plant managers, and even the IMSS (Instituto Mexicano del Seguro Social) the less they do to respect and defend labor rights the better, because it generates better conditions for investment.

One of the few organizations that defends labor rights is linked to the Catholic Church as part of its Labour Ministry. It provides numerous services such as offering legal aid to workers who have been unjustly fired, suggesting alternative ways to make a living, and helping workers defend their social security benefits. The ministry offers free consultations before the IMSS and answers legal questions. It also helps persons age fifty-nine and older who do not qualify for a full pension by providing employment for the number of hours needed to qualify to receive full retirement benefits.

Another organization that defends labor rights is the Centro de Estudios y Taller Laboral A.C. (CETLAC) formed in 1996. It is a community center committed to training, studying, counseling, and organizing maquila workers in Juárez. Its mission is to "take part in the training and education of workers in subjects such as civil, political, labor, and human rights providing legal aid promoting the development of workers' organizations in their working places as well as in their neighborhoods." The Comité Fronterizo de Obrer@s is a grassroots organization that "promotes democratic trade unions and labor rights in seven border cities" and aims to "educate, organize, and empower maquila workers in order to improve their work conditions in the factories and their quality of life." It also gives workshops on union organizing and human and gender rights. This group also provides legal aid regarding collective and individual contracts, seniority bonuses, working hours, and profit sharing, among other topics.

Development of Services to Address and Prevent Violence

A broad spectrum of CSOs work on the ground to address violence and its causes. I will briefly discuss a few of these here. A number of women's organizations offer services, including treatment for women who have been subject to domestic violence. These organizations do the important job of educating and raising awareness about this matter in the maquiladoras. Some organizations support different types of psychological services to address the grieving families of the victims of the femicides. Others support the victims' families by offering different work options.

From the time the government "sealed" the border in 2006 and more drugs like cocaine were sold through the cartels in Mexico, there has been an increase in local drug consumption. It is estimated that in Juárez there are 2,000 to 2,500 drug houses where users regularly receive cocaine injections. Now, several organizations are committed to helping people with addictions in the absence of government actions. Activities with youngsters in neighborhoods carried out by groups such as Casa Aliviani and the OPI are very important. Pacto por la Cultura, a network of artists from Juárez, offers recreational and cultural activities throughout the city, particularly for young children and teens. Outstanding workcare, following the model of community work intervention, is provided for babies and toddlers by the Red de Centros de Aprendizaje y Convivencia para Niños, Niñas y Adolescentes.

Pacto por la Cultura provides the means to create children's orchestras and promote literary work like "Mi Vida en Juárez." It also carries out awareness-raising activities to publicize youth experiences, including media campaigns, a youth journal, and different youth forums.

Social Assessment and Proposal of Public Policies

Both the Instituto Nacional para el Desarrollo Social (INDESOL) and FECHAC have carried out important activities that have brought together a wide range of CSOs in Juárez that offer social assistance services. These groups which include social services and community development agencies, such as those that defend women's rights, children, and indigenous people, among others, have found common ground through these activities. Every year since 2004 INDE-SOL has offered a diploma program for strengthening CSOs in a number of cities across the country, including Juárez. Also, in Juárez they have offered a Diploma on Social Resources through which, weekly, representatives from about forty organizations are able to learn from experts from around the country. FECHAC, for its part, carries out annual meetings of CSOs for the entire state and offers diverse training opportunities for their staff.

As a result of these meetings, which have served to build trust among these groups, the CSOs decided to establish the Consejo Ciudadano para el Desarrollo Social to organize their work according to population groups: children, teenagers, women, elderly, migrants, indigenous, and people with disabilities. The goal was to create an agenda for social development for the city that took into account the needs and interests of different groups and offered options to address the problems of violence and abandonment that these groups have confronted.[3] The Consejo Ciudadano emerged with the goal of analyzing and publicizing the *social reality* of Juárez and to place it on the municipal, state, and national public agendas.

INCIDE Social A.C. was invited to support the work of the Consejo Ciudadano in the construction of a social agenda for the city of Juárez. It agreed to assess the social situation in Juárez as a foundation for building the social agenda. This assessment was based on interviews with experts, government employees, local social activists, and working groups of intellectuals, as well as the review of documents about the social reality in Juárez. INCIDE Social A.C. developed a document assessing social sectors such as education, health, housing, population, and security. The Consejo meanwhile worked to assess the status of various groups in the population. Its findings were then added to the document. The resulting document provided the various CSOs with data as well as indicators and scales for some of the problems in the city, which strengthened their arguments before the government, political parties, funding foundations, FECHAC, and even for the media and international human rights organizations.

Along with this document, Hugo Almada and Linda Delgado of the Instituto Municipal de Investigación y Planeación (IMIP) of Juárez calculated the same indicators broken down by fourteen different areas of the city. Their analysis provided evidence of the enormous inequality within the city and the concentration of poverty in specific neighborhoods. This information was also overlaid with the educational, health, and urban infrastructure data and clearly showed the enormous neglect and even absence of public services in some areas of the city. The results provided clear evidence of the structural problems in social and human development that, in the political and economic context described above, have contributed to the overwhelming and profound violence in the city in the last few years.

In presenting the results of this collective work, the CSOs proposed that Juárez offers a window onto the future for many cities in Mexico whose growth are similar and which have similar structural conditions. They warn about the risk of not strengthening social interventions by governments in other cities to prevent the social disasters found in Juárez by including a list of warning signs or "red flags" for other cities in the appendix to this chapter. Taken as a whole these warning signs point to the complex, interlocking types of structural violence that render so many people vulnerable to human rights abuses.

Conclusions

Ciudad Juárez highlights the consequences of continuing tolerance and impunity toward corruption and criminal elements, as is seen in its history of organized crime and drug dealing, but also in the way in which the maquila model developed. This model results in abuse and violation of human rights of the workers and their families, and in increased inequality and segregation, and distorts the demographic structures in society, especially those of gender and the family. Profound changes occurred in social life in Juárez as a result of the rapid transformation of the economic base, the absence of the rule of law, and the presence of organized crime. Many people work long hours, earn very little, and find it difficult to enjoy and take care of their families, and thus, there is a deep rupture between work and personal and family life. The volatility of employment and the high proportion of migrants in the population also make family life very fragile.

The current situation in Ciudad Juárez also shows the lack of social responsibility and public ethics on the part of the three levels of government, which either did not understand the potential harms or did not want to take up the development of social policies that would lessen the harms produced by rapid population growth and economic transformation. When the social assessment was presented in Ciudad Juárez, Chihuahua, and Mexico City, business leaders and municipal government officials refused to accept the findings, arguing that Ciudad Juárez was a magnificent place to invest and that the women's murders had to do with domestic violence. They argued further that civil organizations were wrong in spreading and exaggerating the deaths, which would produce only a negative image of the city and drive away investors.

On the other hand, the CSOs' vision as reflected in the social agenda sought to convert Juárez into "a city of rights, with quality of life for its inhabitants where society and government together implement and evaluate, public policies." The agenda promoted such values as social compromise, solidarity, diversity, transparency, trust, and professionalism. It included team proposals, specific actions, and systematized programs developed by different working groups of the Consejo, including the elderly, the disabled, indigenous peoples, youth, migrants, and women. These proposals, actions, and programs deal with such urgent issues as culture, health, citizen security, employment, education, housing, and urban infrastructure.[4] A new group called Diálogo Social por la Infancia de Ciudad Juárez was created in connection with UNICEF, in which officials from the three levels of government, private initiatives, and various CSOs participate. Through this dialogue, common goals were established such as a law to protect children and adolescents' rights in the state of Chihuahua; to develop and promote public policy proposals to reconcile employment and family, thus reducing child abuse through actions structuring and generating an intersectoral plan for after-school attention. The process was cut short because the municipal and state authorities were not willing to formalize a Memorandum of Understanding, which was necessary for UNICEF to continue strengthening this process, and because of changes in local administrations.

The current situation in the city can be understood as a result of the historic construction of a space with absence of government, presence of factual powers that privilege accumulation of wealth and private profits, criminal impunity, and the total decay of security and the administration of justice. This responds to a struggle to control regions of the country through organized crime and with the participation of corrupt politicians and structures.

For the first time since I began to observe Ciudad Juárez, I find my friends in civil organizations profoundly discouraged, sad, insecure, and scared, without proposals that they consider feasible and with deep questions about the viability of the city and whether or not they should continue living there.

Some university researchers believe that the presence of the military and organized crime will be temporary and that in one or two years Juárez will be a city where it is possible to live. Since I first wrote this chapter, in March 2009, another 5,332 soldiers have been sent to the city, in addition to the 2,026 that were already there. The military presence is triggering new human rights violations against the inhabitants of Juárez: forced disappearances, invasion of property, torture, impunity, and the absence of due process, among others. Also, the presence of the military is aided by the resources of the municipality itself, lessening other investments that could improve the social conditions of the city. Since then, these conditions have only become worse.

What is left to conclude is that not even such commitment and love for the city, nor the effort, intelligence, and service of civic activists, has been able to counter the greed, evil, lack of humanity, and violence in the city.

Appendix: Warning Signs or "Red Flags" Developed from the Juárez Experience by Consejo Ciudadano para el Desarrollo Social and INCIDE Social A.C.

Population and Families
1. An accelerated increase in population has created new pressures on the expansion of urban and social infrastructure.
2. The number of migrants in the municipality and their rootlessness pose problems of social cohesion.
3. This is a population with a high proportion of young families with small children, who provide the main social pressure for public programs.
4. There is a higher proportion of households headed by women than the national average, reflecting a greater fragility in couple relationships.
5. There has been a failure of both family and institutional support for caretakers in families.

6. There are deficiencies in the provision of infrastructure and services by governments and private and social sector because of the rate of growth of families.

Employment
1. Women bear a work overload. In Juárez four of ten women twelve years and older are working, compared to three of ten at the national level.
2. Women work double shifts with longer working hours. The average is 64.8 hours per week in Chihuahua.
3. The proportion of those who do domestic and extradomestic work is higher in Chihuahua than nationally: 56.6 versus 46.3 percent.
4. The percentage of children and young people who do not study, work, or help at home is higher than the national average.

Export Industry Maquiladoras
1. During the first stage of the maquiladoras, the hiring of women was preferred, creating an imbalance between women's and men's workforce participation.
2. Work at the maquiladoras results in great fragility and volatility in the basic economic sustenance of families.
3. High job instability and low wages that do not meet the basic needs of workers are due to the closure of factories and the outward movement of capital to other regions.
a. Employment instability and high labor rotation prevent workers from acquiring rights of seniority and other associated benefits.
4. The extradomestic service load in Ciudad Juárez is higher than average; more people work and for longer periods.
5. The lack of salary equality between men and women is found in differentiated wages.

Flexible Labor Conditions
1. A high variability in the organization of working hours makes family life and domestic work much more difficult.
2. Payments with performance bonuses for productivity and good behavior generate abuse, wage instability, and frustrations among factory workers.
3. Various labor diseases appear, including mental health problems, as a result of dangerous working conditions at the factories, routine and repetitive

tasks without any development of personal creativity, and pressure to meet productivity goals.

4. Harsh working conditions, the lack of formal mechanisms for recourse, and the lack of representation for workers, cause frustration and resentment, that generate poor working conditions and reduce productivity,

Education

1. Educational services are inadequate and inappropriate.
2. There are deficiencies in attention to the student populations in early childhood education and preschool, elementary, middle, and high school.
3. There is a lack of supply and poor geographic distribution of educational institutions.
4. There is a shortfall in training educators and poor educational capability in the adult population.
5. A high percentage of students are working.
6. Federal programs to support education do not reach Ciudad Juárez, and others are withdrawing.
7. Middle school functions as a filter to further education.
8. Educational plans, programs, and content fail to reflect the reality experienced by children and young people in Ciudad Juárez.
9. There are high dropout rates in education.

Health

1. There is a high incidence of deaths for external reasons (suicides, homicides, etc.). There has also been a very rapid increase in consumption of hard drugs: cocaine and heroin, with increased risk from consumption by injection.
2. There is a high risk to mental health associated with migration and work stress. There is an increased frequency of mental disorders in women due to marked role changes and values determined by migration.
3. There is low investment in the health sector compared to the level of (PIB) GDP of the state of Chihuahua.
4. There is low per capita spending on the insured population compared to the contribution of the state to social security.
5. There is a lack of adequate health facilities in the demographic structure and the geographic distribution of the population (especially maternal, child, and reproductive health services).

Public Security
1. Common delinquency has increased greatly and is now 12.3 percent greater than the annual averages from 1993 to 2003.
2. The number of crimes reported for every 100,000 inhabitants was 2,978, 34 percent higher than that of Chihuahua state.
3. The high crime rate has facilitated the development of drug dealing and the consolidation of the Juárez Cartel as one of the most powerful in the country.
4. Drug dealing is the main cause of homicide among men.
5. Homicides affect mainly populations in productive age groups.
6. In Juárez there are about 2,000 places for the clandestine sale of retail drugs (*picaderos*).
7. Addiction to drugs or alcohol boosts violence in families and also contributes to social violence. In half the cases of child abuse, parents consumed drugs or alcohol.
8. People consider gangs to be the main problem for public security (in 63 percent of homes surveyed).
9. There is systemic gender violence, particularly the victimization of women in homicide.
10. There are high levels of impunity, and a lack of the rule of law.

Housing
1. The annual growth in housing from 1990 to 2000 was 4.9 percent, whereas the national growth rate was 3.3 percent.
2. The city faces a lack of geographic reserves.
3. Land invasions and auto construction with factory waste have led to insecure land tenure.
4. Housing construction is oriented to middle- and high-income sectors.
5. There is a need to relocate 27,000 houses constructed in high-risk zones.
6. There is an 80 percent deficit in green areas and recreational spaces.
7. City segmentation is due to a serious lack of public transportation.
8. About 50 percent of the city lacks paving.
9. There are high rates of pollution in soil, air, and water.

PART IV

Transnational Activism
and Human Rights

CHAPTER 8

The Persistence of Femicide amid Transnational Activist Networks

Kathleen Staudt

Despite the often heard pronouncement that "women's rights are human rights," many women face stark and everyday threats to lives free of violence. In Mexico's fifth largest city, Ciudad Juárez, Chihuahua, bordering the United States, hundreds of women have been murdered since 1993, with over 80 killed in 2008, and every year thereafter amid huge increases in annual murders of men and women that reached 3,100 murders in 2010 alone. Approximately one-third of these women died after sexualized torture and rape, a misogynist crime that Mexican academics and activists named *feminicidio* or femicide (Staudt 2008; Monárrez Fragoso 2002; though see Fregoso and Bejarano 2010 on feminicide). According to Mexican congressional representative Marcela Lagarde, femicide is a "crime of the state" (in Morfín 2004), given widespread police impunity at the state and local levels. Lagarde's strong statement compels the following urgent question. What sorts of laws, human rights principles, and activism will produce state response—particularly from intransigent and problematic local and state law enforcement institutions in a complex federal form of government amid a crowded policy field of drug-related violence associated with organized crime, cartel competition, and militarized responses?

Conceptual Framework: Main Contentions

The conceptual frame for this analysis focuses on transnational human rights activism, context, and the compatibility of human rights language with political realities. Analysts who study international human rights activism assume that transnational activists, allied with local activists, will shame the offending state into reform with humiliating language derived from high-visibility court judgments, media attention, and the mobilization of third-party governments with ostensibly legitimate human rights records (Keck and Sikkink 1998; Sikkink 2004). Initial state backlash and resistance will eventually give way to negotiated compromise (Risse et al. 1999; Aikin Araluce 2009).

Yet the language of shame and communication networks may not resonate either with defensive nationalists at the federal level or with key local and regional stakeholders responsible for police impunity, even as diplomats in the national capital appease and placate critics. Sally Merry's critical research focuses on the discourse of human rights, with analysis that raises questions about the language of shame in the context of unequal north-south relations, historical colonialism, and neocolonial relationships in the global economy. The language of shame and humiliation, Merry argues, resembles the "civilizing norms" that colonizers once used about many countries in the south (2006: 81). Besides Merry, some postcolonial theorists take issue with seemingly universal norms that speak more for Western enlightenment traditions with their emphasis on individual civil rights (Narayan 1997: 15; Estévez 2008 citing Upendra Baxi and Enrique Dussel, both calling for "epistemological decolonization") than for economic and social rights. Most feminists (acknowledging the plurality of feminisms) believe that women cannot exercise political rights without economic and social rights to live without hunger, poverty, and violence. In the Mexican case, human rights considerations are often isolated from economic and trade policies; Estévez, for instance, argues for more attention to global economic structures that shape human rights transnational social movement strategies (2008: 4).[1]

The conceptual language of human rights organizing and its discourse is useful but often does not take regional contexts and political structures into account, as I do in this chapter. Moreover, human rights theorists often do not take the long-standing bureaucratic resistance to feminist perspectives and gender equality into account. Resistance is the product not only of bureaucratic lethargy, but also of personalized identification with, and backlash against, change within institutions founded with masculinist privileges and sustained with masculinist values (Staudt 1982, 1985; see Lovenduski 1998 on masculinist cultures embedded in institutions).

I contend that Mexico has long situated itself as part of the "modern" world in its use of rights-oriented rhetoric and social justice language embedded in its postrevolutionary Constitution of 1917. However, government policy practices—many of which operate outside the "rule of law"—privilege men and wealthy classes and render the economically marginalized majority of women irrelevant to policy priorities, even with robust regional and transnational activism and human rights critiques aimed at ending femicide. Second, one must consider the regional and binational context. Mexico shares a nearly 2,000-mile land border with the United States. This proximity, along with the high U.S. demand for illegal drugs and official U.S. priority to interdict drug supplies through militarized means, renders femicide nearly invisible as a binational human rights issue. Moreover, the regional context requires that human rights activists unpack the nation-state and target pressure on multiple binational decision-makers with authority and resources at local and regional levels; all of this amid a struggle over the demand for illegal drugs in the trafficking corridor centered on Ciudad Juárez and that has recently expanded to and flared in northeastern Mexico, particularly in the state of Tamaulipas.

Governments are not monoliths; they are fragmented and disjointed, not only at and among national-level agencies, but from local to regional, state, and national levels. One agency or official does not speak for the whole, top to bottom, especially the agencies and "street-level bureaucrats" (Lipsky 1980) that enforce procedures involving human rights. Moreover, government administrations change from one election to the next. In Mexico, a new president is elected, without succession possibility, every six years. And presidents bring a host of political appointees with them with priorities for different policies and practices in diverse bureaucratic agencies. At state and local levels, governors are elected on no-succession six-year terms, but municipal elected officials serve only three-year terms on no-succession principles.

Below I develop a situated analysis of femicide and associated human rights activism within current U.S.-Mexico drug-related policy priorities and violence at Mexico's north-central border with the United States, particularly in Ciudad Juárez and the state of Chihuahua with their problematic law enforcement institutions. In this chapter, I examine the reasons why, over a decade of national and transnational feminist and human rights organizing, femicide continues, along with state complicity in these crimes.

The first part addresses the historical context and scope of the femicide problem, followed by attention to local and transnational social movement visibility and pressure, which peaked in 2003–4, with limited achievements since then, despite the continuation of legal strategies and quiet activism in the violent and intimidating atmosphere of Ciudad Juárez. The final section contextualizes Mexico's northern border, specifically the extensive organized crime, especially drug cartels that supply highly profitable illegal substances to meet huge U.S. consumer demand and the globalization of manufacturing industries, both of which have undermined the state's interest in protecting human security and public safety.

After this analysis, readers will identify three factors that explain the persistence of femicide. First, one must distinguish between national and transnational activists and the challenge of dealing with weak or, some might say, "failed" subnational government institutions—namely local and state law enforcement institutions, which are hardly receptive to shame and humiliation, in Mexico's curiously "centralized-federal" government. Second, transnational activists, predictably, moved on to new sites and struggles, and their legal strategies underwhelmed the priorities of both Mexico and the United States to control drug trafficking. Third, drug-related murders and Mexican militarization overwhelm Mexico's northern border. Militarized resources—both from Mexico's federal system and the United States through its Mérida Initiative—ostensibly work to end the drug cartels, but high gender-neutral murder rates continue. Although femicide previewed such violence as early as the early 1990s, the continuing government intransigence and resistance to feminist human rights policies and practices continue in hypermasculine, militarized law enforcement institutions that provide limited-to-no priority to investigating, solving, and stopping women's murders. Extremely high murder rates in 2008–11, approximately two hundred monthly, have created an intimidating shroud that hangs over the city and renders women-killing relatively invisible.

The Problem of Persistent Femicide

From 1993 onward, an onslaught of women-killing began with shocking news media coverage. Many victims, young and poor, had been brutalized before death with signs of rape and torture: breasts cut off, carvings in backs, set aflame while apparently still alive, and so on (for more detail, see Staudt 2008).

Mothers gave testimonies of the tragic deaths of their daughters and their experiences with the police, who gave little priority to investigating the crimes and tracking down the murderers. Lourdes Portillo immortalized the struggles of mothers, searching for justice for their daughters, in her documentary *Señorita Extraviada* (2001).

For nearly a decade, journalists theorized about who was behind the killings. Serial murderers and copycat killers? Organ harvesters? Snuff film-makers? Gangs and drug cartels? *"Los* juniors" (sons of rich families whose wealth can buy protection)? The police themselves? Even Hollywood film-makers entered the fray with conspiracy movies like *The Virgin of Juárez* and *Bordertown*, as did Mexico City filmmakers covering the 1990s period in *Traspatio*. Valiant journalists, such as Sergio Gonzáles Rodríguez (2006) and Diana Washington Valdez (2006), at some threat to their lives, covered the stories and published books; their theories about the murderers are enshrined in the more recent documentary *Bajo Juárez* (2008). The murders of women acquired different names: female homicide, femicide, and *feminicidio*, the term that Mexican feminists developed and use for sexualized killings with a misogynist, hate motive.[2]

Femicide and weak law enforcement institutions in the 1990s, unable or uninterested in investigating and convicting murderers, provided a preview of the current, out-of-control violence that pervades the city.

The Context for Femicide:
A Globalized Manufacturing Site at the Border

Ciudad Juárez, located on Mexico's northern border with the United States, has been a booming manufacturing site at the frontlines of globalized production since the 1960s, when Mexico established the Border Industri-alization Program, which initiated export-processing factories known as maquiladoras. Since then the city has been a magnet for migrants from Mexico's interior.[3] Ciudad Juárez is the largest site for the maquiladora model in the Americas, with approximately three hundred factories and a workforce of 200,000–250,000 employees until, again, the U.S. economic downturn of fall 2008. Its lower demand for subcontracted export-assembly products drastically reduced the number of employees to approximately 160,000, with a rise again to 192,518 in 2011 (Asociación Maquiladora, A.C. 2011). Women have formed the majority of its workforce since the inception of the program, although they now constitute just over half of the assembly line workforce, compared to 80 percent during its early years (Fernández-Kelly 1983; Kopinak 2004). Maquila workers earn, on average, one-to-two legal minimum wages weekly, or approximately U.S.$25–50.[4] In both figurative and literal ways, the city can be called a place of extensive "disposable labor."

Since the early 1990s, Ciudad Juárez has also been the major gateway for drug trafficking into the United States, the world's largest consumer of illegal drugs. Organized criminal cartels once controlled major spaces (*plazas*), tainting and corrupting already weak and unprofessional law enforcement institutions at the municipal and state levels. With the election of president Felipe Calderón in 2006, the federal government moved against these incestuous relationships and sent federal police and military troops to gain control over organized crime. This lethal combination— troops, cartels, and their hit men (*sicarios*)—resulted in the outlier murder rates from 2008 and beyond. With the militarized approach and with numerous complaints to state and national human rights commissions, human rights observers worry that the government is behind some of the murders as well.

Mexico is a federal system of government in which criminal laws are sporadically enforced at the state level and below, with very low levels of public trust in the police and law enforcement institutions all over the country (Staudt 2008: chap. 5; also see selections in Alvarado 2008 and Cornelius and Shirk 2007). Many people are reluctant to report crimes, fearful of the police, corruption, and police complicity with criminals. As women wrote in a group workshop report (in Staudt 2008: 60), "Por lo regular, los funcionarios públicos usan su poder para robar, burlarse, estafar y hasta golpear a la comunidad. Y aunque se oiga feo, hasta violan y matan." (The public authorities usually use their power to rob, ridicule, and even beat the community. And although it sounds ugly, they even rape and kill.)

Feminist and Human Rights Activism

As a response, in the 1990s, feminists and mothers' groups began to network and organize in Ciudad Juárez, seeking justice for their daughters and the grotesque murders of girls and women. Initially, politicians responded by blaming the victims: How were they dressed? Did the girls go out at night, and why? Politicians argued that the murder rates were "normal," calling some of them crimes of passion (for more detail, see Staudt 2008). The authorities put little to no effort into solving the crimes; in fact, some activists were threatened and beaten. In 2001–2, cross-border activism emerged, with solidarity networks in the greater Paso del Norte region. One nonprofit organization based in Las Cruces, New Mexico, Amigos de Mujeres de Juárez, raised funds and worked directly with mothers, going so far as searching in the desert for evidence about which the police had paid little attention. Another network emerged in El Paso-Juárez, known as the Coalition Against Violence toward Women and Families at the U.S.-Mexico Border. A horrifying discovery of eight female corpses in a cotton field in the city itself galvanized activists on both sides of the border to hold solidarity marches and rallies and to memorialize the dead girls and women at shrines during the annual Día de los Muertos celebrations.

National and transnational networks also mobilized to denounce the murders and violence against women. The performance of Eve Ensler's *Vagina Monologues* occurred annually and in multiple locales at the border. Esther Chávez Cano, the founder of Casa Amiga (an antiviolence counseling center in Cd. Juárez), acquired worldwide fame and was named one of "21 women of the 21st century" accompanied with a visit by Eve Ensler in 2003. Ensler added a monologue to the *Vagina Monologues* focused on femicide in Cd. Juárez, performed to audiences around the world and resonating with audiences in Mexico and the United States.

In addition to the cross-border, localized transnational organizing, large international human rights organizations entered the antifemicide political arena. Amnesty International published a monograph entitled *Intolerable Killings* (2003), releasing it via engagement in public dialogue with Chihuahua officials during a U.S. congressional visit in 2003. At different levels of U.S. government, legislators and councilpersons passed resolutions against the femicide, under the leadership of U.S. Representative Hilda Solís (D-Calif.).[5] Alas, while resolution-making activity enhances public awareness, it is largely symbolic, lacking enforcement mechanisms or resources to withhold if the offending government is intransigent.

Activism peaked in 2003–4 with the largest-ever cross-border solidarity march against femicide in Ciudad Juárez, complete with high-profile celebrities from Mexico City and Hollywood. But within a year, Amnesty and other transnational activists began to lose interest in the city, given the even higher rates of femicide in Guatemala (Staudt 2008: chap. 6).

Rhetorical Governmental Responses

The discourse of political authorities changed over the fifteen-year cycle of femicide. As noted earlier, Mexican government officials and politicians initially blamed the victims for their clothing choices or presence on city streets at night. But once activists mobilized and spread awareness of the city's infamy worldwide, officials spoke publicly with greater respect about the victims and their activist mothers. At local, state, and federal levels, officials appointed female special investigators and prosecutors, what I have called "bureaucratic decorations" (Staudt 2008: chap. 5). Even with support from activists, these decorative appointees alone could not forge the "rule of law" or more professional law enforcement institutions.

Corrosive elements within the law enforcement institutions, historically, have reduced overall credibility and integrity, and Mexico is certainly not unique in this regard. In Ciudad Juárez, both residents and experts hold that officials across various layers and agencies within government have long negotiated control over space for narco-trafficking for a price, without recrimination (for academic analysis of the drug corridor, see Payan 2006 among others). One might count politicians' discourse of respect about victims as an achievement, but changed discourse did not transform law enforcement institutions to prioritize crimes of violence against women nor did it reduce corruption.

Furthermore, when President Calderón was elected in 2006, he mobilized the military and federal police forces in attempts to control organized crime. Just after he took office, the Sinaloa cartel began to compete with the Juárez cartel for market share and control over the very profitable border gateway corridor, inevitably bringing these highly armed criminal forces into clashes with the military.[6] Deployment of the military in anticartel activities worsened the situation in Ciudad Juárez, as the military has a long history of corruption and human rights abuses.

In Ciudad Juárez, the conjuncture of these forces produced an unprecedented number of murders: over 1,600 murders in 2008, 2,600 in 2009, 3,100 in 2010, and 2,600 in 2011. Approximately a tenth or more of these involve the murders of women annually within this total, but women's deaths were hardly visible, given the decline in activism and media attention. In fact, official reporting of crime victims has been gender-neutralized. Only feminist scholars like Julia Monárrez at COLEF (Colegio de la Frontera Norte) and Molly Molloy, a moderator of the Frontera List website and Listserv, post regular information on the number of women killed. Previously, the number of women murdered from 1993 to 2007 peaked at 30–40 deaths annually (Staudt 2008), but that number increased fivefold in 2011 (Staudt and Méndez 2014).

Similar research also made the problem of domestic-violence murder visible in Ciudad Juárez (Staudt 2008: chap. 3; also Staudt and Robles 2010). In 2008, Amnesty International produced a monograph about domestic violence and attempted murder in Mexico that focused on three states. The monograph was released with far less fanfare than the 2003 monograph on the femicides and amid quiet, nearly invisible activism in the violent city (see Wright 2010 on the less visible activism). In response, Mexico's congressional representatives pressed for changes toward gender-based language and acknowledgment of femicides around the entire country, producing some procedural change in the federal attorney general's office (Aikin Araluce 2009).

Femicide persists, despite what human rights theorists might view as promising pressure from both internal and external activists, but without effective or meaningful outcomes from sustained pressure on Mexico's law enforcement institutions and/or from the United States. An atmosphere of fear and intimidation exists in Ciudad Juárez, with increasingly cynical sentiments about government-purported "security" in a context of still-ineffective law enforcement institutions.

Activism Continues

After feminist and human rights activism peaked in 2003–4 with high-visibility solidarity marches and celebrities, a "tough organizational act to follow" in any setting (Staudt 2008: chap. 4), a wary, wait-and-see sense prevailed with the arrival of the Mexican military and the federal police in 2008. A new governor was elected in the state of Chihuahua in 2004, and a new president in 2006. Although many Mexican feminists have long been cynical about establishment party politics and co-optation through electoral campaigns, the femicide issue entered some party campaigns. City elites also called for public safety and more professional law enforcement institutions.

But besides the wary watchfulness, there were signs of official backlash and intimidation. Nationalist politicians and the government-influenced media raised questions about corruption and "foreign" influence in activist networks, perfecting their "divide-and-rule" strategies. Nonetheless, feminist and human rights social movement organizing has never been monolithic, given differences about such issues as the priority of violence against women generally versus femicide, fund-raising, and the distribution of funds. Some of the victims' mothers have understandably asked, "Who benefits from our pain?" (for fuller detail, see Staudt 2008: chap. 4). Sustained interest and time for voluntary social movement activism are always potentially problematic, and international NGOs moved on to other locales with femicide rates exceeding that of northern Mexico, such as Guatemala.

Meanwhile, quiet activism persisted as feminists joined with other grassroots activists and pursued action projects despite the atmosphere of fear and intimidation that shrouded the city as cartel violence and crime wrecked the possibility of safe public space. Indeed, notable processes and accomplishments exist, most of them targeted and legalistic, from activism that sought to deny a plum post to a femicide denier to an Inter-American Court of Human Rights case to a readiness on the part of the United States to accept asylum cases based on domestic violence. Three illustrative case vignettes are summarized below.

First, President Calderón named former governor of Chihuahua Francisco Barrio to the plum post of Mexican ambassador to Canada. In the 1990s, Barrio had failed to provide leadership for investigating and prosecuting femicide; instead he blamed the victims. These facts were publicized widely at the time of his appointment in April 2009, and a flurry of transnational electronic communications provided substance for Canadian feminists to successfully challenge Mexico's intended appointment. The appointment was ultimately made, however, but with significant embarrassment.[7]

In April 2008, in the Inter-American Court of Human Rights three mothers sought justice for their daughters, whose corpses had been dumped in a city cotton field (as noted earlier). The court heard testimony from the mothers and expert witnesses. U.S. lawyers also filed amicus briefs documenting international human rights decision precedents. Mexico lost the case, another embarrassment, and it was ordered to make law enforcement implementation changes and to remember the victims at a public site. To date, the government has responded unevenly to these mandates (Staudt and Méndez 2014).

The U.S. government has signaled a readiness to accept domestic violence and police impunity claims as a justification for political asylum. Although it is impossible to know the total number of these cases or their success rate (due to the secrecy of asylum proceedings), I provided affidavits for three such cases in 2009. Three types of organizations provided expertise in these cases, all pro bono and all examples of transnational human rights activism: a law school, a private firm, and a nonprofit organization.

These case vignettes demonstrate the kind of transnational activism around violence against women that continues—an activism that is targeted and efficacious, yet unable to transform perverse law enforcement institutions. In the early twenty-first century, surely no dispute exists about a woman's right to live or about the responsibility of government to provide women with public safety, security, and protection from brutal murders. Yet the challenges to resolving these problems continue to be enormous.

Merry argues that effective pressure over rights and national compliance depends partly on the financial autonomy or dependence of countries; financially dependent countries are more likely to create the appearance of compliance (2006: 32; on Fiji, 89). Although power asymmetries certainly exist, Mexico and the United States share mutual dependencies as important trading partners. Alas, I believe that drug war and free trade policies will likely always trump human rights concerns around femicide.

Below, I discuss the contexts that transnational activists should take into account, woven in with the specific case of Mexico's femicides in Ciudad Juárez.

Human Rights Discourse and the Local Contexts

Many political scientists and most anthropologists know that "context matters," and they build that into their analysis on violence against women (see Staudt 2008; Merry 2006). Moreover, transnational advocacy networks are dynamic and changing, requiring attention to those with sustained interest in the given context versus those that are fickle or zoom in on the issue in other contexts (Staudt 2008 on Amnesty). Merry warns about transnational human rights activity inattentive to the local vernacular (2006: 3), but this has not been as problematic among transnational activists as it has been for state officials whose defensiveness defies human rights claims. The grounded beginnings and invention of the *feminicidio* language plus survey research

(Staudt 2008: chap. 3) show the deep awareness and consciousness that most women have about their human right to live *una vida sin violencia* (a life free of violence), to use the language of recent Mexican congressional (unfunded) mandates.

Numerous official and nongovernmental institutions also operate with a human rights agenda at the global (i.e., United Nations) and regional levels. Many have already issued decisions on femicide, as has Mexico's national human rights commission, to little avail, due to lack of enforcement authority. The Convention on the Elimination of All Forms of Discrimination against Women (CEDAW) provides international norms that some women and human rights advocates have been able to use to foster changes within their countries. In Mexico, civil society activists work to help CEDAW norms trickle down to state and local levels. Transnational activists themselves are shaped by fund-raising strategies and sources of support that are embedded within the international human rights discourse.

Mexico's constitutional and political discourse is eloquent, evoking social justice and rights, despite the distance between discourse and policy implementation in many cases. Kathryn Sikkink (2004) alludes to the way states can co-opt the language of human rights in their discourse yet continue to pursue abusive tendencies—which was common in the national security defenses authoritarian regimes in the Americas used during the Cold War. In the post-Cold War era, the fight against drug cartels now provides the justification for militarization and the human rights abuses that invariably coexist.[8]

To reiterate, we must unpack the nation into its regions, states, and municipalities. National legal discourse and appeasement hardly grapple with "regional patriarchies" (on the concept, see López-González 2005). To strengthen transnational activism in ways that better address the context of Mexico's femicide, I discuss critical local and transnational contexts below.

The Law Enforcement Context

The adoption of international human rights norms requires the existence of the "rule of law" and of professional law enforcement institutions. Police impunity and unjust courts are common and widespread, a continuing legacy of colonial control systems in independent countries, which were hardly addressed to justice in historical and contemporary terms.[9] The state of

Chihuahua may be an egregious, outlier case of police impunity, but such practices exist in other parts of the world. Indeed, unnamed femicide likely also exists in many places, without the advantage of the relatively free expression that exists in Mexico to communicate human rights abuses, albeit with ongoing assassinations of journalists.

In federal systems of government, with their division of law enforcement functions and responsibilities, advocates must take into account the multiple targets and levels of authority in complex governance. Even if the federal or national government responds to and acknowledges international norms in its rhetoric, such rhetoric does not mean that decision makers will generate the political will and budgetary resources to require change at the state and local levels. Indeed, until 2003, Mexico's federal government cited jurisdictional problems in its ability to act on femicide in Chihuahua—the "it's not our problem" defense for inaction. Human rights action depends on whether federal or national mandates (funded or unfunded) actually change practices.

In the United States, local police intransigence on domestic violence and rape began to change after a thirty-year project of pressure from feminist groups in the 1960s and 1970s, increased professionalism and accountability in the criminal justice system, and *funded* mandates from the U.S. Congress for victim-friendly law enforcement, now with bipartisan political support— albeit in a bureaucratic and fragmented system in which victims/survivors do not always report crimes and/or fall through the cracks of justice (fully developed in Staudt 2008: chap. 5). Hopefully, it will not take thirty years of sustained activism for municipal and state governments to comply with the laws in Mexico.

Transnational activism occurs within global and local economic contexts that aggravate the abuse of comprehensive rights, not only civil and political, but also social. Shifting global conditions, recessions, and polarizing growth can aggravate people's ability to maintain their livelihoods, such as the NAFTA-induced devastation of small-scale agriculture, and peso devaluations that cheapened maquila wages amid rising costs of living.

Transnational activists' interests shift, undermining local grassroots activists' energy, funds, and successes to sustain the pressure with limited resources, time, and power. Like any organizations—governmental and nongovernmental—transnational activism changes with new leadership, fundraising strategies, and emergent political opportunities. Local activists' ability to sustain their work requires nonthreatening, nonintimidating political space and occasional successes to avoid burnout and fatigue. The prevailing atmosphere of fear deters some potential activists in northern Mexico, whether fear emanates from the political authorities, the narcos, and/or the military, but courageous people express their activism through social media and on the streets (Staudt and Méndez 2014). Newspapers exercise caution, and some have eliminated coverage of murders, but in Ciudad Juárez, the *Diario* removed journalists' "by-lines," given assassinations and revenge killings.

The Binational Context

Intransigence emanates not only from offender countries, but also from supposed exemplar countries. Subsequent nuances in human rights theorizing call attention to "mixed signals" that supposed national allies or exemplars of human rights practices emit (Sikkink 2004). Here, we must insert the United States into the analysis, a nation often considered an ally of human rights principles.[10] The United States sends multiple signals to Mexico, the most important of which have to do with trade relations and drug interdiction and the least of which have to do with stopping femicide and women's everyday insecurities. Resolutions, gestures done in good faith, have virtually no impact on policy priorities.

Contrast those antifemicide resolutions to programs associated with the high-profile War on Drugs and the budgeted money attached to that "war." In 2009, the U.S. delayed release of some funding for the U.S. Mérida Initiative to support Mexico's antidrug cartel mobilizations, alleging human rights abuses (Booth and Fainaru 2009). As with other "conditional" funding and the potential humiliation associated with economic assistance or dependency, Mexican reaction is largely nationalistic. Compare this to the femicide resolution: U.S. congressional representatives unanimously agreed that women-killing must stop, but they provided no funding, no follow-up, and no conditions associated with the eradication of femicide that held all levels of Mexican government accountable, especially the state of Chihuahua and the municipality of Ciudad Juárez.

Politicians in Mexico's Congress also passed resolutions and new laws focused on women "living lives free of violence." But Mexico is a federal system of government, with jurisdictional territorial issues. Laws without resources that do not compel state governments to change can be called "unfunded mandates."

Although most attention is focused on Mexico on the issue of femicide, U.S. complicity in the overall lawless context must be acknowledged. Rather than an independent, exemplary, third-party government ally of human rights, U.S. policies helped create and sustain a "drug economy," complete with powerful stakeholders, in addition to the illegal distribution networks: (1) drug consumers and their massive demand for highly profitable commodities; (2) law enforcement bureaucracies with material stakes in perpetuating jobs; (3) private prison industries that profit from the market niche of an overcriminalized population (on comparative figures, Staudt 2009), including marijuana users convicted for possession of small amounts serving jail terms (that often exceed those for sexual assault and domestic violence crimes). In budgetary terms, a forty-year "War on Drugs" overcapitalized the criminalization strategies and undercapitalized the medical problems of abuse and addiction. Less U.S. demand for all drugs would reduce the profitability of drug cartels. Moreover, the end to "prohibition"—that is, decriminalization or legalization of "soft" drugs like marijuana, and regulating the substance like alcohol—would undercut the cartel economy. The U.S. prohibition era, 1920–33, amid weak and corrupt law enforcement institutions, gave rise to massive organized crime, much of which has morphed into organized crime in this era.

The Patriarchal Context

Domestic violence murders produce the same dead victims as sexualized murders. Whether government officials or activists, people should recognize the fine line that separates sensationalized sexualized hate killings from the torture and misogyny of "ordinary" domestic violence killings. The term domestic hardly addresses the terror such crimes can mean for everyday life.

Activists should recognize the special, personalized resistance to feminist and violence against women abuses, compared with other policies and bureaucratic lethargy. The history of the state is a history of patriarchy, in ideological and institutional terms. Many institutions, but especially law enforcement institutions, reek of traditional masculinism. Changes have certainly occurred with the spread of civil, political, and labor rights to women, and with the concept of women's rights as human rights, but resistance to gender equality continues, particularly in "masculinist" institutions: those organizations dominated by men and so-called masculine values that prize control, aggression, and military strength. Law enforcement institutions are primary examples of such institutions. The tragic irony of persistent femicide is that the success of targeted human rights activism depends primarily on the long-term project of reforming and transforming these near-incorrigible masculinist institutions and the misogyny that sustains them.

CHAPTER 9

Transnational Advocacy for Human Rights in Contemporary Mexico

Alejandro Anaya Muñoz

Throughout the past six decades, as the international human rights regime has developed, as a growing number of international human rights non-governmental organizations (NGOs) have emerged and consolidated, and as more countries have included the promotion and protection of human rights in their foreign policy objectives, the behavior of rights-violating governments has been increasingly scrutinized by weary international eyes. Indeed, more than six decades after the adoption of the Universal Declaration of Human Rights in 1948, the involvement of international actors in domestic human rights processes is taken for granted. A growing literature has studied the way international advocates (nongovernmental, intergovernmental, and governmental) monitor, scrutinize, and take action in response to human rights violations in different countries, showing that, through the exertion of pressure, they influence the development of domestic politics and thus the behavior of rights-violating governments (see, for example, Anaya Muñoz 2009a; Brysk 1994; Cardenas 2007; Thomas 2002; Keck and Sikkink 1998; Burgerman 2001; Risse et al. 1999). This literature, however, has tended to focus on the exertion of pressure on openly repressive authoritarian regimes. Lesser attention has been given to the dynamics of transnational pressure in countries that overcome authoritarianism and systematic repression.

Mexico experienced a long period of authoritarian rule that lasted for seven decades (1929–2000). Even if it experienced different human rights

crises throughout this time—notably, the repression of the student movement in the late 1960s and the "dirty war" against leftist guerrilla movements
in the state of Guerrero during the 1970s—the situation in the country did
not attract the attention of transnational human rights advocates until the
second half of the 1990s, when the government response to indigenous and
peasant insurgency in Chiapas and other southern states generated a significant human rights crisis (Anaya Muñoz 2009b; Keck and Sikkink 1998).
Soon after, in 2000, a painstaking transition to a competitive multiparty political system culminated with the election of the first opposition president
in seventy years, Vicente Fox (president 2000–2006). The resulting "democratic bonus" and new approach to human rights in foreign policy promoted
by President Fox—characterized by opening the country to international
monitoring and assistance—radically improved Mexico's human rights reputation at the international level. But human rights problems persisted, in
spite of changes in policies and discourse (Anaya Muñoz 2007). Has Mexico
been the target of transnational human rights pressure after its political
transition in 2000 and the ensuing improvement of its international human
rights reputation? This chapter focuses on three high profile human rights
problems in this period—the systematic disappearances and killings of
women in Ciudad Juárez, the severe social conflict in Oaxaca in 2006, and
the militarization of the struggle against drug cartels during the presidency of Felipe Calderón (2006–2012). On the basis of these three situations,
this chapter explores the point at which serious human rights shortcomings have generated processes of transnational pressure on the Mexican
government.

This chapter shows that Mexico has continued to be the target of transnational ideational pressure or shaming after the 2000 transition, with two
interrelated caveats. First, the levels of shaming vary substantially across the
three situations studied here. Indeed, not all the situations generated the
same amount of transnational human rights pressure against the Mexican
government. Second, intergovernmental and government actors have not
always been ready to join NGOs in the exertion of ideational pressure on
Mexico. The chapter concludes with a preliminary discussion of two questions that derive from its central findings. Does the exertion of transnational
ideational pressure or shaming matter at the end of the day? (What kind of
impact does it have in the human rights situation in practice?) And under
what conditions are intergovernmental entities and government actors from

developed democracies more likely to join NGOs in the exertion of pressure on rights-violating governments?

Transnational Advocates and the Exertion of Ideational Pressure

NGOs, intergovernmental organizations, and Western governments—the more relevant actors in the transnational advocacy of human rights[1]—attempt to influence the behavior of governments that violate human rights by exerting pressure—that is, by affecting the latter's material and/or ideational interests. Material pressure targets interests related to trade, aid, investment, and the like. For example, preferential trade agreements, loans, or investment funds can be conditioned to changes in human rights practices. Ideational pressure, on the other hand, is exerted by questioning a country's status as a "civilized state" or as a "worthy member" of the international community (Hawkins 2002, 2004; Khagram, Riker, and Sikkink 2002). Ideational pressure is implemented through the tactic of "shaming"—that is, the explicit public denunciation of a gap between behavior and accepted norms (Hawkins 2004; Lebovic and Voeten 2006). This chapter focuses on ideational pressure because shaming is by far more common than material sanctions in the international politics of human rights. In practice, the latter type of pressure has been largely irrelevant for a country like Mexico; NGOs, intergovernmental entities, and other governments shamed Mexico because of grave human rights shortcomings, but material sanctions were not pursued (Anaya Muñoz 2009a, c).[2]

Human rights NGOs are crucial for the transnational advocacy of human rights because they often initiate the whole process, exerting pressure directly on rights-violating governments, but also introducing issues or situations to the agenda of intergovernmental and governmental actors, urging them to take action (Keck and Sikkink 1998). It should not be surprising that human rights NGOs exert pressure on rights-violating governments; after all, that is what they do.[3] In this sense, it is particularly relevant to carefully examine whether NGOs are joined by intergovernmental entities and government actors in acts of shaming. Indeed, human rights bodies and organs of intergovernmental organizations are *also supposed* to monitor the human rights situation in specific countries, and some of them are even mandated to authoritatively conclude whether violations have taken place. But, as they are immersed in inter*governmental* organizations, we can expect them to be more cautious than NGOs in criticizing or condemning specific governments. For obvious reasons, government actors are likely to be the most reluctant to exert shaming—the diplomatic principle of reciprocity and the need to achieve security or economic interests trumps, in practice, the promotion of human rights in foreign policy.

In cases like Mexico, in which the main mechanism of pressure is ideational, shaming by intergovernmental bodies and governments of powerful democracies is particularly relevant. If a particular country aspires to be accepted as a worthy member of the international community, then the opinion of the leaders of that community (developed democracies) and the organizations in which it is embodied is particularly important.[4] Checkel (2001) has argued that a social agent is more likely to be persuaded by new arguments if "the persuader is an authoritative member of the in-group to which the persuadee belongs or wants to belong" (54). In other words, the exertion of shame will only be consequential if it is undertaken by governments with "social" ascendancy over the target. Of course, legislative bodies and not only executive branches are potential participants in shaming activities— congresses and parliaments can (and often do) impose sanctions or establish conditions for the distribution of aid to foreign governments and express concern about or even criticize and condemn the violation of human rights in specific countries (Burgerman 2001: 11–15).

Taking all these factors into account, this chapter looks at the acts of shaming against Mexico carried out by international NGOs, intergovernmental bodies, and governments of developed democracies. More specifically, the focus is on two leading international human rights NGOs, Amnesty International (AI) and Human Rights Watch (HRW), although other organizations or networks of activists are also considered when necessary. As for intergovernmental actors, particular attention is given to the specialized human rights organs and bodies of the UN and the Organization of American States (OAS). However, as will be shown here, other intergovernmental organizations, in particular the Council of Europe, have been relevant players in recent processes of shaming of Mexico. Finally, the chapter looks at government actors from the United States and Europe. The United States is evidently the international actor with most ascendance over Mexico. European countries and the European Union also have diplomatic and, to some degree, economic ascendance over Mexico. In addition, they have shown a particular concern about human rights in Mexico in the recent past (Anaya Muñoz 2009c).

Disappearances and Killings of Women in Ciudad Juárez

Toward the mid- to late 1990s, civil society groups from Ciudad Juárez and El Paso (Texas) began to denounce the growing number of disappearances and killings of women on the Mexican side of the border. A few years later, they were joined by a few NGOs based in Mexico City and eventually by important international NGOs, such as AI (AI 2003a; for a detailed account of this process, see Staudt and Coronado 2007). August 2003 marked a very important moment, when a high-level delegation from AI (led by its secretary-general, Irene Kahn) visited Mexico and met with local actors, including the families of the victims, and high-ranking government officials. As expected, Kahn's public appraisal of the situation was explicitly critical (AI 2003a, b). In this context, AI released its report *Mexico: Intolerable Killings: Ten Years of Abductions and Murders in Ciudad Juárez and Chihuahua* (AI 2003c), in which it documented 370 murders of women over a ten-year period. The report denounced abductions, torture, and "horrific sexual violence" against scores of women, together with discrimination against the victims and their families and blatant failure to investigate the crimes.

Since 2004, HRW had also emphasized in its annual reports that a "dramatic" and "paradigmatic" example of the overall failure of the justice system in Mexico was "the unsolved murders of hundreds of young women and girls" in Ciudad Juárez (HRW 2004). In its 2006 special report on human rights in Mexico, *Lost in Transition*, HRW (2006b) recalled that the human rights issue that attracted most international attention during Fox's tenure in office was the murder and disappearance of over four hundred women in Ciudad Juárez, and HRW criticized the inadequate government response. The NGO underlined how state-level law enforcement agencies attempted to "solve" these cases by resorting to the entrenched practice of forced confessions (resulting from torture) from "scapegoats."

Since the late 1990s, numerous human rights bodies and UN procedures started to pay explicit attention to the disappearances and killings of women in Ciudad Juárez. The situation was explicitly addressed and critically assessed by the special rapporteurs on extrajudicial, summary, or arbitrary executions; on independence of judges and lawyers; and on violence against women. The Committee Against Torture (CAT) and particularly the Committee on the Elimination of Discrimination Against Women (CEDAW) included critical appraisals of the situation in Ciudad Juárez in their "concluding observations" reports on Mexico (CEDAW 2002, 2006; CAT 2006). Very important in this respect was CEDAW's special inquiry under article 8 of the Optional Protocol to the Convention on the Elimination of All Forms of Discrimination Against Women, undertaken in 2003 and 2004.[5] The inquiry included a fact-finding mission in 2003 and resulted in the release of a critical special report in 2005 (CEDAW 2005).

In addition, during different official visits to Mexico, both Mary Robinson (UN high commissioner for human rights, 1997–2002) and Louise Arbour (high commissioner, 2004–8) explicitly expressed their concern about the scores of unsolved killings and disappearances of women in Ciudad Juárez and criticized the behavior of both state (Chihuahua) and federal authorities (Saliba 2002; Ballinas 2002; Becerril et al. 2005). Last, with respect to the UN bodies and procedures, the examination of the human rights situation in Mexico by the UN Human Rights Council (through its Universal Periodic Review mechanism) in 2009 resulted in a number of recommendations pertaining to violence against women, some of which specifically addressed the case of Ciudad Juárez (Human Rights Council 2009).

Within the sphere of the OAS, the Inter-American Commission on Human Rights (IACHR) also gave special attention to the situation in Ciudad Juárez. In 2003, the IACHR special rapporteur on the rights of women conducted an in loco mission and published a critical special report that concluded that despite the government's efforts, the Mexican state had not fulfilled its international obligations to prevent and eradicate violence against women and to investigate, prosecute, and punish the perpetrators of the violent crimes against women in Ciudad Juárez (IAHCR 2002, 2003). In 2009, the Inter-American Court of Human Rights adopted a milestone ruling in the "Cotton Field" case, in which it concluded, inter alia, that the Mexican state had violated the rights to life, personal liberty, and personal integrity and failed in its obligation to investigate (Inter-American Court 2009a). Indeed, the "Cotton Field" ruling has been one of the most important acts of shaming over the Mexican government around the systematic disappearances and killings of women in Ciudad Juárez.

The disappearances and brutal killings of women in Ciudad Juárez also made it to the agenda of a regional intergovernmental organization to which Mexico is not a member, the Council of Europe.[6] The situation was addressed by both the Council's main organs—the Parliamentary Assembly and the Committee of Ministers. The Parliamentary Assembly appointed a special rapporteur who conducted two fact-finding missions to the country and produced a thorough and critical report (Council of Europe-Parliamentary Assembly 2005a). On the basis of this report, the Parliamentary Assembly and the Council of Ministers adopted sharply critical resolutions (Council of Europe-Parliamentary Assembly 2005b; Council of Europe-Committee of Ministers 2005). The resolution by the Parliamentary Assembly concluded unabashedly that

> The reaction of the authorities can only be considered insufficient and leads to the impression that the authorities are still not fully in control of the situation. The Assembly calls on President Fox to reiterate his 2004 statement that the fight against feminicides is the state's top priority. It is urgent to move from audit to action in order to end the climate of impunity for gender-based violence still prevalent in the region. Each branch of power has to face up to its responsibilities and tackle urgent tasks in order to produce rapid results and thus regain the trust of victims' families and of civil society as a whole. (Council of Europe-Committee of Ministers 2005)

Within the framework of the European Union,[7] the killings of women in Ciudad Juárez started to appear on the agenda of the European Parliament in 2005. In subsequent years, the Parliament held an audience on the situation, appointed a rapporteur (who elaborated a harsh special report), and adopted a resolution that underlined that the sexual violence suffered by the victims constituted a form of cruel, inhumane, and degrading treatment, and that recalled "the failure to investigate or sanction the acts . . . and the frequent obstacles to access to justice encountered by female victims and their relatives" (European Parliament 2007a, b).

In addition, cross-border activism by civil society groups from Ciudad Juárez and El Paso generated the involvement of different city (El Paso), state (Texas), and federal legislative actors in the United States. The results of this activism included (1) a joint resolution by the Texas legislature relating to the "plague" of "sexual assault and brutal slaying" of women in Ciudad Juárez (78th Legislature of the State of Texas, 2003; cf. Staudt and Coronado 2007: 360–61); (2) a visit to Ciudad Juárez by a delegation of members of Congress; (3) a formal letter by ninety-four legislators to President Calderón;

and (4) a joint congressional resolution that condemned "the ongoing abductions and murders of young women in Ciudad Juárez and the city of Chihuahua" (*Notimex* 2003; WOLA 2007).

Partly as a response to all this transnational pressure, the federal and Chihuahua governments implemented a number of legal and institutional reforms. At first, the state government denied that the systematic disappearances and killings of women was a human rights issue, and even blamed the victims and their families. The federal government, on the other hand, alleged that this was a local problem, beyond its jurisdiction. But as the transnational pressure accumulated, both levels of governments started to adopt a human rights discourse and to implement reforms. The state government, for example, established the Chihuahua Institute of Women's Affairs and a Deputy Attorney's Office for Human Rights and the Support for the Victims of Crime, and it included the crime of intrafamily violence in the state civil and penal codes. On the other hand, the federal government, inter alia, ratified the Optional Protocol to the Convention on the Elimination of Discrimination Against Women, established the Commission to Prevent and Eliminate Violence Against Women in Ciudad Juárez and a Special Attorney's Office for crimes against women, and adopted the General Law for Women's Access to a Life Free from Violence.[8]

Human Rights Violations During the Conflict in Oaxaca

The social conflict that took place in Oaxaca throughout most of 2006 was a source of permanent preoccupation for AI, which repeatedly expressed its concern about the human rights violations that were taking place. Researchers from AI's international secretariat in London visited Oaxaca in both June and November 2006 and met with the Oaxaca dissidents who suffered police repression and their families, civil society organizations, and government officials. In late July to early August 2007, AI undertook a high-level visit to Mexico (again led by Irene Khan). The delegation traveled to Oaxaca, where it met with the dissidents, civil society organizations, and government officials, including governor Ulises Ruiz. In Oaxaca, Khan presented the highly critical report *Mexico: Oaxaca—Clamor for Justice* (AI 2007c) and made a strong public condemnation of the violations, underlining the prevailing impunity. She also met with the secretary of the interior, secretary of public security, members of Congress, and, for the first time ever, magistrates of the National Supreme Court of Justice. In these meetings, she stressed repeatedly the issue of impunity (Catillo García 2007: Vélez Ascencio 2007; R. Garduño 2007). In addition, Khan held a long meeting with Felipe Calderón in which they discussed the situation in Oaxaca, among other issues. Her conclusion was that "Felipe Calderón's commitment to human rights will be tested by his will to take decisive action to break the impunity circle that has persisted in situations such as Oaxaca" (AI 2007b; Presidencia de la República 2007b).

For its part, in its 2006 and 2007 annual human rights reports, HRW emphasized that "Mexican police forces routinely employ excessive force when carrying out crowd-control operations," resulting in some cases in the death of protesters (HRW 2008a: 220). After a violent clash between police and protesters in Oaxaca in July 2007, HRW urged the government of the state to "ensure that alleged brutality by the police is thoroughly investigated and that those responsible are prosecuted" (HRW 2007a).

In addition to AI and HRW, the actions of the International Civil Commission of Human Rights Observation (Comisión Civil Internacional de Observación de Derechos Humanos, CCIODH) must be considered, given the network's systematic reporting and intense activism around the situation in Oaxaca. The members of the CCIODH—made up of activists from numerous European and Latin American countries—visited Oaxaca from mid-December 2006 to late January 2007. They conducted hundreds of interviews, particularly with members of the dissident group Popular Assembly of the Peoples of Oaxaca (Asamblea Popular de los Pueblos de Oaxaca, APPO), including those under arrest, their families and local NGOs. From the outset, the CCIODH declared: "the situation is much more profound and grave than we imagined," noting in particular the lack of effective investigations into the more than twenty deaths that occurred during the conflict (Olivares Alonso 2006). The CCIODH's lengthy and extremely critical final report was issued in February 2007. The report was distributed in Mexico and presented to the European Parliament and high-level officials of the UN High Commissioner for Human Rights (UNHCHR) in Geneva (CCIODH 2007b). In 2008, the CCIODH denounced the continuing human rights violations and the harassment suffered by social movements in Oaxaca, issuing another thorough report on the situation (CCIODH 2008).

In summer 2006, NGOs from Oaxaca and Washington requested a hearing before the IACHR in relation to the general human rights situation and the crisis of the rule of law in Oaxaca (Due Process of Law Foundation

2006).[9] The IACHR, in turn, expressed "its profound concern over the violent events that have taken place in recent days in the State of Oaxaca" and urged the Mexican government "to adopt all necessary measures to resolve the critical situation affecting citizen security in Oaxaca, with absolute respect for its international human rights obligations" (Inter-American Commission on Human Rights 2006). In March 2007, local NGOs requested another hearing, which focused on the plight of the scores of dissidents who remained in prison. The new president of the IACHR and rapporteur for Mexico, Florentín Meléndez, called for respect for the legal order, but within the framework of "strict respect for human rights" (IAHCR 2007d). In April 2007 he visited Mexico, including Oaxaca, where he met with victims, NGOs, and government officials. In July 2007, after new clashes between the police and APPO protesters, the IACHR publicly regretted the renewed violence and expressed its "deep concern" for the human rights situation in Oaxaca, urging Mexico's government to "promote a process of dialogue that allows for the solution of the conflict in the context of a democratic society and with full respect to human rights" (IACHR 2007b).

Commissioner Meléndez again visited Mexico in August 2007. In Oaxaca, he met with APPO detainees and NGOs and received numerous reports of human rights violations. On this occasion, Meléndez expressed his "deep concern for the acts of violence and the violations of human rights" and urged "the government of Oaxaca and the federal government to investigate in an objective and impartial way the human rights violations perpetrated during the violent repression of public rallies, to compensate the victims and to assure that no human rights violation remains in impunity." Immediately after the visit, he announced he would issue a special report in which he would summarize his view on the situation in Oaxaca and present specific recommendations to the government (IACHR 2007c). This report, however, never materialized. Furthermore, the IACHR denied a hearing requested by Oaxacan NGOs in October 2007, while it held a private meeting with representatives from the Oaxaca and federal governments (Edgar and Maza 2007). After that meeting, the president of the IACHR expressed "his satisfaction concerning the information provided by authorities of the state government of Oaxaca on the implementation of the recommendations he made during his [last] visit to Mexico" (Inter-American Commission on Human Rights 2007a).

The UNHCHR representative in Mexico, on different occasions, expressed concern about the violence and the violations of human rights that took place during the social conflict in Oaxaca. He urged the federal government to take action and pursue a negotiated settlement, and to clarify the alleged participation of "paramilitary" groups in acts of violence against protesters. In October 2006, for example, after a particularly violent incident in Oaxaca, he condemned the incident and stressed that "violence is not justified by any means," called on the government and the dissidents to cooperate and find a negotiated solution, and urged the authorities to undertake a prompt, efficient, and impartial investigation (Naciones Unidas 2006a, b).

The 2007 U.S. Department of State *Human Rights Report* noted that "the *allegations* of official abuses or killings related to the 2006 violence" in Oaxaca have not been solved, making specific reference to the murder of an American journalist, who was killed while covering the conflict (U.S. Department of State 2007, emphasis added). Regarding the scores of arbitrary detentions conducted by security forces on different occasions, the 2007 *Report* stated: "While many associated with the Oaxaca demonstrators were legitimately arrested for criminal offenses, such as vandalism and assault, human rights groups expressed concern that charges against some lacked merit and that authorities failed to follow due process." The State Department report, however, reproduces only the concerns or "allegations" of human rights groups. In this way, it is not a means through which the U.S. government elaborates formal denunciations or criticisms of the Mexican government's behavior.

A network of German NGOs and solidarity groups attracted the attention of Erika Mann (member of the European Parliament and president of the European Parliament Delegation to the EU/Mexico Joint Parliamentary Committee) regarding the human rights situation in Oaxaca. In September 2006, in the context of an official visit to Mexico, and encouraged by the aforementioned network of German NGOs, she visited Oaxaca and met with local NGOs, political dissidents, local journalists, and representatives from the tourism industry. A detailed report of her visit was sent to the European Parliament Committee on Foreign Affairs in October 2006 (Mann 2006; cf. Ávila 2007). However, as noted by Teresa Ávila (former director of the German Coordination for Human Rights in Mexico), the report did not present a strong condemnation or a clear critique of the human rights situation in Oaxaca (Ávila 2007).

A few days after a visit to Europe by President Calderón in 2007, Mann (again encouraged by the German NGO network) called for an extraordinary session of the European Parliament Delegation to the EU/Mexico Joint Parliamentary Committee to receive members of the CCIODH, who presented the conclusions of their report on Oaxaca. The European parliamentarians asked to be kept informed and expressed their interest in visiting Oaxaca in the near future (CCIODH 2007a; Ávila 2007). However, this visit did not take place and the European Parliament never issued a resolution or any other formal statement about the situation.

The government responded to this limited transnational pressure by resorting to a human rights discourse and claiming it would investigate all cases of alleged violations of human rights and punish those responsible. In time, most of the dissidents arrested during the conflict were released from prison. But there were no further actions; the government, overall, did not change its behavior in practice. In fact, in summer 2007, one year after the climax of the abuses, police forces brutally crushed another public protest by APPO sympathizers (Anaya Muñoz 2012). International pressure, on the other hand, faded away. By 2008, the Oaxaca situation had lost considerable prominence in the agenda of most of the international actors that had advocated on its behalf during the previous two years.

Human Rights Violations in the Struggle Against Drug Cartels During the Calderón Presidency

AI and HRW have shown particular concern about military involvement in public security tasks in Mexico. From the first year of the presidency of Felipe Calderón, AI representatives warned that the "armed forces are not qualified or designed to undertake [. . . policing] functions, so there is a risk that grave human rights violations occur" (*El Universal* 2007). AI also stressed that President Calderón was "prioritizing a very narrow view of public security" (Reuters 2007). During a visit to Mexico in 2007, Irene Kahn argued that AI's "experience around the world and decades of work on Mexico show that public security cannot be achieved on a sustainable, effective basis without respect for human rights," and criticized the government's approach to security, stating that the "decision to extend the role and function of military personnel in law enforcement increases the risk of human rights violations and impunity" (AI 2007a).

In 2008, AI reported that "Military personnel performing policing functions killed several people and committed other serious human rights violations" such as arbitrary detention and torture (AI 2008a). In addition, AI urged the U.S. Congress to include human rights safeguards in the U.S.-Mexico cooperation plan on security—the "Mérida Initiative" (AI 2008c; cf. 2008b). Furthermore, in 2009 AI published its special report *Mexico: New Reports of Human Rights Violations by the Military*, in which it claimed to have identified a pattern of human rights violations by members of the armed forces in law enforcement actions against organized crime (AI 2009).

In its 2006 report *Lost in Transition*, HRW denounced that Mexico failed "to integrate human rights and public security into a single coherent agenda" (2006a). More recently, HRW criticized the "egregious abuses" committed by the military in the struggle against drug traffickers, and the impunity the perpetrators enjoy. In a similar approach to that taken by AI, HRW stressed that, taking into consideration the evidence of human rights violations perpetrated by Mexico's security forces (including the military), "The U.S. Congress should oppose counternarcotics assistance to Mexico unless it includes strong conditions aimed at ending abuses by Mexican security forces" (HRW 2007b). In 2009, HRW published its special report *Uniform Impunity: Mexico's Misuse of Military Justice to Prosecute Abuses in Counternarcotics and Public Security Operations* (HRW 2009c), in which it underlined that "while engaging in law enforcement activities, Mexico's armed forces have committed serious human rights violations, including enforced disappearances, killings, torture, rapes, and arbitrary detentions." The main focus of this special investigation is not the human rights violations as such, but military jurisdiction over them: "An important reason such abuses continue is that they go unpunished. And they go unpunished in significant part because most cases end up being investigated and prosecuted by the military itself." More recently, HRW published yet another special report on this situation in which it documents over two hundred specific cases of human rights violations perpetrated by members of the armed forces in the struggle against drug cartels (HRW 2011).

Since the late 1990s and early 2000s the UNHCHR manifested concern about two features of the security agenda in Mexico—the growing direct military involvement in public security activities, and the prosecution of human rights violations presumably perpetrated by members of the armed forces through the system of criminal military justice. In this sense, the UNHCHR *Diagnóstico sobre la situación de los derechos humanos en México* concluded that prosecution through the system of military justice of alleged human rights violations perpetrated by military personnel affected the human rights of the victims, particularly because military courts do not meet the principles of independence and impartiality (UNHCHR 2003). This position was informed by explicit criticisms of the military justice system in Mexico previously made by UN special rapporteurs.

More recently, after a military patrol killed a group of unarmed civilians in the state of Sinaloa in 2007, the UNHCHR representative in Mexico argued that the soldiers involved should be prosecuted and tried under the civil system of criminal justice, and not by military courts. In this context, he stressed his overall concern about military participation in Mexico's strategy to combat drug traffickers (Salgado 2007). In a similar vein, during a visit to Mexico in early 2008, Louise Arbour explicitly rejected that human rights and security are opposite or competing goals, and expressed that "Foremost amongst the issues brought to my attention has been the question of the use of the military to engage in law enforcement activities" (Ballinas, Becceril, and Aranda 2008). Again, she argued that the human rights violations perpetrated by the military must be investigated by the civil justice system, and not the military justice regime. Similarly, military participation in law enforcement activities and the issue of military jurisdiction were explicitly criticized by the UN Human Rights Council, in 2009, and by the UN Human Rights Committee, in 2010 (Human Rights Council 2009; Human Rights Committee 2010).

Leading Mexican human rights NGOs have attempted to bring the issue of the human rights violations perpetrated in the framework of the government's militarized security strategy to the attention of the IACHR. At the request of a number of Mexican NGOs and the Washington-based Center for Justice and International Law (CEJIL), the IACHR held a public hearing on the issue in October 2008. In this hearing, the IACHR suggested only some concern about military jurisdiction (IACHR 2008b). In this respect, the IACHR declared that it follows "with particular attention the state of citizen insecurity in the region [i.e., the Americas], as well as the respect for human rights as an essential component of all public policies to address the problem" (2008a). In March 2009, the IACHR held a second public hearing, this one centered on military jurisdiction, and expressed "its concern over the fact that in some countries of the region the military justice system continues to be used to investigate and prosecute common crimes committed by members of the armed forces or the police" (2009).

Perhaps the most authoritative condemnation has come from the Inter-American Court of Human Rights, which in four separate rulings (one adopted in 2009 and three more in 2010) explicitly concluded that "in the face of situations that violate the human rights of civilians, *under no circum-*

stances can military jurisdiction operate," determining that Mexico must make legislative reforms in order to address this point (Inter-American Court 2009b, 2010a, b, c).

The U.S. Department of State *Human Rights Country Report* on Mexico published from 2008 to 2011 (covering events taking place in 2007–2010) make reference to reported killings, illegal searches, rape, arbitrary detentions, and torture committed by the military in the struggle against drug trafficking. The reports also suggest that the system of military jurisdiction is not generating the conviction of members of the military for cases of violations of human rights. However, the "signals" sent by these reports are "mixed" at best (Sikkink 2004). For example, the 2009 report states that the National Human Rights Commission "and NGOs also expressed concern about *alleged* human rights abuses committed by some military units deployed in counternarcotics operations and cited several incidents implicating military units in killings, illegal searches, rapes, and arbitrary detentions of individuals" (U.S. Department of State 2008a, emphasis added). The report does not subscribe (or deny) the merits of these "allegations." In addition, the Department of State does not use language that explicitly condemns the reported killings and other violations. Indeed, the U.S. government has clearly been concerned about insecurity in Mexico and commended Calderón's efforts against drug traffickers. President George W. Bush stated, in this respect: "I am deeply concerned about how lethal and how brutal these drug lords are. I have watched with admiration how President Calderón has taken a firm hand in making sure his society is free of these drug lords" (U.S. Department of State 2008b).[10]

In mid-2008, the U.S. Congress approved a cooperation plan (the aforementioned "Mérida Initiative") to buttress Mexico's "war on drugs." A small fraction of the funds (15 percent) were conditioned on human rights considerations, including that civilian judicial bodies have jurisdiction over cases of human rights violations allegedly perpetrated by military personnel. In 2009, growing reports of human rights violations by the Mexican military in the fight against drug traffickers raised some expectations that the U.S. Congress could withhold over $100 million of the Mérida Initiative funds (Fainaru and Booth 2009; Brook 2009). In 2010, some funds were temporarily withheld, but they were eventually released. Indeed, at the end of the day, no Mérida funds have been canceled on account of human rights considerations (for further analysis see Meyer, this volume).

The human rights concerns raised by Mexico's security policies during the Calderón period did not reach the agenda of the different bodies of the

European Union in any significant manner. The exception may be the European Commission *Country Strategy Paper (2002–2006)* (European Commission 2001) on Mexico, which concluded that the "expansion of the [Mexican] army's mandate to tasks which should in theory be the responsibility of the civilian authorities have led to human rights excesses and violations, which generally remain unpunished." Such an appraisal, however, is not present in the *Country Strategy Paper (2007–2013)* or in the recent annual human rights reports of the Commission.

Various officials from European countries and the European Union nevertheless expressed concern about the respect of human rights in the framework of the security agenda in Mexico under Calderón. For example, in the summer of 2007, President Calderón attended the "G-8 plus five" meeting in Germany and visited other countries in Europe, promoting Mexico's image as an attractive investment destination. In his speeches and presentations to heads of state, government officials, and private investors, Calderón emphasized his security efforts, attempting to convey the message that European investment would be secure in Mexico. Military involvement in Calderón's security strategy was explicitly endorsed by most of his European counterparts and interlocutors. However, they all also stressed that human rights should not be compromised. Javier Solana, High Representative for the Common Foreign and Security Policy of the EU, commended Calderón's approach but reminded that "The principle of respect for human rights is that upon which all strategies of struggle against organized crime shall be based, otherwise, the fight would be lost" (AFP 2007; cf. Bugarin 2007). Similarly, Italy's prime minister, Romano Prodi, declared: "We express Italy's support for the fight on which president [Calderón] has embarked against organized crime, always with respect to human rights, which is very important" (Presidencia de la República 2007a). Finally, in a visit to Mexico in 2008, José Manuel Durao Barroso, president of the European Commission, acknowledged the importance of fighting drug trafficking and supported Mexico's efforts. But he stressed that "It is essential that this fight be taken with full respect for human rights" (S. Garduño 2008).

So, as shown in the previous paragraphs, the transnational pressure on Mexico around this situation accumulated during the Calderón period, eliciting some responses from the Mexican government. The government's discourse on the issue of military jurisdiction changed over time. In late 2010, and explicitly as a response to the aforementioned rulings by the Inter-American Court of Human Rights, the Calderón government sent to Congress a bill to reform the system of military jurisdiction so that cases of torture, disappearances, and rape by members of the armed forces are investigated and prosecuted through the civil or ordinary system of criminal justice. The bill, however, lingered in Congress, and it seems that the Calderón government did not do much in order to push it forward. So it seems that the reform bill proposed by the Calderón government was only a discursive concession that did not change much in practice. In December 2011, in a speech during the annual National Human Rights Award ceremony, and making an explicit reference to the government commitment to the implementation of the recent rulings by the Inter-American Court of Human Rights, President Calderón declared that he had instructed the minister of the interior and the legal counsel of the presidency to give new arguments to Congress in order to enrich the ongoing debate on the reform of military jurisdiction. In addition, he claimed to have instructed the Attorney General's Office and the Ministries of Defense and the Navy to (in the absence of a reform) find administrative ways to transfer all cases of alleged violations of human rights perpetrated by members of the armed forces to civilian prosecutors and courts (Presidencia de la República 2011). Although the formal legal framework of military jurisdiction was not reformed, towards the end of the Calderón period, numerous cases were indeed being transferred to civilian courts. In addition, the Supreme Court made a series of landmark decisions in specific cases in which it adopted the position established by the Inter-American Court of Human Rights—that cases of the presumed violation of human rights by members of the armed forces should be tried by civil courts.

Conclusions

Mexico has continued to be the target of transnational human rights ideational pressure or shaming. The human rights violations addressed in this chapter have generated numerous critical reports by international NGOs. They have been monitored by specialized bodies and procedures of intergovernmental organizations, which have also elaborated numerous (again, critical) reports. They have even resulted in rulings by authoritative bodies (i.e., the Inter-American Court of Human Rights) and different critical actions by foreign legislative bodies and supranational organs. Mexico's transition to electoral democracy and the sharp improvement in its international human rights reputation after 2000 did not fully insulate it from transnational

Table 1. Ideational Pressure by International Actors Against Mexico

Issue	NGO actions	Intergovernmental actions	Governmental actions
Femicides in Ciudad Juárez	Annual reports *In-loco* visits Special report by AI	Reports by special rapporteurs, CEDAW, and Committee against Torture Special report by IACHR Ruling by Inter-American Court of Human Rights Special report by CEDAW (chapter 8, Optional Protocol) Hearing, appointment of special rapporteur, special report, and resolution by Parliamentary Assembly, Council of Europe	Hearing and resolution by Texas Legislature Hearing, *in-loco* visit, resolution and letters to Vicente Fox by U.S. Congress Hearing, appointment of special rapporteur, special report and resolution by European Parliament
Social conflict in Oaxaca	Annual reports *In-loco* visits Special report by AI Report by CCIODH	Hearings in IACHR *In-loco* visits by IACHR	*In-loco* visit and (uncritical) report by president of European Parliamentary Delegation to EU/Mexico Joint Parliamentary Committee
Struggle against drug cartels	Annual reports *In-loco* visits Special reports by HRW and AI	Mentions of concern and recommendations by UNHCHR Reports by UN Human Rights Council and Human Rights Committee Hearings in IACHR Four rulings by Inter-American Court of Human Rights	Mentions of concern by some European officials Human rights conditions inserted in Mérida Initiative and some funds temporarily withheld "Mixed signals" in State Department *Country Reports*

shaming. In other words, the human rights shortcomings that persist in Mexico still generate critical reactions by external actors involved in transnational advocacy of human rights. Indeed, transnational ideational pressure and shaming do not end after the transition to democracy, particularly if the transition leads to "illiberal" or "low quality" democracy, as in the Mexican case (Cansino and Covarrubias 2007; Smith and Ziegler 2008).

As summarized in Table 1, the levels of pressure generated around specific human rights situations are not identical. It is clear that the situation in Ciudad Juárez generated a much broader and deeper process of shaming. Not only NGOs, but also numerous intergovernmental organs and bodies and even some legislative actors from the United States and the European Union, have explicitly noted, criticized, and condemned the gap between expected and actual behavior by the Mexican authorities.[11]

Government responses have been more numerous and more meaningful as the pressure has increased. But even in the Ciudad Juárez case, in which the pressure has been greatest, have the government responses meant significant improvements in respect for human rights in practice? The government undertook a lot of actions that signal its commitment to human rights norms, but at the same time the violations continue to take place (Cardenas 2007). Thus, the reader might wonder what is the point of transnational advocacy of human rights; or more specifically, what is the point of shaming rights-violating countries if even after the exertion of very high levels of pressure, "commitment actions" are all we can expect?

The main response of the academic international relations literature is that transnational advocacy makes a difference in practice; that it generates responses from target governments. If transnational pressure did not matter, why bother to systematically observe a country like Mexico and its continued targeting by international advocates of human rights? As already acknowledged, the high levels of ideational pressure generated by international advocates have not solved the deeply entrenched problem of violence against women in Ciudad Juárez, nor have they solved the historical flaws of the system of administration of justice in the state of Chihuahua, let alone Mexico as a whole. Tragically, women continue to be killed and impunity remains pervasive in Ciudad Juárez, the state of Chihuaha, and Mexico. But one must not overlook that the legal and institutional reforms that (at least in part) resulted from transnational pressures have significantly increased the potential leverage of local activists. This is, as shown by Simmons, the most valuable result of the transnational advocacy of human rights—the modification of the domestic rules of the game, so that opportunities for effective litigation and social mobilization improve (Simmons 2009). In the case of Ciudad Juárez, the federal and state governments undertook several measures to modify the legal framework and the institutional machinery for the administration of justice and for the prevention and elimination of violence against women, not only in Ciudad Juárez or Chihuahua, but in the whole country. The new legal and institutional context is more conducive to successful litigation and social mobilization. In addition, transnational pressure has been conductive to the adoption of a clear human rights (and women's rights) discourse by Mexican authorities at all levels. The long-term importance of discursive changes must not be minimized; changes in discourse constrain actors' policy options and might even contribute to deeper processes of internalization of norms. In this sense, it is true that the pressure exerted by international advocates of human rights documented in this chapter has not eliminated the shameful disappearances and killings of women, but it has made an important contribution to that end. Unfortunately, such a contribution by international advocates has been considerably less significant in relation to the struggle against drugs and more so in the human rights violations perpetrated in Oaxaca.

This systematic study of transnational human rights shaming by specific actors around concrete situations also shows that intergovernmental and government actors are not always willing to join NGOs in the explicit criticism or condemnation of rights-violating governments. Certainly, the critical or condemnatory reactions to the violations of human rights in Oaxaca by UN and OAS human rights bodies and, particularly, by government actors from the United States and Europe have been rather shy—particularly if compared to those undertaken in relation to the Ciudad Juárez situation. In the same sense, government actors have not joined NGOs in the exertion of pressure on the Mexican government around the violations of human rights perpetrated in the war against drug cartels. This finding is of course not a novelty. But it is important to underline that such an empirical observation has not been explicitly studied and theorized. The academic literature notes that activists from civil society tend to start and drive the advocacy process, and that intergovernmental and government actors will then follow. As noted in this chapter, this is not always the case.

So, a key question is under what conditions are intergovernmental and, even more so, government actors willing to join NGOs in the exertion of pressure on rights-violating governments? An attempt to answer such a question falls beyond the scope and possibilities of this chapter, which pursued a more modest objective—the description of the transnational shaming activity that has been generated around different high-profile situations of violation of human rights in Mexico. A blueprint for an analytical framework for such a question, however, has been suggested by the literature, which has identified different elements related to the characteristics of advocacy networks themselves and to the nature of the situations around which they mobilize (see, for example, Keck and Sikkink 1998: Burgerman 2001) that have an influence on the generation of successful advocacy initiatives. In this sense, *denser* networks seem to be more likely to generate deeper and broader transnational advocacy campaigns against rights-violating governments. On the other hand, situations that can be presented as *credible and dramatic* instances of the violation of human rights will be more likely to trigger criticism and condemnation by all sorts of international actors. More specifically, situations appear to be more amenable to being presented as credible and dramatic stories if (a) sufficient evidence can be collected; (b) bodily harm is systematically inflicted on innocent and/or vulnerable individuals; and (c) the situation resonates clearly with existing international norms (Anaya Muñoz 2011). This *suggests* that the disappearances and killings of women in Ciudad Juárez have generated shaming actions not only by NGOs but also by numerous intergovernmental and important governmental entities because this situation has been advocated by a very dense network, and because its inherent characteristics facilitated its presentation as a credible and particularly dramatic story—sufficient evidence could be amassed, bodily harm was perpetrated against vulnerable or innocent individuals, and the situation clearly resonated with international norms. But, again, the objective of this chapter has not been to "test" this framework. Such an endeavor, of course, would need to be explored in a more systematic and detailed fashion in future research.

CHAPTER 10

Restrictions on U.S. Security Assistance and Their Limitations in Promoting Changes to the Human Rights Situation in Mexico

Maureen Meyer

At the outset of his administration in 2006, Mexican president Felipe Calderón launched a massive deployment of soldiers and federal police in counter-drug operations in several parts of the country while also implementing a series of initiatives to strengthen Mexico's public security and justice institutions. President Calderón also affirmed shortly after assuming office that, parallel to these national efforts, "the U.S. is jointly responsible for what is happening to us . . . in that joint responsibility the American government has a lot of work to do. We cannot confront this problem alone" (Thomson 2007). This call for greater counter-drug cooperation and acknowledgment of binational sources of the illicit drug trade culminated in the announcement of a U.S. foreign assistance package to Mexico that would become known as the Mérida Initiative. As of fiscal 2012, the Mérida Initiative had provided Mexico with over $1.9 billion in assistance, with the Obama administration requesting $234 million in assistance for fiscal 2013.

This chapter describes the development of U.S. assistance to Mexico under the Mérida Initiative and examines language in the aid package that permits the U.S. Congress to withhold part of the funding based on Mexico's progress in investigating and prosecuting human rights abuses by federal police and the military. This is followed by a description of the partnerships formed between U.S. and Mexican organizations on this issue and the advocacy strategies they have implemented for work with both governments. The chapter discusses the impact of the organizations' efforts to ensure that human rights are on the agenda of U.S.-Mexico relations, and presents preliminary conclusions on the limits of the strings attached to this assistance in promoting systemic changes to the human rights situation in Mexico. Because the significant expansion in U.S. security cooperation with Mexico occurred during former President Calderon's administration, the analysis focuses on the time period of his administration which ended on November 30, 2012. Current President Enrique Peña Nieto took office on December 1, 2012. In the first few months of his administration, very little changed regarding the security strategy in Mexico and human rights violations continue to occur at alarming levels.

Overview of the Security Situation in Mexico

In spite of, or because of, President Calderón's large-scale efforts to combat organized crime, there has been a dramatic increase in drug-related violence in Mexico since the beginning of his administration in December 2006. According to media reports, as of July 2012, over 60,000 people had been killed in drug-related killings since the beginning of Calderón's government (Booth and Miroff 2012). The expansion of organized criminal activities to include not only drug trafficking but also extortion, kidnapping, human trafficking, and other illicit activities; the arrests of several government officials for passing on information to or working with drug trafficking organizations; reports of campaign financing by drug traffickers in state and local elections; and widespread corruption among federal, state, and local police agents illustrate the penetration of organized criminal groups into state structures and the daunting challenges that the Mexican government faces in effectively addressing the security crisis.

To respond to this situation, the Calderón administration enacted a series of initiatives to strengthen its public security institutions. In early 2009, President Calderón announced the creation of the Federal Police, mainly composed of agents from the defunct Federal Preventative Police (Policía Federal Preventiva, PFP) and Federal Investigative Police (Agencia Federal de Investigación, AFI). Under the guidance of the Public Security Ministry (Secretaría de Seguridad Pública, SSP), there were concerted efforts to improve the training, professionalization, and modernization of Mexico's federal police force. There were also initiatives to combat police corruption, such as the creation of the National Center for Evaluation and Trust Control (Centro Nacional de Evaluación y Control de Confianza) and the promotion of the establishment of such centers at the state level (E. Olson 2009). However, Mexican experts on police reform note with concern that the law that created the federal police did not include provisions to strengthen the accountability and transparency of the force. Parallel to these efforts, the SSP created an Internet-based communications platform known as Plataforma México, designed to facilitate coordination and communication of the federal police, who are stationed throughout the country. In the long term, the Plataforma will also incorporate state and municipal police. The federal government also provided limited resources to support state and municipal public security efforts.[1]

Historic constitutional reforms to Mexico's justice system and in public security institutions also went into effect in June 2008. These judicial reforms represent a significant transformation from a primarily inquisitorial system to an adversarial system, which includes oral trials and alternative means of conflict resolution in criminal procedures. The reforms aim to strengthen the rule of law, put pressure on law enforcement agents to carry out more professional investigations, and address corruption. Given the extent of the judicial reforms being undertaken, the Mexican government established an eight-year transition period for the reforms to be completed. So far very little progress has been made to implement the necessary changes, and governors in several states have expressed concern about the lack of political will and resources to ensure that they will be effectively implemented (Justice in Mexico Project 2010). According to the federal government's technical secretary for the implementation of the justice reform, four years into the reform process only three of Mexico's thirty-one states (Chihuahua, the state of Mexico, and Morelos) are fully operating under the new justice system, and just seven additional states are partially operational (Meyer 2012).

While these efforts to strengthen Mexico's police and judicial institutions are important, the predominant element of Mexico's security strategy during the Calderón administration was large-scale counter-drug operations, which were launched throughout Mexico; this strategy has continued during the Peña administration. The military dominates these operations with the participation of approximately 45,000 soldiers, and the Mexican military increasingly becoming involved in other public security tasks. As of July 2012, ten of Mexico's thirty-one states had appointed retired military officials as ministers of public security, and multiple municipal public security ministries were led by military officials.

President Calderón originally stated that use of the military to combat organized crime was a temporary solution. However, it became clear that the armed forces would not be removed from public security tasks linked to combating organized crime during his administration in spite of the fact that promoting this transfer of responsibilities was included as a strategy in the government National Human Rights Program for 2008–12.[2] In fact, the Sectoral Program for National Defense 2007–2012 of the Ministry of Defense (Secretaría de la Defensa Nacional, Sedena) affirmed the armed forces' role in supporting the government's public security tasks and confronting organized crime (Programa Sectorial de Defensa Nacional, 2007). The only significant change in President Calderón's strategy was the decision to shift control of the counter-drug operation in the state of Chihuahua from the military to the federal police. This transfer of powers took place in early April 2010, and the military's role in the state became and continues to be primarily patrolling and monitoring the rural parts of the state, intelligence work, and maintaining military checkpoints. The federal police assumed leadership in security and counter-drug efforts in Ciudad Juárez, the state's largest and most violent city, but the municipal and state police are also slowly regaining their public security responsibilities, particularly after the appointment of Julian Leyzaola as the head of the municipal police in March 2011 (Dudley 2013). With the exception of Ciudad Juárez, the military continues to dominate the counter-drug operations, and the Peña administration has not made any clear announcements as to when or how a similar shift in responsibilities to civilian law enforcement agencies will take place in other parts of the country.

While the Mexican government's original decision to give the military the lead role in counter-drug operations was understandable given the level of violence and the enduring problems of police corruption and lack of training, the human cost of the military's increased interaction with Mexican society has been high. According to Mexico's National Commission on Human Rights (Comisión Nacional de Derechos Humanos, CNDH), complaints against the Mexican military increased from 398 in 2007 to 1921, in 2012.[3] In 2010 and 2011, one-third of the recommendations issued by the Commission were directed at Sedena and the Mexican Navy (Secretaría de Marina, Semar).[4] The majority of these recommendations were made in response to human rights violations committed in the context of counter-drug operations. Reported abuses included arbitrary detentions, torture, illegal imprisonment, forced disappearances, and extrajudicial executions.

U.S.-Mexico Security Cooperation and Human Rights

There have been unprecedented levels of security cooperation between Mexico and the United States since former President Calderón assumed office in December 2006. In March 2007, Calderón and U.S. President Bush met in the city of Mérida, where they agreed to expand bilateral and regional counter-drug and security cooperation. In a news conference at the North American Summit in Quebec, Canada, on August 21, 2007, both Bush and Calderón referred to the U.S. security assistance package negotiated as the development of a common strategy to deal with the shared problem of drug trafficking and violence along the U.S.-Mexico border (White House Press Office 2007).

The ongoing negotiations between the United States and Mexico culminated in the announcement on October 22, 2007, of the Mérida Initiative, which was originally presented as a three-year U.S. security assistance program for Mexico and Central America. This assistance has now gone beyond the original three years. As of fiscal year 2012, the United States had provided Mexico over $1.9 billion in assistance to combat drug trafficking and related violence as well as to support judicial reform, institution building, anticorruption efforts, and rule of law activities.[5] The Obama administration requested $234 million in Merida Initiative assistance for Mexico in fiscal year 2013. A significant amount of the allocated funds—$428.8 million—have been designated to purchase transport helicopters for Sedena, surveillance planes for Semar, and inspection equipment and other technology for the Mexican military. While the first three funding cycles were heavily focused on military equipment and technology, a shift has taken place in the pillars of U.S. assistance. Currently the Mérida Initiative still funds efforts to combat organized crime in Mexico, but there is a greater focus on supporting institution building and training than supplying hardware. Since 2010, a significant portion of the funds have gone specifically to judicial reform, institution building, anticorruption, and rule of law activities. Current programs also support human rights organizations and violence prevention programs, particularly for at-risk youth.

Throughout the initial budget process in 2008, organizations like the Washington Office on Latin America (WOLA) expressed concerns regarding U.S. assistance to the Mexican military, the imbalance in funding for equipment and hardware versus support for structural reforms to Mexico's security and justice institutions, and the need for accountability with regard to human rights. Regarding the latter, international human rights organizations, such as Amnesty International and Human Rights Watch (HRW), as well as U.S.-based organizations, including WOLA and the Latin America Working Group (LAWG), all weighed in on the need to include human rights language in the assistance package.

After tense negotiations between the Mexican and U.S. governments, and because of the interest of key members of Congress in placing human rights conditions on the agenda, the first funding allocated to Mexico in the FY 2008 Supplemental Appropriations Act provided for the possibility of withholding 15 percent of the funds under the International Narcotics Control and Law Enforcement (INCLE) and Foreign Military Financing (FMF) accounts until the State Department reported in writing that the government of Mexico is

(1) Improving the transparency and accountability of federal police forces and working with state and municipal authorities to improve the transparency and accountability of state and municipal police forces through mechanisms including establishing police complaints commissions with authority and independence to receive complaints and carry out effective investigations;

(2) Establishing a mechanism for regular consultations among relevant Mexican Government authorities, Mexican human rights organizations and other relevant Mexican civil society organizations, to make recommendations concerning implementation of the Mérida Initiative in accordance with Mexican and international law;

(3) Ensuring that civilian prosecutors and judicial authorities are investigating and prosecuting, in accordance with Mexican and international law, members of the federal police and military forces who have been credibly alleged to have committed violations of human rights, and the federal police and military forces are fully cooperating with the investigations;

(4) Enforcing the prohibition, in accordance with Mexican and international law, on the use of testimony obtained through torture or other ill-treatment. (U.S. Congress 2008)

It should be noted that these conditions differed from the version of the legislation originally approved by the U.S. Senate, which conditioned 25 percent of the funding and would have required the Mexican government to try military officials accused of human rights violations in civilian, not military courts. These conditions were changed because of Mexico's rejection of the language and claims that the requirement to try the military in civilian courts would violate its national sovereignty (Seelke 2009). On several occasions during the original and subsequent negotiations of the Mérida Initiative, Mexican officials reached the point of suggesting that Mexico would reject the aid package if the conditions were too stringent. In fact, in the weeks leading up to U.S. Congress approval of the first year of the aid package, the Permanent Commission of the Mexican Congress (Comisión Permanente del Congreso de la Unión) issued a statement supporting the Mexican government's position of not accepting assistance that included any conditions (*Milenio* 2008). After the first legislation was passed, additional references to the human rights conditions, or poor choices of words by U.S. officials, such as referring to the reporting process as "certification" (which many Mexicans link to the contentious U.S. drug certification process in place in 1986–2002), have prompted a similar response from Mexican legislators (e.g., Robles de la Rosa 2009).

Tracking the amount subject to the 15 percent human rights reporting requirements is complicated because different amounts and accounts have been subject to the conditions for different budget cycles. Table 2 shows the total amount allocated for Mexico under the Mérida Initiative from FY 2008 to FY 2012. In the first budget allocation, the FY 2008 Supplemental, the human rights conditions applied to 15 percent of the funding for INCLE and FMF, or approximately $57 million. For the FY 2009 budget, the 15 percent conditions applied to all of the funding accounts but excluded the $75 million allocated for judicial reform, institution building, anticorruption, and rule of law activities; this means that roughly $33.75 million could be withheld. In the FY 2009 Supplemental, the conditions applied only to the $160 million in the INCLE account, or $24 million, while the $260 million in FMF designated for aircraft for the Mexican navy was excluded in order to expedite the assistance. In the FY 2010 budget, the 15 percent withholding applied to all the accounts, but it excluded assistance for judicial reform, institution building, anticorruption, and rule of law activities; the State Department determined that the conditions applied to $12 million in assistance. For the FY 2010 Supplemental funds, as will be described below, the State Department

Table 2. FY 2008–2012 Funding for Mérida Initiative by Aid Account ($ millions)

Account	2008 Supp.	2009	2009 Supp.	2010	2010 Supp.	2011	2012 est.	Acct. total	2013 request
Economic Support Fund	20.0	15.0	0.0	15.0*	0.0	18.0	33.3	101.3	35.0
Narcotics Control and Law Enforcement	263.5	246.0	160.0	190.0	175.0	117.0	248.5	1,400.0	199.0
Foreign Military Financing	116.5	39.0	260.0	5.3	0.0	8.0	NA**	428.8	NA
Total	400.0	300.0	420.0	210.3	175.0	143.0	281.8	1,930.1	234.0

Source: Seelke and Finklea (2012) ** As of FY2012, FMF is no longer included as part of the Mérida Initiative.

decided to withhold $26 million. For FY 2011, approximately $3.5 million in funds could be withheld (Seelke and Finklea 2012). Last, the requirements were altered in FY 2012 and do not apply to assistance to promote transparency, anticorruption, and the rule of law in the military and police forces; the amount conditioned is approximately $18 million in assistance. Similar to its actions regarding the FY 2010 Supplemental funds, the State Department decided to withhold this assistance from FY 2012 until certain agreements to collaborate on human rights priorities could be reached with the Mexican government.[6]

Human Rights Monitoring of the Mérida Initiative

Following the approval of the first year of Mérida Initiative funding, U.S.-based organizations felt the need to provide Mexican colleagues with information to understand the components of the aid package and the possibilities to make use of the human rights reporting requirements. Through dialogues with counterpart organizations in Mexico, a workshop was organized for Mexican human rights organizations and other interested actors in Mexico City in September 2008.[7]

The workshop resulted in the creation of an informal working group of organizations in both countries with interest in monitoring the human rights requirements in the Mérida Initiative and assessing the reach of the requirements in pushing for change in the human rights situation in Mexico.[8] The overall objectives have been to secure withholding conditioned funds until the Mexican government has made real progress toward fulfilling the human rights requirements, and to use the requirements to encourage more pressure from U.S. officials regarding the human rights situation in Mexico. The following account details the many ways these organizations have worked to influence the State Department annual report on the Mérida Initiative requirements and to engage the U.S. Congress more in the human rights situation in Mexico.[9]

The informal group of U.S.-based and Mexican human rights organizations decided in late 2008 to submit to the State Department a memo with an analysis and exemplary cases to inform their assessment on the human rights requirements established in the Mérida Initiative. The first memo was sent to the State Department in January 2009. Key congressional offices, such as the Appropriations Subcommittees on Foreign Operations, also received copies. Four additional memos were issued in July 2009, October 2009, May 2010, and June 2012. Publicly, the organizations circulated a joint statement on July 16, 2009, calling on the U.S. government to withhold the funding for Mexico under the Mérida Initiative. The statement asserts that

> Based on our organizations' collective work and documentation in the area of human rights, we can affirm that the Mexican government has failed to meaningfully advance the investigation, prosecution or sanction of human rights violations, particularly abuses committed by members of the Mexican military against civilians. In light of the Mexican government's failure to meet these critical commitments, the United States should not release to Mexico the portion of Mérida Initiative funding withheld under the Initiative's human rights reporting requirements. (WOLA 2009)

A similar statement was issued on September 14, 2010, after the State Department issued its second favorable report to Congress on the human rights requirements in the Mérida Initiative (WOLA 2010).

Apart from these memos, the organizations also held a series of meetings with congressional offices and representatives of the State Department to discuss the human rights situation in Mexico, the increase in abuses by the military against civilians in the context of the counter-drug operations, and the persisting impunity for these abuses. These meetings have been held jointly between U.S. and Mexican organizations in the context of visits of Mexican organizations to Washington, D.C., to participate in hearings before the Inter-American Commission on Human Rights. Human rights organizations, including members of WOLA, have also met on separate occasions with personnel at the Mexico Desk of the State Department to discuss human rights in Mexico.

In Congress, the directors of WOLA and LAWG, along with a Mexican human rights defender, provided testimony for a hearing on the Mérida Initiative in the House Appropriations Committee Subcommittee on State, Foreign Operations, and Related Programs in March 2010. All three testimonies expressed concern for the human rights situation in Mexico and called for the human rights requirements included in the Mérida Initiative to be more than "simple window dressing" (J. Olson 2009).

In July 2009, HRW also sent a public letter to secretary of state Hillary Clinton that stated that "the U.S. State Department should not certify Mexico's compliance with the Mérida Initiative's human rights requirements so long as Mexican army abuses continue to be tried in military rather than civilian courts" (HRW 2009b). Mexican human rights organizations have also published a series of articles on the Mérida Initiative and human rights in Mexico, and several organizations have participated in the consultation mechanism established by the Mexican government as part of the reporting requirements included in the Mérida Initiative.

The first statement made by a member of Congress on the human rights requirements in the Mérida Initiative was by Senator Patrick Leahy, chairman of the Senate Appropriations Subcommittee on State Department and Foreign Operations. On August 5, 2009, Senator Leahy issued a statement on the provisions in the law he authored:

> The law withholds 15 percent of the Mérida funds until the Secretary of State reports to Congress that the Mexican Government is meeting four requirements, including prosecuting military and police officers who violate human rights. The Congress provides 85 percent of the aid without conditions, but there needs to be evidence that the military is accountable to the rule of law. Those requirements have not been met, so it is premature to send the report to Congress. We had good faith discussions with Mexican and U.S. officials in reaching these requirements in the law, and I hope we can continue in that spirit. (Leahy 2009)

In spite of Leahy's statement and the call from the human rights community in the United States and Mexico to withhold funding, the State Department quietly issued to Congress during the 2009 August recess the "Mexico-Mérida Initiative Report," which triggered the release of most of the funds withheld from the FY 2008 Supplemental Appropriations Act and the FY 2009 Appropriations Act, totaling approximately $90 million. Contrary to what is stipulated in the law, the State Department's report did not explicitly state whether Mexico had or had not met the requirements, and merely detailed a series of initiatives being undertaken by the Mexican government in the four reporting areas. Of note was the inclusion of information from Mexico's Defense Ministry regarding investigations into army abuses against civilians that had yet to be substantiated when the report was issued.

As described above, subsequent to this first report, U.S. and Mexican human rights organizations continued their work to document human rights violations in Mexico and provide assessments to the U.S. Congress and the State Department on issues related to the four human rights requirements established in the Mérida Initiative. From the period between August 2009 and September 2010, when the State Department submitted its second report on the requirements to Congress, two joint memos were written, in October 2009 and May 2010, and numerous meetings were held with congressional staffers to discuss Mexico's failure to fulfill the requirements laid out in the Mérida Initiative and the need for Congress to closely examine the State Department's upcoming report on the requirements.

Nonetheless, in early September 2010, the State Department issued its second report on the human rights requirements in the Mérida Initiative and again determined that the Mexican government had met the requirements and that it was going to obligate the $36 million in withheld funds from the FY 2009 Supplemental and FY 2012 Appropriations Act. However, in this same report, the State Department announced its own internal decision to withhold funding from the FY 2010 Supplemental, some $26 million, until progress was made in Mexico on two issues: passage by the Mexican Congress of human rights reforms to the Constitution, and introduction of legislation to reform Mexico's Military Code of Justice "to limit the crimes falling under the jurisdiction of military courts" (U.S. Department of State 2010).

After the report was presented, WOLA, together with partner organizations, issued a public memo to the U.S. Congress that reiterated that the human rights requirements had not been met and that the funds should have been withheld. The memo states that while the State Department decision to press for the passage of important constitutional reforms in Mexico and to address the need to reform Mexico's military jurisdiction was positive, "neither of these steps will alone ensure fulfillment of the human rights requirements. Therefore, we believe that the funds in the 2010 Supplemental budget should also be pegged to compliance with the four human rights requirements—which measure not only changes in law, but in practice" (WOLA 2010).

In June 2012, WOLA, together with partner organizations, issued another memo to the State Department on the human rights requirements in the Merida Initiative, again reiterating that requirements had not been met. The memo affirmed that "the best way for the U.S. to reinforce the importance of human rights, accountability, and transparency in its bilateral relations with Mexico, and advance the interests of both countries, is to enforce the conditions it has set out (WOLA et al. 2012).

In August 2012, the State Department issued its third report on the human rights requirements in Merida. As with previous reports, the Department expressed its intentions to obligate the withheld funds from the FY 2011 and FY 2012 budget. At the same time, it decided to withhold the FY 2012 funds until it could work with Mexican authorities to identify areas of collaboration on human rights. These included "enhancing the capability of civilian prosecutors to investigate and prosecute cases of human rights abuses," enforcing prohibitions on the use of torture, and strengthening efforts to protect human rights defenders (U.S. Department of State 2012).

Impact of the Reporting Requirements on Human Rights in Mexico

The joint advocacy work by U.S.-based and Mexican human rights organizations detailed above is an example of indirect pressure on the Mexican government. We have knowledge that the Mexican government obtained copies of both public and private memos, but the target of this work has been the U.S. Department of State and the U.S. Congress to inform the State Department's own report, to provide Congress with information for its examination of the State Department report, and to highlight the Mexican government's failure to advance on the investigation and prosecution of human rights abuses.

Given its ongoing nature and the fact that as of the writing of this chapter the State Department had issued only three reports on the requirements, it is still premature to conduct an overall assessment of how the possibility of withholding funds may promote systemic changes to the human rights situation in Mexico. Nonetheless, the results of the work to date suggest that while inadequate, the human rights reporting requirements do serve as a useful additional tool to press for change regarding the human rights situation in Mexico.

For example, some Mérida Initiative funds have in fact been withheld from Mexico, suggesting that that this could be a useful mechanism for promoting progress on certain cases of human rights violations. In an August 2009 report, the Congressional Research Service stated that some $2.8 million in FY 2008 was on hold at the time "until Congress is certain that the Mexican Attorney General is thoroughly investigating the murder of Bradley Will, an American journalist killed while covering a protest in Oaxaca in

2006" (Seelke 2009). Likewise, a small amount of FY 2008 military funding was withheld until the State Department could substantiate the claim in its August 2009 Mérida Initiative report regarding Mexican military personnel who had been convicted or were being investigated for human rights abuses. More recently, Senator Leahy put a hold on $95 million in International Narcotics and Law Enforcement funds for Mexico for FY 2013 based on the lack of clarity about how the funds would be spent and due to human rights concerns. Leahy indicated to *CQ Roll Call* that in part he was using the hold to pressure the Mexican military and federal police to stop human rights violations: "I hope to get some responses on it. If I don't, I'll continue the hold" (Broder 2013).

The very fact that the State Department also decided on its own to withhold select funds from the FY 2010 Supplemental and FY 2012 budget sent an important message to Mexico regarding U.S. government concern about human rights. While not in line with the original requirements, press coverage in the United States and Mexico about the 2010 report focused on the State Department decision to withhold some funds from Mexico because of human rights abuses, not the technicalities of the justification used to withhold the funds (see, for example, Mendoza 2010; Diaz Briseño 2010).

At the same time, the conference report for the FY 2010 Appropriations Bill made clear Congress's frustration with the way the State Department had issued its first report on the Mérida Initiative human rights requirements. The conference report expresses concerns that the State Department's report regarding human rights in Mexico

> did not include the requisite findings by the Secretary of State that the Government of Mexico had met the requirements in the law. The conferees remain concerned with the lack of progress on these issues, and the lack of transparency in cases involving allegations against Mexican military personnel, and direct that future reports submitted pursuant to section 7045(e)(2) of this Act include the necessary findings. (U.S. House 2009)

Subsequently, in March 2011 and July 2012, members of the House of Representatives sent letters to Secretary of State Clinton on the importance of withholding the conditioned funds if the human rights requirements in the Mérida Initiative were not met (WOLA 2012). This pressure from Congress on the State Department to produce more accurate reports may be a mechanism on its own to press the Mexican government for more concrete results in its efforts to investigate and prosecute perpetrators of human rights abuses.

On the advocacy front, before the Mérida Initiative was negotiated, work on Mexico for organizations such as WOLA was limited in Congress to the murders of women and girls in Ciudad Juárez and select human rights cases, including the social conflicts in Oaxaca in 2006 (see Anaya Muñoz 2009). As the human rights reporting requirements are part of U.S. legislation and linked to U.S. financial support for Mexico's counter-drug operations, they have been used as an effective way to raise awareness with U.S. policymakers of the increase in abuses that have occurred as a result of the counter-drug operations and the ongoing failure of the Mexican government to investigate and hold soldiers and police responsible for human rights violations. For example, in 2009 there were at least sixteen hearings in the U.S. Congress on increased drug-related violence in Mexico, U.S. foreign assistance, and border security programs. The reporting requirements provided the opening to discuss human rights in the March 2009 hearing on the Mérida Initiative held by the House Appropriations Subcommittee on State, Foreign Operations, and Related Programs that was discussed above. Likewise, on May 10, 2012, the House of Representatives Tom Lantos Human Rights Commission held the first hearing specifically on human rights in Mexico since the Mérida Initiative began in 2008. The pending report from the State Department on the human rights requirements was a topic of discussion at the hearing, and the three testimonies from representatives of human rights organizations, including WOLA, again called on the State Department to withhold Mérida Initiative funds until meaningful progress is made by the Mexican government in fulfilling the human rights requirements included in the aid package (Tom Lantos Human Rights Commission, May 10, 2012).

In terms of the executive branch, the U.S. Embassy in Mexico in fall 2009 began a series of meetings with Mexican human rights organizations to discuss recurring human rights issues and to develop recommendations in areas such as improvement of mechanisms to investigate and prosecute human rights abuses committed by the police and the military, and development of benchmarks to measure progress on human rights cases. This is the first time in memory that the U.S. Embassy has established a regular and formal dialogue with the Mexican human rights community. The embassy has also started a Bilateral Human Rights Dialogue with the Mexican government, which consists of a series of meetings to discuss various human rights concerns, including abuses by the Mexican military. While the human rights situation in Mexico certainly merits concern in and of itself, it can be surmised that these discussions are also taking place in part because of the State Department need to report on progress being made on human rights in Mexico.

As for the media, while many stories discuss U.S. funding for Mexico's "war on drugs," the Mérida Initiative requirements have provided an additional opportunity to discuss the human rights situation in Mexico because it is now linked to U.S. funding, and U.S. and Mexican organizations have been able to work with the media to get more coverage of certain situations. For example, in July 2009 the *Washington Post* ran a front page article on allegations of torture being used by the Mexican army that included a discussion of the human rights requirements in the Mérida Initiative.[10] While it was clearly not planned, the same day this story ran there was a hearing by the House Committee on Oversight and Government Reform titled "The Rise of the Mexican Drug Cartels and U.S. National Security." Prompted by the *Washington Post* article, Committee Chair Edolphus Towns stated in his opening remarks, "As the effort in Mexico to address the drug threat continues, we must be mindful that abuses from the state are equally intolerable" (Towns 2009).

Finally, it would appear that that the Mexican government, particularly the Defense Ministry, is now more transparent in providing information—albeit minimal and incomplete—on investigations regarding soldiers' abuse.[11] While this shift is also due to the increasing national and international pressure and coverage regarding human rights violations by the military in Mexico, the fact that the State Department must report on Mexico's efforts to investigate and prosecute soldiers allegedly involved in human rights abuses has also increased the pressure on Sedena to be more transparent in its investigations.

The Political Reality and Limitations to Conditions

The fact that to date the majority of the conditioned funds have been released for Mexico, including the $26 million the State Department had withheld from the FY 2010 Supplemental, should come as no surprise on the diplomatic level, since, as Anaya Muñoz has affirmed, "Overall, binational cooperation against drug trafficking is much more important to the U.S. executive branch of government than general or specific human rights considerations" (Anaya Muñoz 2009a). However, based on the advocacy work of different organizations on the human rights certification under Plan Colombia, the U.S. funded antinarcotics strategy launched in Colombia in the late 1990s, there was some expectation of more pushback from the U.S. Congress on the State Department's initial report and the report's failure to provide specific information on progress being made to investigate and prosecute documented cases of human rights abuses. While the issue of human rights has come up in a limited manner at Mérida Initiative hearings, it has not been a priority for members of the U.S. Congress when discussing security in Mexico. As the advocacy work of U.S., Mexican, and international human rights organizations continues, it is hoped that there will be more public voices in the U.S. Congress regarding the grave situation in Mexico. One positive sign was the remark made by Senator Richard Durbin in his opening statement for the Senate Judiciary Committee Subcommittee on Human Rights and the Law hearing "Drug Enforcement and the Rule of Law: Mexico and Colombia" in May 2010 that criticized the Mexican military's human rights record: "the military in Mexico operates with virtual impunity—resulting in limited success in stemming drug violence and human rights abuses that rival and surpass the corruption of the law enforcement system they were tasked to replace" (Durbin 2010). The two congressional letters to Secretary Clinton specifically on the human rights requirements in the Mérida Initiative, as well as other congressional letters to Secretary Clinton on related human rights concerns in Mexico that reference U.S. cooperation through the Mérida Initiative,[12] also suggest that there is a growing recognition in Congress of the grave human rights situation in Mexico and of the need to use U.S. assistance as leverage for change in Mexico.

Given Mexico's strategic importance to the United States as a key ally in the region and our 2,000-mile shared border, administration officials are also reluctant to address human rights issues, at least not publically. Instead, when Calderón was president, they publicly lavished him with praise regarding his "heroic" efforts to tackle drug trafficking.[13] In fact, the sole mention of human rights in any of the public encounters between the two presidents while Calderón was in office was in response to a media question during a press conference held in Mexico in August 2009. The statement is telling of the care that Obama has taken not to criticize the country's southern neighbor:

I have great confidence in President Calderón's Administration applying the law enforcement techniques that are necessary to curb the power of the cartels but doing so in a way that is consistent with human rights . . . . I am confident that as national police are trained and coordination between the military and local police officials is improved there is going to be increased transparency and accountability and that human rights will be observed. The biggest by far violators of human rights right now are the cartels themselves that are kidnapping people, extorting people and encouraging corruption in these regions, that's what needs to be stopped. (White House, Office of the Press Secretary 2009)

Conclusions

The above analysis illustrates that in spite of the limitations on the use of conditions as a mechanism to promote changes in the human rights situation in Mexico, the reporting requirements have contributed to ensuring that human rights remain a part of the bilateral discussions between the United States and Mexico. The insertion of human rights conditions in U.S. legislation has also opened the door for increased joint advocacy work by U.S. and Mexican organizations, and by international organizations such as Human Rights Watch and Amnesty International, to provide congressional offices with evidence of the Mexican government's failure to adequately investigate and prosecute human rights abuses committed by security bodies, particularly the military, and the failure of the State Department to adequately address this situation in its own reports.

A reflection on the experience with Plan Colombia, which began in 2000, is also helpful in assessing the effectiveness of these types of requirements. Lisa Haugaard, LAWG executive director, affirmed in her March 2009 testimony before Congress on the Mérida Initiative that

The saving grace in the Colombia experience was the existence of human rights conditions within the package. . . . Without the human rights conditions and the willingness of the Congress, particularly the foreign operations subcommittees, to insist that the State Department take the conditions seriously, human rights groups in the United States and Colombia would not have been able to get the attention of

the State Department and the U.S. Embassy, and the wide scale killings of civilians by the Colombian army would have passed virtually
without U.S. comment and probably would have continued unchecked.
(Haugaard 2009)

While there are many differences between the situations in Mexico and
Colombia and in the relations between the United States and these countries,
the Colombia experience does suggest that over time, and through the ongoing
work on this issue by U.S. and Mexican organizations, there will be more
U.S. policymakers and elected officials who will be willing to put pressure
on the Mexican government regarding the human rights situation, and thus
contribute to positive change.

Conclusion: Multiple States of Exception, Structural Violences, and Prospects for Change

William Paul Simmons

This volume has covered a range of human rights abuses and their binational causes. Indeed, the volume can be read as a sustained indictment of Mexican and U.S. policies on immigration, drug interdiction, gun possession, trade, and security for fueling human rights abuses, including the criminal violence perpetrated by cartels, *bajadores*, and other extralegal actors.

Taken as a whole, the contributions in this volume provide a sobering outlook on the ways forward to address these crises. The main solutions proposed so far by the Mexican and U.S. governments—more border enforcement and a stepped up war on drugs—will most likely lead to increased human rights abuses. The fact that these human rights abuses have increased exponentially despite generally good objective conditions for human rights protection also suggests very few good steps forward, at least in the short term. Traditional human rights tools for drawing attention to these issues have already been used to little effect. The media are covering these issues. Transnational activist networks have come and gone. Cases are being brought to human rights tribunals. The Mexican government has already passed or considered a plethora of laws to address these situations, and set up independent human rights commissions. The United States has attached human rights conditions to aid packages to Mexico.

Clearly, the human rights abuses are rooted in deeper and more intractable causes—enormous profits from illicit activity, poverty, income inequality, misogyny, corruption, xenophobia, racism—and so they will not go away any time soon. Poverty will continue to fuel massive migration and the cartel war by providing a constant flow of immigrants traveling to the United

States and producing thousands of foot soldiers to be arrested or killed in the cartel wars. As long as it is profitable for the cartels and others, migrants will be treated as commodities and be branded as inferior. Indeed, these chapters show that there is a self-sustaining quality to many of these abuses. Immigration enforcement is hailed as working if more migrants are apprehended, or if the numbers decrease, and thus, the argument for more enforcement is easy to promote, despite the human consequences. The drug war has made drug trafficking even more profitable and the cartels more powerful and fueled an arms race among the cartels and between the cartels and the government.

As noted in the Introduction, the binational human rights situation is quite fluid and complex. Indeed, as I write this in June 2013 several significant events have occurred, many of them positive for human rights. After sketching some of these events, I conclude by asking whether they should cause us to temper the pessimistic conclusions listed above; are they significant enough to change the underlying structures fueling the human rights crises?

Recent Binational Events

In the United States the past two years witnessed a number of significant events at both national and local levels. President Obama outlined a "Blueprint" for comprehensive immigration reform very similar to that pursued by President Bush in 2005 and 2006. Many saw this as more of a political ploy to curry favor with the rapidly growing Latino electorate, and the president spent little political capital on the issue. However, in June 2012 the president issued a memorandum entitled "Deferred Action for Childhood Arrivals," which instructed agents of the Department of Homeland Security to use their prosecutorial discretion to grant "Deferred Action" status to those undocumented individuals who came to the United States as children and who are in school or have graduated from high school or college or are currently serving or have served in the U.S. armed forces. Basically, this memorandum enacted the main principles of the DREAM Act without requiring congressional approval. During the 2012 presidential campaign, President Obama reiterated his support for comprehensive immigration reform, while Governor Romney, at least during the primary season, embraced harsher policies and called for "self-deportation"—that is, making life in the United States so difficult that undocumented immigrants will voluntarily leave the country. In the election's postmortem, numerous commentators attributed President Obama's reelection to his significant advantage among the growing Latino population, support that stems in good part from his less strident position on immigration.

In the aftermath of President Obama's reelection, there has been much talk of the Republican Party undergoing serious reflection about its opposition to comprehensive immigration reform. And, a group of eight senators proposed a bill that lays out a comprehensive immigration reform package, including a path to citizenship for undocumented migrants. It remains to be seen if such efforts will be any more successful than those in 2005 and 2006, when conservative talk radio and other forces were able to defeat any immigration measure that included a path to citizenship for undocumented migrants already in the United States. Has the political discourse shifted enough so that policies that include humanitarian measures will not be trumped by policies focused on securitization and militarization? Although the bill passed the Senate, there is substantial doubt whether such a package will ultimately be approved by the House of Representatives. In fact, the House Republicans continued their anti-immigration actions by passing a bill to reverse President Obama's executive action that granted deferred removal to young people who were brought illegally to the United States by their parents.

In addition, at the national level, U.S. support for Mexico's drug war has been refocused and is now labeled "Beyond Mérida." It includes a more balanced approach to fighting the drug war, including targeting much of the money for judicial reform and a sizable amount for "strengthening communities." The Obama administration also proposed an increase in spending for fighting the "war on drugs" within the United States, with increases in funding for programs to reduce demand through prevention and treatment.

At the state level, potentially revolutionary initiatives were approved in 2012 in Colorado and the state of Washington to legalize the recreational use of marijuana. Medical marijuana has also been legalized in eighteen states and the District of Columbia. However, since these laws are at odds with the national Controlled Substance Act, it will probably take several years of legal battles before they have a substantial effect on the cartels' profits. Nonetheless, such a change in popular opinion toward decriminalization of drug use could ultimately have effects that reverberate throughout the hemisphere.[1]

In my home state of Arizona, several major provisions of the infamous SB 1070 were deemed unconstitutional by the U.S. Supreme Court in 2012

(*Arizona v. United States* 132 S. Ct. 2492 (2012)). The "show your papers" provision that allows local law enforcement officers to ask for proof of citizenship when there is a reasonable suspicion that someone is undocumented was upheld but is being closely monitored by local activist groups who claim that it will lead to unconstitutional racial profiling. While similar legislation was enacted or strongly considered in a number of states, including Alabama, Georgia, Tennessee, and Utah, the Supreme Court ruling should blunt the momentum for such draconian legislation. Arizona's lesser-known employer sanctions act, which fines companies knowingly hiring undocumented workers, has been upheld by the Supreme Court, though there seems to be little political will to enforce it.

Notorious sheriff Joe Arpaio of Maricopa County, famous for his roundups of suspected undocumented migrants, found himself embroiled in several scandals and faces his most serious legal challenges to date. A class-action suit by Latino drivers who were stopped and detained by the sheriff's office at any time since 2007 has been successful in U.S. District Court with the judge prohibiting the Sheriff's office from stopping and detaining anyone based on the suspicion of being in the country illegally. The judge has also ordered unprecedented measures such as the appointment of an independent monitor to oversee the Sheriff's office and the installation of video cameras in all patrol cars to document all stops. At the same time, the U.S. Justice Department issued a report that found racial profiling and "a culture of bias against Latinos" in the sheriff's office. The Justice Department filed a wide-ranging civil rights suit against Sheriff Arpaio that has yet to be decided. Despite these cases and a series of other revelations—including mismanagement of funds, intimidating county supervisors and state judges, and failure to properly investigate dozens of cases of sexual assault—Sheriff Arpaio remains very popular with large segments of the population and won reelection in 2012 by about 10 percentage points. The head of Arizona's state senate, Russell Pearce, who proposed dozens of controversial anti-immigrant bills in the past few years and was the chief sponsor of SB 1070, lost a recall election in early 2012 and was the first state senate president recalled in U.S. history. He failed in his 2012 election bid to reclaim his seat.

Undocumented migration has drastically reduced in Arizona and other border states, though as Consul Escobar-Valdez discusses in his chapter, this is probably due just as much to the severe economic recession as to border enforcement or anti-immigrant measures. And yet, the dynamic predicted by INS Commissioner Meisner continues: increased border enforcement will push migrants to more remote and more dangerous areas. While this strategy may dissuade some from migrating, its main effect has been to make the journey more dangerous. For example, the humanitarian group No More Deaths now patrols public lands nearly eighty miles from the Sonora-Arizona border. This area has become a major route for human smugglers and drug smugglers. It appears that more accessible pickup areas for migrants closer to the border are now so heavily patrolled by the Border Patrol that the smugglers have decided to move their pickup spots farther north, thus necessitating the additional risk for migrants and smugglers of several more days of walking in the scorching Arizona desert. Migrant trails strewn with empty water bottles and backpacks crisscross a large area. One volunteer encountered two migrants who had been lost and wandered in the desert for fifteen days. No More Deaths volunteers have already found one "rape tree" a mere ten miles from the burgeoning town of Casa Grande and its shopping malls, and forty miles from the southern outskirts of Phoenix. Numerous major drug busts have also occurred in this corridor.

The deaths of migrants in the desert continue. The remains of 192 migrants were found in Arizona in 2011 (Gonzáles 2011). Parts of southern Texas have seen record numbers of migrant deaths (almost 150 in the first nine months of 2012) due to extensive drought and extreme heat and possibly as a result of more migrants crossing in the area in response to the increased enforcement in Arizona (Rappleye and Seville 2012).

In December 2012, Enrique Peña Nieto of the PRI became president of Mexico. Peña Nieto has sketched a much different vision for fighting the cartels than Calderón, moving away from direct attacks on the cartels and their kingpins to taking coordinated steps to reduce the violent crime rate. He has proposed a new federal police force and a nationwide centralized command for local police forces. Peña Nieto has claimed that his policies will reduce the country's murder rate by 50 percent by the end of his six-year term.

Nonetheless, the drug war continues unabated, with massacres of cartel members reported in a litany of places around the country including Ciudad Mante, Nuevo Laredo, Chapala, Cadereyta Jiménez, Jalisco, and Guadalajara. The total death toll from the Mexican drug war exceeded 60,000 in 2012. Also, well-publicized reports have estimated that 1,000 children have been killed since the start of the drug wars.

While there have been some arrests in the 2010 Tamaulipas massacre, nearby another massacre or series of massacres took place in spring 2011 with close to 200 bodies found in mass graves. Apparently most of the victims were migrants pulled off buses traveling through the area. While unclaimed baggage piled up in the bus station, neither the bus companies nor the police investigated the disappearances. Sixteen police officers were later arrested for aiding the killings. In June 2013, the Mexican military raided a house in northern Tamaulipas and rescued 165 migrants, mostly from Central America, who had been kidnapped and were being held hostage. These massacres and other reports of maltreatment of migrants from Central America, including the discovery of 513 migrants crammed into two semitrailers in southern Mexico, have been well publicized and have led to a fairly significant conversation about potential means to ameliorate their plight. President Calderón signed a much-heralded law that granted some rights for transmigrants. The law decriminalizes entering the country without papers, allows immigrants to receive education and health care, and increases training of Mexican migration officers. The bill also allows undocumented migrants to receive papers that might include something similar to a humanitarian visa.[2]

Several significant figures in the drug cartels have been arrested or killed recently. The founder of La Familia Michoacana, Nazario Moreno Gonzalez, known as "El Mas Loco" (The Craziest), was killed by Mexican security forces in December 2010. The cartel, which was most active in western Mexico, then splintered, and the head of one of the strongest factions, José de Jesús Méndez Vargas, "El Chango" (The Monkey), was captured in June 2011. In May 2011, Martín Beltrán Coronel, one of the leading figures in the Sinaloa cartel, was arrested near Guadalajara. A founding member of the Zetas, Flavio Méndez Santiago, was arrested in Oaxaca. And in October of 2012 Salvador Alfonso Martínez Escobedo, a leading figure in the Zetas who likely was responsible for the Tamaulipas massacres, was arrested. On the same day Heriberto Lazcano Lazcano, generally credited as the leader of the Zetas, was gunned down by Mexican naval forces.

Few commentators see these arrests or killings as seriously weakening the cartels. The killings continue. The cartels continue to expand their influence, aided by corruption and botched or ill-conceived policies. Most notoriously, the U.S. Bureau of Alcohol, Tobacco, and Firearms (ATF) came under intense scrutiny for a failed operation that provided high-powered weapons to the cartels. In Operation Gunrunner, of which Operation Fast and Furious was a part, the ATF allowed members of Mexican cartels to purchase more than 2,500 weapons, including AK-47s and .50 caliber rifles, from gun dealers in the United States, in an attempt to track down the leaders of the cartels. However, the operation appears to have been bungled, with little communication with Mexican officials. Numerous guns supplied by the ATF are now unaccounted for, and some have been used in high-profile killings, including the murders of a U.S. Border Patrol agent and a prominent Mexican attorney.

Meanwhile several high-profile reports called into question the overall war on drugs. The Global Commission on Drug Policy, chaired by the former president of Brazil and with numerous prestigious members, including Kofi Annan, former secretary general of the United Nations, and the former presidents of Mexico and Colombia, issued a report in June that called for governments to experiment with legalizing drugs in order to stop the funding of organized crime. A report issued by a U.S. Senate subcommittee argued that the United States was unable to show a significant effect from the billions of dollars it has spent on antidrug efforts in Latin America. The report was especially critical of paying billions of dollars to U.S. private contractors, especially five large companies—DynCorp, Lockheed Martin, Raytheon, ITT, and ARINC—for eradicating drug crops, operating surveillance equipment, and training Latin American officials. And in the 2012 U.S. elections, proponents of the decriminalization of marijuana argued that such a policy would have the effect of reducing cartel violence in Mexico.

Multiple Interlocking States of Exception

The updates listed above may sound like significant changes, but in many ways, they mirror activities and initiatives of the past decade, with little evidence of substantial improvement in human rights. The underlying dynamics outlined in this volume's Introduction remain. The human rights abuses are the result of an interlocking (see Razack 2005; Morales and Bejarano 2009) series of states of exception where vulnerable people are made more vulnerable by the interplay of structural violence, cauterization, and public policies. If anything the contributions to this volume show the myriad manifestations of states of exception as well as their fluidity and self-perpetuating nature. They also show that in the U.S.-Mexico context multiple actors have assumed sovereignty in Mbembe's terms of assuming the right to kill. There are multiple deployers of violence often acting with impunity.

To better illustrate the underlying dynamics of these human rights abuses I want to outline four types of states of exception that appear in this volume, all of which are interlocking and thus mutually reinforcing. First, we have the states of exception that are created by various forms of structural violence that exclude many individuals from the law or the full protection of the law. Obvious examples here would include poor women in Ciudad Juárez who are made more vulnerable by such structural factors as misogyny, poverty, and neoliberal trade policies. Other vulnerable groups discussed in this volume, such as Central American migrants in Mexico or undocumented migrants in the United States, face structural violence in the form of xenophobia and racism. Second, a state of exception exists where there is too much law, a state of law-fullness. This is found in the militarized borders in the region, where officers can often take the law into their own hands with impunity. On a more subtle level, an emphasis on securitization means that human rights victims such as the migrants who suffer sexual violence are treated not as victims but as "illegals" or as a security risk and thus should be deported as quickly as possible. Third, there are areas where the law is suspended, zones of official impunity, where extralegal actors have assumed power, such as the areas of Mexico where the cartels have taken almost complete control. This category would also include the drop houses in Phoenix and Tucson as well as the situation of migrants as they are led by smugglers on the journey to the United States. Finally, there are those instances where the law has been suspended at more of a microlevel, where individuals are free to act because they are not bound by the dictates of law. These are areas that are known as interstices in the law or what Honig (2009; borrowing from philosopher Bernard Williams) calls a tragic situation, where a decision must be made, but there is little or no law or moral theory to guide the choice. For instance, an immigration judge has a great deal of discretion in asylum cases and can give the benefit of doubt to an applicant or can deny the applicant's claim on a technicality. In the Arizona desert, ranchers, Border Patrol officers, and hikers routinely encounter struggling migrants. They can choose to aid them, report them, ignore them, berate them, or take them into custody. The decision and the action can be done with impunity.

While most scholars assume that states of exception are unusual and rare, especially in democratic regimes, political theorist Bonnie Honig (2009) has recently argued that states of exception are more the norm than the exception. In Honig's theory democratic regimes have numerous spaces that allow for oppressed groups to create their own law or at least forge modifications in the existing law. For Honig, states of emergency are also states of emergence. In my previous work (Simmons 2011), I too have stressed the pervasive nature of states of exception, but I remain less sanguine about the potential for the hegemonic system to respond to marginalized groups. Too often actors encountering marginalized groups in a state of exception are shaped by structural violence and invisible ideologies—the same hegemonic power structures that created the states of exception in the first place. Thus, most ranchers encountering migrants will see them not as victims needing aid but as trespassers or drug smugglers, while immigration judges will be tainted by ideologies that portray asylum seekers as lawbreakers, opportunists, and, in general, not deserving of asylum in the United States.

The four types of states of exception—the structural violence in existing law that excludes some vulnerable individuals, lawfullness and securitization, zones of lawlessness filled by extralegal actors, and the interstices of the law—are interlocking in the sense developed by Sherene Razack (2005). She argues that hegemonic power structures do not merely intersect, but "multiple systems of oppression come into existence through each other" (343), and, I would add, they feed off each other.

The site where these power structures intersect and reveal their interlocking nature is the marginalized individual who is branded by the law as inferior, as a second-class citizen or noncitizen. The same individuals are also more likely to be the victims of a militarized place like the border, where the law is ever present, so that the victim is unable to find recourse in law. The marginalized are also more likely to be seen as commodities or foot soldiers in the havens carved out by the cartels and other extralegal actors. Finally, those who are branded or cauterized by the hegemonic system or by the law are less likely to be beneficiaries of immigration judges' discretion in their tragic situation, the moment of decision in the interstices of the law.

Pessimistic conclusions about the U.S.-Mexico case are reinforced because the current states of exception are advantageous financially and politically for a number of key actors. The cartels as rational actors desire to maintain zones of impunity, but they do not want lawlessness to spread too much. They want the violence contained. For instance, if violence were to spill over in a significant way across the U.S. border it would involve U.S. law enforcement in a more immediate and sustained way, which would be bad for cartel business.[3] Further, the cartels do not seek to destabilize the Mexican government itself. Indeed, it could be argued that the Mexican government and proponents of militarized border enforcement are in favor of a state of exception. Members of the "crimmigration" industrial complex—such as private prisons, private transport companies, Border Patrol leaders, and politicians—owe their positions to their anti-immigrant or antidrug stances and are rewarded by the chaos.

Not only do these actors benefit from the states of exception; they have the resources and the will to adapt to changing circumstances. Drug cartels adapted to the decline in power of the Colombian cartels by ramping up production in Mexico and elsewhere. Smugglers have adopted numerous innovative means for transporting people, drugs, money, and guns across an unprecedented militarized border. When smuggling migrants became quite profitable, the cartels were able to move in to that new business arena. To increase profits, organized crime groups kidnapped loads of migrants and held them for ransom in drop houses in Phoenix and elsewhere. When the drop houses were raided in Phoenix, the cartels successfully moved most of their kidnapping operations south into Mexico. When the Mexican government attempted to crack down, the cartels had the means to obtain higher-powered weaponry and to infiltrate the ranks of law enforcement, political, and legal agencies. Now, President Peña Nieto's proposed initiatives to reduce the murder rate in Mexico will most likely be successful, but their success will require making an uneasy peace with major cartel figures who will agree only as long as the peace terms are good for business. Of course, such a truce would preserve a whole set of entrenched violences that would keep marginalized groups vulnerable.

Similarly, there may be renewed momentum for comprehensive immigration reform in the United States, but has the anemic public discourse changed dramatically enough? Will comprehensive immigration reform, if it is passed, be watered down significantly in the legislative bargaining process or because of external events related to the wars on terrorism and drugs?

A New Grassroots Mobilization

Anaya Muñoz's and Meyer's chapters argue that the groundwork for future human rights promotion is being constructed in Mexico with the growth of civil society organizations, judicial reform, the battle against corruption, and the conditionalities of the Mérida Initiative. These factors could improve the already existing conducive environment for human rights in Mexico that we discussed in the Introduction: democratization, civil society, human rights commissions, and a fairly successful globalized economy. The long-term future has substantial promise. The human rights infrastructure will be in place when it is desired, perhaps when it can serve a political function. The above analysis indicates that radical changes in structural factors will be needed to address many of the human rights abuses, and perhaps the elections of 2012 marked a turning point, when human rights can regain some traction in public discourse.

Such a turning point will also require brave individuals on the ground who use the multiple states of exception for good ends. There are scattered signs of a nascent form of grassroots resistance. For instance, one new force has appeared that could ultimately be an important factor leading to major change in Mexico. A peace movement has developed that has staged several protests against the violence of the drug war. Father Alejandro Solalinde from Oaxaca has been leading a series of protests in southern Mexico and at the Mexican Congress. Noted poet Javier Sicilia, whose son and six others were tortured and killed by the cartels in March 2011, led a peace caravan across Mexico in June 2011 that ended in El Paso. In a speech he implicated the United States in the cartel war, especially the funding and training of the Mexican army through the Mérida Initiative, as well as those individuals in the United States who use illicit drugs: "Americans have to realize that behind every puff of pot, every line of coke there is death, there are shattered families" (BBC News 2011d).

But those who speak out remain at great risk. An aid caravan headed toward a besieged indigenous community in Oaxaca was attacked by gunmen, with two killed and more than a dozen missing. And in the state of Chihuahua two leading female activists were killed. Marisela Escobedo had investigated and tracked down her daughter's killer and had provided evidence at trial. The perpetrator was initially acquitted for "lack of evidence" but then found guilty a week later. By then, he had fled, and law enforcement refused to enforce a warrant for his arrest. The initial three judges who acquitted for lack of evidence are now being investigated and may be tried for ignoring the evidence in reaching their verdict. Escobedo was leading a protest in front of the governor's office when someone associated with the suspect appeared, chased her down, and killed her in broad daylight. At the protest she and others were chanting the slogan "Ni Una Más" (Not one more [death]), which has long been a mantra among those protesting the feminicides and was coined by Susana Chávez, a poet-activist. A month later Chávez was found in a street in Juárez; she had been tortured, killed, and had one of her hands cut off. An initial police report that she had befriended the killers and was drinking with them has since been discounted. Her murder remains unsolved.

Nevertheless, whether or not the near future will witness significant structural change, Mexico will not become an exemplar for human rights any time soon. The abuses will continue in the short term, at least for several years, and there are many indications some will get worse before they get better. The abuses will grind on and on. The marginalized Other, be it the migrant, the poor woman in Juárez, the indigenous person, will continue to be cauterized.

NOTES

Introduction

1. Of course, many other human rights tragedies are occurring, including abuses against indigenous peoples, continuing tensions in Chiapas and Oaxaca, sex tourism, and human trafficking.

2. Following Fregoso and Bejarano (2010), we employ the term "feminicide" as opposed to "femicide" in both the Introduction and the Conclusion. "Feminicide" connotes the structural violence and gender hierarchies that support the killing of women and girls.

3. We focus here on the United States and Mexico, though a larger study examining the larger region would be helpful.

4. Until 2010, Mexico rated "free" according to Freedom House, but now it is considered "partly free."

5. Mexico ranks 56th on the Human Development Index (2010), considered a country with high development, which measures health, education, and income, and 5th among major Latin American countries, trailing only Argentina, Chile, Uruguay, and Panama and well ahead of most Central American countries.

6. Schmitt defined sovereignty as the power to declare an exception to the law (see Agamben 2005: 1).

7. Of course, this logic lurks behind almost every ideology that has supported genocide, colonization, xenophobia, or slavery. Examples abound. African slaves brought to the Americas were often physically branded on their faces or shoulders. Even after that practice was banned in much of the United States, less physical but very real legal branding was perpetrated by legislation and legal opinions. Once branded rightless, as beneath rights, those marginalized would no longer be granted access to the courts and could not even testify in the courts in any state, as if their voices, their perspectives literally did not exist (see, for example, Cogan 1989). Such branding and exclusion contributed in no small part to the brutality the rightless suffered at the hands of genteel slave owners and "courageous" captains of death boats, who were deadened to the immense suffering of the rightless.

8. One law enforcement official described this as "an out and out shoot out." Notwithstanding the exponential increase in violence during the Mexican drug war, this

seems to be somewhat sensationalized, as such a business enterprise would not be sustainable.

9. Her analysis relies on Risse and Sikkink's (1999) sequence of socialization steps for TANs.

Chapter 1. Reflections on Immigration, Binational Policies, and Human Rights Tragedies

1. "Attrition" was a concept widely used during the Vietnam War. It did not work in Southeast Asia, and I do not think it will work in North America.

2. Jiménez and López-Sanders (2011) also label as "schizophrenic" the NAFTA policies that allow free transit of capital, goods, and services between the two countries, while penalizing the flow of workers that tends to follow the same capital and products.

Chapter 2. Sexual Violence Against Migrant Women and Children

1. We use the term "victimization" with much hesitation, and only to be consistent with the prevailing literature. These women and children should not be seen merely as victims—to do so would be to reduce them to experiences that were imposed on them, and to revictimize them. They are survivors—resilient, autonomous people trying to make the best of a tragic situation.

2. We are grateful for the excellent research assistance of several graduate students from ASU's Master's Program in Social Justice and Human Rights, especially Marla Conrad, Katie Norberg, Courtney Anderson, and Layal Rabat.

3. Ruiz Marrujo (2009) reports "between 80 and 90 percent of migrant women have suffered sexual violence" (citing La Jornada 2003).

4. We have a better sense of the conditions at home from those working with girls in the process of applying for an SIJ (Special Immigrant Juvenile) visa. These children have to show that they have been abused, abandoned, or neglected and have no home to return to. Because they must provide subjective accounts of their conditions at home, they give us the most complete account of their conditions.

5. The award-winning documentary film De Nadie as well as the 2006 best-selling book Enrique's Journey provide harrowing pictures of what these migrants face as they travel through Mexico.

6. Falcón (2007: 203) concluded that "rape is routinely and systematically used by the state in its militarization efforts at the U.S.-Mexico border." We definitely agree with her findings that the border, especially the culture of law enforcement officials, has become an area of militarization, hypermasculinity, and patriarchy.

Chapter 3. Immigration Enforcement at the U.S.-Mexico Border

1. Of course, there are some important exceptions, such as within the EU, though "fortress Europe" confronts those from outside it.

2. It is rooted in part in a successful federal lawsuit alleging widespread civil rights abuses by Border Patrol agents against Hispanic citizens and legal resident immigrants (see Dunn 2009; *Murillo, et al. v. Musegades, INS, et al.*, 809 F.Supp. 487 (W.D. Tex. 1992)).

3. Nonetheless, much of this view is based on erroneous stereotypes and misinformation. For example, studies of the economic fiscal impact of unauthorized immigration to the U.S. tend to find very mixed or ambivalent impacts in recent decades—some negative, some positive (Council of Economic Advisors 2007; Congressional Budget Office 2007)—though the hardships are clearer in times of economic recession. And though immigrants commit crimes, overall rates of criminal offending are lower for immigrants (including the unauthorized) than for native-born citizens, especially among Hispanic immigrants (Portes and Rumbaut 2006: 194–97; Sampson 2008). As for terrorism, the FBI proposed that the Canadian border poses a greater threat than does the U.S.-Mexico border, as a 2006 study found no evidence of Muslim terrorists having crossing the latter from 1993 to 2004 (Leiken and Brooke 2006). Thus, unauthorized immigration appears to pose little threat to U.S. residents. Furthermore, the ever-increasing immigration enforcement along the U.S.-Mexico border does little to aid the public, nor does it contribute to a heightened sense of national sovereignty.

Chapter 4. Politics of Death in the Drug War

1. The phrase and concept of "the right to kill" originate first with Foucault (1977). See also Mbembe 2003: 16.

2. For the estimate of more than 55,000 dead, see Reuters 2012. The highest estimate is 99,667 as of June 2012 (see O'Reilly 2012, citing Molly Molloy of New Mexico State University). I owe this notion of multiple sovereignties in Mexico to Fregoso (2006).

3. The Mexican Secretariat of Public Security (SSP) is responsible for designating these "zones of impunity."

4. Award-winning Mexican journalist Anabel Hernandez, an investigative reporter who has spent five years researching a book about the Sinaloa cartel and its leader Chapo Guzman, offers a more nuanced narrative about the ties between former president Fox and El Chapo. She claims in her 2010 book, *Los señores del narco*, that the DEA in Mexico obtained information that President Fox received a bribe of $40 million in exchange for political protection for El Chapo's escape from prison (320). She also claims that El Chapo talked about his escape to other gang members and that

the laundry-cart episode was a diversion. According to her DEA-derived story (2010: 321–22), El Chapo walked out of the prison dressed in full Federal Preventive Police (PFP) uniform escorted by PFP envoys sent by the Fox administration after the prison escape alarms had sounded. Hernandez summarizes her analysis of the alleged relationship between the Mexican military and the Sinaloa "cartel" this way: "The [Mexican] government went from being a controller of narco-trafficking to the armed wing of the cartels." Hernandez declares further, "This is what's happening here. Portions or sectors of the military, the Federal Investigations Agency, the federal police, and Secretariat of Public Security, are at the service of the cartel of Sinaloa . . . Guzman and the Sinaloans have been protected for the past nine years [2001–10] by the federal government" (Livesey 2010, citing Hernandez).

5. U.S. and Mexican national drug policies of criminalizing marijuana persist even while other governments across the hemisphere advocate legalizing marijuana nationally and regulating its use to undercut drug gang profits (Cave 2012b; see also Nadelman 2012). Although Mexican presidents Vicente Fox and Ernesto Zedillo publicly favored regional legalization of marijuana in the Americas, neither Calderón nor his PRI successor, Peña Nieto, has publicly pressured the U.S. government to legalize marijuana nationally in the United States (Archibold 2012; Rodriguez and Weissenstein 2012).

6. This report cites figures released by the Secretariat of Public Security (SSP) in June 2009.

7. One short-lived exception is perhaps General Francisco (Pancho) Villa's raid on the border town of Columbus, New Mexico, and the aftermath in 1916–17.

Chapter 5. Migration, Violence, and "Security Primacy" at the Guatemala-Mexico Border

1. "Glocal" refers here to the intersection of local and global phenomena. For one of the earliest comprehensive elaborations on this matter, see Robertson 1995.

2. For the purposes of my analysis, the reader should keep in mind that one distinguishing characteristic of DTOs is that they challenge state authority without necessarily, or purposely, seeking to take over the establishment or overthrow the state. Some of the major drug trade organizations in Mexico can be categorized as transnational crime syndicates.

3. The project studied migration of Mexican border populations within Mexico and out-migration to the United States as well as the flow of foreign migrants passing through Mexican territory on their way to the United States; project title: "Social and Economic Consequences as a Result of Migration Processes at the Balancán-Tenosique/Petén border" (Code: TAB-C09-2007-75064). Funding for this initiative came from the government of the state of Tabasco and Mexico's National Council on Science and Technology.

4. The Sinaloa DTO, in particular, has been actively involved in drug transshipments through many other points along the Mexico-Guatemala border for a number of years. The Zetas have only recently become an independent group, after breaking away from their former employer, the Gulf DTO. Cook (2007) offers a history of the Zetas as seen from an official U.S. perspective. A contrasting and concise profile of Zetas' evolution can be found in an article on a website with right-wing leanings, which houses an online newsletter published by Security International Solutions (*Counter Terrorist* 2010)

5. Geographer Victor Konrad uses the term in reference to expanded enforcement at the U.S.-Canada boundary, but it is equally applicable to what may happen at the Mexico-Guatemala border.

6. In support of this argument, let us consider the following. The presentation of the paper from which this chapter evolved coincided with a high-level meeting of the Mexican Defense Secretariat, the director of Mexico's National Institute on Migration, the U.S. Defense Department chief of staff, the respective heads of the Northern and Southern U.S. Commands, the head of Canada's Department of Defense, the chief of staff of the Guatemalan Defense Ministry and the Defense Ministry of Belize, among other officials. The group convened in Mexico City on April 15, 2011, to discuss "shared border issues" (*Prensa Libre* 2011b; *La Jornada* 2011a).

7. In a provocative article in *Nexos*, a well-regarded Mexican magazine, a public policy analyst has argued that the dispersal of violence through many states in Mexico is a result of Felipe Calderón's all-out war on drug trafficking organizations and also a consequence of the diminished well-structured, hierarchical status certain DTOs have experienced, which is the result of internal disputes. The split between the Zetas and the Gulf groups and the locations where these DTOs have found weak local governments, smaller networks of organized crime groups and cultivation of illicit drugs, says this source, set the right conditions to trigger and fuel turf battles for the control of a wide repertoire of illicit business (Guerrero 2011).

8. Precise dating is a matter of debate because the split between the Zetas and the Gulf DTO began around 2008, perhaps earlier. An ex-*coyote* told me that he had stopped delivering groups to northern Mexico as of 2005 because the Zetas began inquiring about his whereabouts (Mayate, pseudonym, personal communication, June 2010). A local resident and trusted confidant, someone who in the past had contact with this organization, stated that the Zetas arrived around 2005 (Pacho, pseudonym, personal communication, February 2010).

9. Maras are gang cliques. While certainly posing serious security concerns, the reality of Maras as a sociological product of the circumstances in which they have emerged and evolved is far more complex. For a detailed discussion of this issue, see Washington Office on Latin America 2006. The work of Dennis Rodgers (2009) sets the Maras' problematic in a wider Central American context. Thus far nothing, that I am aware of, has been published on Maras in connection with transit migration. For a fairly balanced, recent assessment of Central American Maras, see Bruneau, Lammert and Skinner (2011).

10. Overall, I agree with Dudley (2011: 42) when he asserts that "assumptions that these gangs are at the heart of this violence [the high level of violence in Central America and Mexico] is somewhat flawed, and the belief that they play a significant role in drug trafficking is exaggerated."

11. I say "this way" because other explanations should be considered. Pacho told me once that mass killings could be a way to show what DTO A is capable of doing to DTO B should the latter decide to interfere in the former's dealings. Another possibility is that if something goes wrong, as when a double-crossing deal bursts open, or if someone decides to switch sides, for example, executions serve as a way to take revenge and/or eliminate possible informers.

12. This magazine provided a summary of the original report, which was published in a digital weekly (Martínez 2009b), coming out of El Salvador.

13. The academic community now widely accepts the waning of Mexican migration to the United States over the last years, particularly after the onset of the economic crisis in 2007. This is not the case for Central American flows, however. Statistics generated by the Department of Homeland Security (see ProPublica.org 2012) concur with the trend that comes from ground data I have gathered at the Catholic Church-supported migrant shelter in Tenosique. The shelter's database indicates that Salvadorans, Hondurans, and Guatemalans, specifically, have continued to pass through in larger numbers over the last two years (Archives, Casa-Albergue La 72, Tenosique, Tabasco, information retrieved through 2011 and 2012).

14. For examples of such accounts, see BBC News 2010a; *El Periódico* (2010, 2012).

15. Despite serious shortcomings (the first document is rather descriptive and includes some inaccuracies, whereas the second lacks properly referenced sources), both investigations contain firsthand, valuable information on Petén's situation. InSight Crime, a research think tank with offices in Bogotá and Washington, D.C., sponsored the unsigned investigation. The organization's objective is "to increase the level of research, analysis and investigation on organized crime in Latin America and the Caribbean" (www.insightcrime.org/about-us).

16. Noño, pseudonym, personal communication, June 2011. This point has been noticed among other experts. Guerrero (2011) refers to the split-off groups from major DTOs as "second generation" organizations. He adds, concerning the Zetas: "It is possible that some of these cells have deserted from Zetas ranks or [have become] gangs passing as Zetas that take advantage of Zetas' reputation [to engage in criminal activities]" (my translation).

17. Calderon's administration claimed it had made important progress by showing off statistics such as the claim to have seized thirty high-profile drug lords from 2007 to April 2011 (Guerrero 2011). Capturing leaders is one (partial) way of measuring success and, supposedly, solving the problem; the dismantling of entire structures is a whole different matter, something far from happening. Wide sectors of Mexican

society question outright President Calderón's strategy to fight the DTOs because of the high cost and collateral damage associated with it. Up until 2012, the most visible and outspoken public initiative along these lines, though as yet one loosely assembled, is the Movement for Peace and Justice with Dignity. The clearest statement regarding the movement's guiding principles can be found in a manifesto delivered at Ciudad Juárez, Chihuahua, on June 10, 2011. At a different level, this resonates with claims about the way the Mexican government has purposely magnified its successes, instead of delivering a more balanced account (see InSight Crime 2011b).

18. See Liotta (2002) for a substantial discussion of the core issues regarding a human security approach similar to the perspective I outline here. Additional commentary is in order to briefly address what some authors may consider the overlapping bases, in both conceptual and discursive terms, between the human security perspective and the human rights approach. The matter is a topic of lively debate. Examples from two disciplinary arenas illustrate the point. For the sake of brevity I offer the following excerpt as one way to illuminate a broader discussion within the field of development studies: "human security is the fulfilment of basic human rights that are in turn the fulfilment of basic human needs. In [Galtung's] model these are survival, wellness, freedom and identity" (Galtung 2005, quoted in Gasper 2005: 233). Interested readers can find a comprehensive treatment of the topic in a special issue of the *Journal of Human Development*, published in July 2003. In the area of international law there is also a wealth of material on the human rights-human security nexus. Benedek (2008), to cite one source, asserts that the foundational, common ground that human security and human rights share is human dignity (13), a notion emanating from the Universal Declaration of Human Rights. He points out that the two concepts are "intertwined, interrelated, mutually reinforcing and contingent upon each other" (13); while this relationship is not downright simple, this author suggests that human rights is subsumed to human security: "A secure environment is a prerequisite for enjoying human rights. Living conditions that violate human dignity make people prone to violations of human rights" (12). Critiques of the human security perspective and its utility abound. See, among others, Oberleitner 2005 and Ryerson 2008.

19. Many other dignitaries, among them President Calderón, attended this meeting (BBC News 2011b; Radio Netherlands Worldwide 2011; *Prensa Libre* 2011a).

Chapter 6. The Binational Roots of the Femicides in Ciudad Juárez

The author is grateful to John Robert McCarty, Kassandra Goffena, and Christina Fraga for their research assistance for this chapter.

1. Despite the difficulties in getting an accurate count because of the drug cartels' largely successful muzzling of local media, the major source of information on the deaths that has been compiled by activists since the mid-1990s, research by Collins

and Mueller (2009), indicates an ongoing high level of women's murders throughout the last twenty years, which has continued through at least 2010 (see Figure 3; cf. Amnesty International 2012).

2. It was only in the recent past (1998) that rape was defined as a "crime against humanity" by the International Criminal Tribunal for Rwanda (Ellis 2007).

3. By the twenty-first century, the magnitude of the Juárez femicide had been overshadowed by ten times that rate of murder of Guatemalan women (Amnesty International 2005). But the Juárez femicide was first and continues.

4. There are other explanations. Wright (2011, 2007), for instance, offers a compelling analysis, extending the idea of "necropolitics." She argues that official Mexican discourse attempts to justify the femicide as the logical outcome of women's failure to maintain traditional roles in the family. By becoming "public"—in employment, recreation, consumption—women are simply asking for trouble and thus justify the inaction of officials and impunity of law enforcement. While this is a persuasive argument, it does not explain why these same changes that were happening along the border originally and eventually throughout the country did not lead to the femicide that happened in Ciudad Juárez. This explanation also fails to acknowledge the culpability of Mexico's northern neighbor.

5. Mexico experienced two devastating economic crises in the latter half of the twentieth century. The first was the crisis of 1982, which was a consequence of the variable income from the petroleum industry. The second was the "Peso Crisis of 1994," which led to devaluation of the peso. In both of these instances, Mexico relied on the international community to support its currency and credit worthiness. In exchange, Mexico committed to "structural adjustment programs" with their emphasis on privatization, decreased social services, and development of the export sector, to meet the terms of refinanced loans (Watkins 2009).

6. Maquiladoras are the foreign-owned manufacturing plants that primarily occupy the Export Processing Zone (EPZ) on the northern border of Mexico with the United States. Like EPZs the world over, they are designed to take advantage of low wages and favorable tax policies. Maquilas are taxed only on the value added by Mexican labor to unfinished goods brought into the country by foreign corporations, primarily from the United States (Torres Ruiz 2011).

7. The rise of the maquiladoras in border towns, including Ciudad Juárez, has been compared to the earlier industrial revolution of the Western powers (Landau 2005). The ability of corporations to find low wages, little or no taxes, very weak environmental laws, and a state willing to cooperate to the fullest extent created an environment of declining health standards for the workers migrating to these areas. This industrialized area, with a population that grew exponentially, became slums with houses made out of cardboard boxes and tin sheets, poor sewage, and little access to water or electricity (Landau 2005).

8. Wright (2001) argues that it was the discourse characterizing women as undependable and subject to high rates of turnover that led to extra training for men and

the defeminization of the labor force when civic leaders sought to attract more high tech industry to Ciudad Juárez. But this is also a global trend (see also Torres Ruiz 2011).

9. In the Set of Principles for the Protection and Promotion of Human Rights Through Action to Combat Impunity, submitted to the United Nations Commission on Human Rights, impunity is defined as "the impossibility, *de jure* or *de facto*, of bringing the perpetrators of violations to account—whether in criminal, civil, administrative or disciplinary proceedings—since they are not subject to any inquiry that might lead to their being accused, arrested, tried and, if found guilty, sentenced to appropriate penalties, and to making reparations to their victims" (UN Commission on Human Rights 2005).

10. "Cartel" is a misnomer for this type of criminal organization, since they resort to open warfare rather than control of supply and price fixing. Nevertheless, we follow the common nomenclature. The most direct case against the cartels for the killings as well as corruption of law enforcement is made by Diana Washington Valdez, prize-winning reporter for the *El Paso Times*. Her assertions and evidence are presented in Washington Valdez 2006.

11. It is often pointed out that illegal drugs are one of the few commodities for which third-world countries have a superior trade balance with first-world countries.

12. The states of Chihuahua, Sinaloa, and Baja accounted for 66 percent of the 2008 murders (Williams 2009a). Over the next two years, the epicenter of violence shifted to the Zetas' new stronghold in northeastern Mexico, across the border from Texas, as of 2013 the most violent region in Mexico (Grillo 2012). At this point, however, different sources report varying accounts of the current levels of violence on the border. Based on reports from Mexico City's Lantia Consultores, a consulting firm, by mid-May 2012 there had been 685 drug-related killings in the state of Nuevo León. That placed it ahead of Chihuahua with 560, although Ciudad Juárez, with 510 organized crime-related murders in the first six months of 2012, still remains the most murderous city in Mexico (Corcoran 2012).

The Mexican army, however, says that killings by criminal gangs in Ciudad Juárez have fallen 42 percent in the first six months of 2012, from 1,642 in 2011 to 952 in 2012 (Chavez 2012). Chihuahua state prosecutors, using other figures, indicated a decline from 1,322 in the first half of 2011 to 653 in the first half of 2012 (Martínez-Cabrera 2012). Only one thing is clear: regardless of the source, drug-related homicide is down from its murderous high when Juárez led the world in killings for three years in a row according to the Chihuahua attorney general's office. All sources attribute the decline to the increasing weakness of the Juarez Cartel and growing control by Sinaloa forces.

13. In March 2007, when President Bush met with newly elected Mexican president Calderón to address efforts to combat drug and weapons trafficking, the Mexican president stated that it would be difficult to reduce supply from his country without a reduction of demand from the United States (Sullivan and Beittel 2008).

14. The street price for trafficked narcotics increases substantially as it crosses the border but also increases rapidly in relation to the distance from the source to the consumer. Methamphetamine and cocaine have a street price of $100 per gram in the state of Arizona (private communication by Detective J. R. Eccles of the Maricopa County Sheriff's Office with Kassandra Goffena, March 27, 2009). See also Keefe 2012. By the time a gram of methamphetamine or cocaine reaches New York it brings a street price of $300 to $500 because it has been trafficked through seven or eight groups before reaching its final consumer. Each trafficking group has put their "tax" on it. Similarly, a kilogram of heroin is worth $12,000 to $18,000 in Mexico, but $200,000 in New York. Rising costs reflect increased risk of apprehension.

15. The U.S. Office of National Drug Control Policy (ONDCP) released a 2008 report naming marijuana as the number one cause of illegal drug abuse within the United States. This report states that 14.8 million Americans were current users in 2006, and by 2008, 2 million more had begun using marijuana in the past year. While our major concern is not the influence of illegal drugs on life in the United States, it is important to note that the vast majority of both juvenile and adults arrested for stolen vehicles, robbery, and burglary test positive for drugs (U.S. ONDCP 2008). Also, according to U.S. Bureau of Justice Statistics (BJS) at the end of 2001, 55 percent of the federal prison population, and 21 percent of state prison populations, were incarcerated on drug offenses (U.S. BJS 2007). From 1990 to 1998 the federal prison population almost doubled, and the state prison population increased 35 percent. Drug charges were primarily responsible for these increases.

16. The percentage of cartel weapons actually obtained from the United States is the subject of considerable dispute, as I will discuss below. Although a valid estimate of the actual number may be impossible to determine, it appears unlikely that the cartels could maintain their commanding role in corrupting Mexican law enforcement without them.

17. The actual costs of corruption to the cartels should not be underestimated. The Sinaloa Cartel estimates that bribing just municipal police costs $1 billion a year. President Calderón's drug czar, Noe Ramirez, was charged with accepting $450,000 per month (Keefe 2012).

18. To qualify for the legal purchase of a gun in Mexico, customers first gain approval from the government through the acquisition of a permit, which may take months to attain. After purchasing a gun, restrictions are placed on how much ammunition can legally be purchased monthly and where the gun can be taken (Hawley 2009). Permits are required, and strict regulations placed on the possession of any firearm above .22 caliber (Kopel 2009).

19. The Mexican drug cartels are not providing the sole demand for trafficked weapons. The increase in violent criminal activity, such as armed robberies, muggings, kidnappings, torture, and killings, has resulted in an increase in demand for restricted weapons as well as a boom in demand for armored cars and executive

protection security companies, as wealthy people living in Mexico want security for themselves and their families. "Not all illegal guns are in the hands of cartel members and street criminals. A healthy percentage of them are purchased by affluent Mexicans who . . . own prohibited [weapons] for self defense" (Burton and Stewart 2007).

20. The intractability of the gun supply problem has long daunted the U.S. Department of Justice, which is faced with a powerful pro-gun lobby that inhibits control of gun sales even within the United States. This frustration contributed most recently to the "Fast and Furious" fiasco and, ultimately, the highly partisan vote by the U.S. House of Representatives to hold attorney general Eric Holder in contempt of Congress (Weisman and Savage 2012).

21. "Globalization has indeed made the world a 'smaller place' as it has allowed rapid transport of human beings, resources and information. It has opened up the sex trade and increased the scope for violent men to evade risks associated with crime control policies on violence against women at home by enabling them to entice, entrap or force women in the 'periphery' into abuse and exploitation" (Radford and Tsutsumi 2008).

22. See Hausmann's excellent review of the literature on geographic influences on economic development in his 2001 article. Hausmann served formerly as chief economist of the Inter-American Development Bank.

Chapter 7. Reflections on Antiviolence Civil Society Organizations in Ciudad Juárez

1. In 2006, CSOs, along with several businessmen and the academic community, strongly opposed the San Jerónimo project that was promoted and supported by mayor Héctor Murguía, The first stage planned to urbanize 20,000 acres belonging to Eloy Vallina—the richest man in Chihuahua, whose land borders the state of New Mexico. This project was promoted by businessmen, many of them also politicians. Even the governor of New Mexico, Bill Richardson, was interested. This project would generate enormous earnings for just a few, and it would duplicate in a couple of years the size of a city that clearly already suffers deficiencies at many sites, as was demonstrated in the geographic diagnosis. Organizations were opposed to assigning the city's public resources for the benefit of private groups that produce only private profits. They also highlighted the elevated human costs associated with doubling the size of Ciudad Juárez. The government had already shown an inability to promote harmonious development that would absorb the thousands of new workers and their families who would be attracted by the opening of new maquiladoras in the area. Unfortunately, the project is under way. The "Camino Real," at a cost of 1.3 million pesos, "leads to nowhere" according to Juárez citizens, although the owners of Juárez are clear that it

leads to Santa Teresa, New Mexico. Despite the 50,000 signatures gathered by people and organizations opposed to San Jerónimo in a referendum, the project continues. In 2009, the government authorized 130 billion pesos for the construction of a road linking Anapra, a suburb at the edge of Juárez with little infrastructure, to Ciudad Vallina (or San Jerónimo).

2. Civic activists have also fought to prevent the Zaragoza family from expelling poor citizens in Lomas de Poleo in order to take over those lands, the property of the Reforma Agraria, which is still in dispute. Villagers have enjoyed the possession of that land for several decades. The Zaragoza family laid siege to this neighborhood, with permanent armed guards at its entrance; although this action is illegal, it has been protected by the authorities. Of the eighty-five families that inhabited this area originally, only twenty-five now remain in the fight.

3. Juárez has traditionally only been seen from the perspective of its potential economic growth and as a source of employment and development for the maquiladoras. Certainly, the levels of social abandonment and the absence of investment in the development of the population were not a concern until the violence spread in the 1990s.

4. For instance, the working group that deals with children, including Catalina Castillo from the OPI, Lourdes Almada from Casas de Cuidado Diario, and Luz Maria Villalva from Techo Comunitario, together with the Pacto por la Cultura with Wilicaldo Delgadillo, explored the possibility of bringing together citizens to develop a strategy to make Ciudad Juárez a place for children, taking into consideration that infants are the most vulnerable group in a context of violence.

Chapter 8. The Persistence of Femicide amid Transnational Activist Networks

1. Estévez analyzes the devastating effects of NAFTA on Mexico's agricultural sector (amid continuing U.S. subsidies for its farmers), and on women in low-wage manufacturing such as textiles (2008: chap. 1, esp. 3–8).

2. The phrase has not yet become a legal term used in prosecution, and in U.S. prosecutorial strategies hate and misogyny are difficult motives to establish and for which to generate evidence and proof beyond a reasonable doubt. A raped and mutilated corpse alone, also common in some domestic violence murders, would not likely constitute evidence for hate murder charges.

3. For comprehensive analysis of the transnational metropolitan Paso del Norte urban region, see Staudt, Fuentes, and Monárrez Fragoso 2010.

4. Of course, such estimates depend on the peso-dollar exchange, with the peso plummeting from 10:1 to 15:1 after the late 2008 U.S. economic recession, and in mid-2012 resting at 13.8:1.

5. Solís was subsequently an Obama cabinet appointee as U.S. secretary of labor.

6. Most arms confiscated are traced to U.S. origins; the infamous Alcohol, Tobacco, and Firearms (ATF) "Fast and Furious" gun smuggling/trafficking program, started under the Bush administration and continued under the Obama administration, brought reckless bureaucratic bungling to light.

7. PRI president Peña Nieto (2012–18) has appointed a new ambassador to Canada: Francisco Suárez.

8. Written by a group of academics and ex-presidents in the Americas, the Latin American Commission on Drugs and Democracy report (2009) warned about threats to democracy and called for a paradigm shift in regulation of drugs, as did the Global Commission on Drug Policy report (2011).

9. Samantha Power reports that the UNDP documents how "four billion people live in places with dysfunctional justice systems—abusive police, entrenched bribery, mismanaged courts" (2009: 52).

10. Let me state that I do not view the United States as an exemplar, given widespread abuses of civil and political rights in the United States (witness the plight of immigrant detainees, deportations, and raids) and U.S. inattention to social and economic rights (once considered the agenda of the "enemy" in the Cold War era, with long-lasting consequences).

Chapter 9. Transnational Advocacy for Human Rights in Contemporary Mexico

1. Other actors, such as funding agencies, churches, and trade unions, are also relevant but not as important as NGOs, intergovernmental organizations, and Western governments.

2. See Meyer's chapter in this volume on the economic conditions in the Mérida Initiative. Potential reasons for lack of material pressure on Mexico might be related to its importance as a trading partner for the United States and Europe and as an important site for Western investment.

3. It is not always evident, however, why NGOs privilege some issues while neglecting others (Carpenter 2007).

4. A recent study (Franklin 2008) on seven Latin American countries (Mexico included) concludes that criticism made by international NGOs and foreign governments reduces repression, *particularly in countries that rely on foreign aid and investment*. The statistical analysis made in that study concludes that shaming by NGOs is the most significant, followed closely by that of governments, while criticism by intergovernmental organizations is almost irrelevant. The author recognizes that these findings are "somewhat surprising." About governments, he speculates that the impact of their shaming is not greater than that by NGOs because the U.S. government

tends to send "mixed signals" about the human rights situation in other countries—some officials might be critical, while others might be apologetic. A possibility not contemplated by the author is that his analysis does not appear to take into consideration the characteristics of the relationship between the country that criticizes and that which is the target of criticism. That is, the effect of a specific criticism is likely to depend on the level of "social" ascendancy the country that criticizes has over the target country. In relation to the very weak effect of criticism by international human rights organs and bodies, he suggests that "international power relations have limited the scope of IGOs," especially the UN Commission on Human Rights (Franklin 2008: 4). If this is true, that would be even more the case for NGOs. In addition, if criticism by the now extinct UN Commission on Human Rights was so unimportant, why did states devote so much diplomatic energy to avoid being targeted by its resolutions (Forsythe 2000: 70–71; Lebovic and Voeten 2006: 861–65)?

5. Article 8 of the Optional Protocol states that "If the Committee receives reliable information indicating grave or systematic violations by a State party of rights set forth in the Convention . . . the Committee may designate one or more of its members to conduct an inquiry and to report urgently to the Committee. Where warranted and with the consent of the State Party, the inquiry may include a visit to its territory."

6. Mexico holds observer status in the Council of Europe.

7. The Council of Europe and the European Union are independent entities. The former is an intergovernmental organization; the latter is a supranational entity.

8. See the introductory chapter to this volume. Also see Aikin Araluce 2011; Anaya Muñoz 2012.

9. Two hearings focusing on the situation in Oaxaca took place in 2005.

10. Traditionally, U.S. foreign policy about drug trafficking in Latin America has actively endorsed, promoted, and supported an approach based on militarization of antidrug efforts, without showing significant concern for human rights (Isacson 2005; Freeman and Sierra 2005).

11. For an explicit discussion of why the Ciudad Juárez situation generated such high levels of transnational human rights shaming, see Anaya Muñoz 2011.

Chapter 10. Restrictions on U.S. Security Assistance and
Their Limitations in Promoting Changes to the
Human Rights Situation in Mexico

1. The Municipal Public Security Subsidy began in 2008 to support police professionalization; in 2011 only 220 of Mexico's 2,440 municipalities received this subsidy. Municipalities are also eligible for funding through the Contribution Fund for Public Security for the states and Federal District. However, state congresses determine how the funds are distributed to the municipalities, and there is no control mechanism monitoring how the funds are spent.

2. Strategy 2.4 of the Program includes as an area of action: "Promote the progressive and verifiable substitution of the Armed Forces in public security tasks, particularly those that correspond to police activities," http://www.gobernacion.gob.mx/work /models/SEGOB/Resource/620/1/images/PROGRAMA_NACIONAL_DE_ DERECHOS_HUMANOS_2008-2012.pdf.

3. This includes complaints against the Ministry of Defense (Sedena) as well as the Mexican navy (Semar). See CNDH annual reports for 2007 and 2012, www.cndh. org.mx.

4. In 2010, the total number of recommendations was 86, of which Sedena received 22, and Semar 6. In 2011 the total was 95, with 25 for Sedena and 6 for Semar. The level of complaints against the military at the state level is even higher. Chihuahua's state human rights commission received over 1,300 complaints of human rights violations by the military between March 2008 and September 2009. In Michoacán the number reported for 2009 was more than 400, while the Commission received 84 complaints in the first three months of 2012 alone. See Amnesty International 2009; Gil 2009; Comisión Estatal de Derechos Humanos en Michoacán, Informe Estadístico (issued monthly) http://www.cedhmichoacan.org/Documentos/Difusion/estadistico_quejas_ Marzo_2012.pdf .

5. On June 30, 2008, the U.S. Congress approved $400 million in assistance in the first tranche of funding for Mexico, in the Supplemental Appropriations Act of 2008. On March 11, 2009, Mexico received an additional $300 million in Mérida funds through the FY 2009 Omnibus Appropriations Act. In the 2009 Supplemental Appropriations Act, signed into law on June 24, Mexico received $420 million in assistance. On December 16, the FY 2010 Omnibus Appropriations Act was signed into law, and Mexico received $210,250,000 in assistance under the Mérida Initiative. On July 21, 2010, the FY 2010 Supplemental Appropriations Act was signed into law, and Mexico received $175 million in assistance under the Initiative. It then received $143 million in Mérida assistance through the FY 2011 Appropriations Act, signed into law April 15, 2011. Last, Mexico received $281.9 million in the FY 2012 Appropriations Act, signed into law December 23, 2011.

6. The language from the FY 2012 Appropriations Bill read: "Prior to the obligation of 15 percent of the funds appropriated by this Act that are available for assistance for Mexican military and police forces, the Secretary of State shall report in writing to the Committees on Appropriations that: the Government of Mexico is investigating and prosecuting in the civilian justice system, in accordance with Mexican and international law, military and police personnel who are credibly alleged to have violated human rights; is enforcing prohibitions on the use of testimony obtained through torture; and the Mexican military and police are cooperating with civilian judicial authorities in such cases."

7. From the United States, WOLA, LAWG, Amnesty International-U.S.A, the Due Process of Law Foundation, and HRW participated in different stages of the organization for the workshop, as did the Mexico-based Miguel Agustin Pro Juarez Human Rights

Center, the National Network of Human Rights Organizations "All Rights for All," Fundar: Research and Analysis, and Amnesty International-Mexico.

8. This coalition was originally made up of WOLA, LAWG, Fundar, and the Miguel Agustin Pro Juárez Human Rights Center. The Mexico-based Tlachinollan Human Rights Center and Amnesty International-U.S.A began participation in 2009. HRW and the Civilian Monitor of the Police and Security Forces in the mountain region of the state of Guerrero joined in 2010, and the Robert F. Kennedy Center for Justice and Human Rights has participated since 2011.

9. The author wishes to note that these joint efforts are by no means the only work by U.S. and Mexican human rights organizations and others regarding the Mérida Initiative and the human rights requirements in the aid package. This chapter describes one specific experience based particularly on her organization's own involvement in the work.

10. Fainaru and Booth 2009.

11. For example, on June 11, 2009, during Mexico's Universal Periodic Review (UPR) before the UN Human Rights Commission, officials from the Mexican Ministry of Foreign Affairs affirmed that the "The Military Justice system currently investigates 6 cases that are in the preliminary investigation phase, 3 cases in which 32 military personnel have been brought before the authorities, and there are 9 registered convictions against 14 military personnel" (Government of Mexico 2009, para. 16). On July 8, 2009, HRW issued a letter to the Mexican secretary of the interior, Fernando Francisco Gómez-Mont Urueta, requesting information about these cases, such as copies of the charges, indictments, court records, transcripts, and judgments, including sentencing. In the response, Gomez-Mont affirmed that fourteen soldiers were condemned for human rights abuses. However, according to HRW, the letter did not provide any of the information it had requested, such as copies of the documentation, nor did it provide enough information to affirm that the Mexican government is effectively prosecuting human rights abuses committed by the military (HRW 2009a).

12. See the March 2012 letter from Representative Raul Grijalva (Grijalva 2012); the letter sent by members of Congress to Secretary Clinton on human rights defenders in Mexico (Latin America Working Group 2011); and the letter from members of Congress on human rights violations against migrants in transit in Mexico (Grijalva 2011).

13. Although as illustrated through the cables released by WikiLeaks, internally, U.S. officials expressed multiple concerns about President Calderón and his security strategy.

Conclusion. Multiple States of Exception, Structural
Violence, and Prospects for Change

1. One early study showed that just the initiatives in Colorado and Washington could reduce cartel profits by over $2 billion (Ramsey 2012, but see Kilmer et al. 2010).

2. There has also been a push emanating from the Rafto Symposium in Norway in November 2010, which the author was part of, for a transmigrant visa, but that has yet to gain traction in the Mexican Congress.

3. This theory would explain why El Paso, Texas, remains one of the safest big cities in the United States, while its sister city across the river, Ciudad Juárez, experiences record numbers of murders.

REFERENCES

ABC News. 2009. "Kidnapping Capital of the U.S.A." February 11.

AFP. 2007. "Pide Felipe apoyo en lucha contra narco." *Reforma*, June 6.

Agamben, Giorgio. 1995. *Homo Sacer: Sovereign Power and Bare Life*. Trans. Daniel Heller-Roazen. Stanford, Calif.: Stanford University Press.

———. 2000. *Means Without End: Notes on Politics*. Trans. Vincenzo Binetti and Cesare Casarino. Minneapolis: University of Minnesota Press.

———. 2005. *State of Exception*. Chicago: University of Chicago Press.

Aguayo Quezada, Sergio. 1995. "A Mexican Milestone." *Journal of Democracy* 6, 2: 157–67.

Aguilar, Ruben, and Jorge G. Castaneda. 2009. *El narco: La guerra fallida*. Mexico City: Punto de Lectura, 2009.

Aikin Araluce, Olga. 2009. "Transnational Advocacy Networks and Political Change in Mexico: Towards a Process of Socialization of International Norms of Violence Against Women in the Case of Murdered Women in Ciudad Juárez, Chihuahua." In *Human Rights Along the U.S.-Mexico Border*, ed. Kathleen Staudt, Tony Payan, and Z. Anthony Kruszewski. Tucson: University of Arizona Press, 150–67.

———. 2011. *Activismo social transnacional: Un análisis en torno a los feminicidios en Ciudad Juárez*. Mexico City: ITESO, Universidad Autónoma de Ciudad Juárez and Colegio de la Frontera Norte.

Alvarado, Arturo, ed. 2008. *La reforma de la justicia en México*. Mexico City: Colegio de México.

American Friends Service Committee. 1998. *Sealing Our Borders: The Human Toll*. Fourth Report of the Immigration Law Enforcement Monitoring Project. Houston: ILEMP.

American Public Health Association (APHA). 2009. "APHA Policy Statement: Border Crossing Deaths; A Public Health Crisis Along the U.S.-Mexico Border." Washington, D.C.: APHA, November 11.

Amnesty International (AI). 1998. *United States of America: Human Rights Concerns in the Border Region with Mexico*. London: AI.

———. 2003a. "Mexico: Amnesty International Secretary General Visits Mexico Saturday 9–Wednesday 13." Media advisory, August 5.

————. 2003b. "Mexico: Despite Promises on Juárez, Doubts Remain about Government's True Commitment to Human Rights." Press release, August 13.

————. 2003c. *Mexico: Intolerable Killings: Ten Years of Abductions and Murders in Ciudad Juárez and Chihuahua.* AMR 41/026.

————. 2005. *No Protection, No Justice: Killings of Women in Guatemala.* AMR 34/017/2005.

————. 2007a. "Mexico: Amnesty International Completes High Level Mission; Presidencia de la República—Press Room, President Calderón Receives Amnesty International Secretary General." Press release, August 7.

————. 2007b. "Mexico: Amnesty International Completes High Level Mission; President Calderón Commits to Human Rights." Press release, August 8.

————. 2007c. *Mexico: Oaxaca—Clamor for Justice* AMR 41/031/2007, July 31.

————. 2008a. *Amnesty International Report 2008: State of the World's Human Rights, Mexico.* London: AI.

————. 2008b. "Amnesty International Urges U.S. and Mexican Lawmakers to Vigilantly Consult on Anti-Drug Aid Package: Human Rights Protections Must Be Incorporated into the Package." Public statement, October 5.

————. 2008c. "Mexico: Mérida Initiative Can Only Deliver Security with Human Rights." Press release, June 4.

————. 2009. *Mexico: New Reports of Human Rights Violations by the Military.* London: AI, December.

————. 2010. *Invisible Victims: Migrants on the Move in Mexico.* London: AI.

————. 2012. Mexico: Briefing to UN Committee on the Elimination of Discrimination Against Women. http://www2.ohchr.org/english/bodies/cedaw/docs/ngos/AmnestyInternationalForTheSessionMexico_CEDAW52.pdf.

Anaya Muñoz, Alejandro. 2007. "Calidad de la democracia y derechos humanos en México." In *Por una democracia de calidad: México después de la transición,* ed. César Cansino and Israel Covarrubias. Mexico City: Centro de Estudios de Política Comparada/Ediciones de Educación y Cultura. 161–74.

————. 2009a. "The Influence of Issue-Characteristics on the Levels of International 'Shaming' over Mexico: Comparing the Femicides in Ciudad Juárez and Security-Related Violations of Human Rights." Paper presented at 2009 Annual Convention of the International Studies Association, New York.

————. 2009b. "Mexico After the Institutional Revolutionary Party." In *Encyclopedia of Human Rights,* ed. David Forsythe. New York: Oxford University Press. 3: 495–506.

————. 2009c. "Transnational and Domestic Processes in the Definition of Human Rights Policies in Mexico." *Human Rights Quarterly* 31: 35–58.

————. 2011. "Explaining High Levels of Transnational Pressure over Mexico: The Case of the Disappearances and Killings of Women in Ciudad Juárez." *International Journal of Human Rights* 15, 3: 339–58.

———. 2012. *El país bajo presión: Debatiendo el papel del escrutinio internacional de derechos humanos sobre México*. Mexico City: Centro de Investigación y Docencia Económicas.

Anderson, Stuart. 2013. *How Many More Deaths? The Moral Case for a Temporary Worker Program*. Washington, D.C.: National Foundation for American Policy.

Andreas, Peter. 1999. "When Policies Collide: Market Reform, Market Prohibition, and the Narcotization of the Mexican Economy." In *The Illicit Global Economy and State Power*, ed. H. Richard Friman and Peter Andreas. Lanham, Md.: Rowman and Littlefield. 125–41.

———. 2000. *Border Games: Policing the U.S.-Mexico Divide*. Ithaca, N.Y.: Cornell University Press.

———. 2003. "Redrawing the Line: Borders and Security in the Twenty-First Century." *International Security* 28, 2: 78–111.

Annan, Sandra L. 2006. "Sexual Violence in Rural Areas: A Review of the Literature." *Family Community Health* 29, 3: 164–68.

Archibold, Randal C. 2010a. "Budget Cut for Fence on U.S.-Mexico Border." *New York Times*, March 16.

———. 2010b. "A Proposal to Address Rights Abuse in Mexico." *New York Times*, October 20.

———. 2012. "U.S. Remains Opposed to Drug Legalization, Biden Tells Region." *New York Times*, March 5.

Arendt, Hannah. 1951. *The Origins of Totalitarianism*. New York: Harcourt.

Arnson, Cynthia J., and Eric L. Olson, eds. 2011. *Organized Crime in Central America: The Northern Triangle*. Woodrow Wilson Center Report on the Americas 29. Washington, D.C., November.

Arriola, Luis. 2010. "Reconfiguración de la frontera Tabasco-Petén y migración al inicio del siglo XXI." *In Migraciones contemporáneas en la región sur-sureste de México*, ed. Hugo Angeles, Mario Ortiz, Martha Rojas, and Donato Ramos. Mexico City: Universidad Autónoma Benito Juárez de Oaxaca and El Colegio de la Frontera Sur. 169–88.

———. 2012. *Human Agency and the Making of Territoriality at the Frontier: A Case Study from Northern Petén, Guatemala*. Saarbrücken: Lambert Academic Publishing.

Asociación Maquiladora, A.C. 2011. "AMAC 2011 General Statistics." http://www.slideshare.net/elperrote/juarez-amac-datos-estadisticos.

Associated Press. 2012. "Mexico Files Drug Charges Against 3 Generals." *New York Times*, August 1.

Ávila, Teresa. 2007. "German Coordination for Human Rights in Mexico." Telephone interview by Alejandro Anaya Muñoz, August 3.

Aviña, Alexander. 2012. "Seizing Hold of Memories in Moments of Danger: Guerrillas and Revolution in Guerrero, Mexico." In *Challenging Authoritarianism in Mexico:*

Revolutionary Struggles and the Dirty War, 1964–1982, ed. Adela Cedillo and Fernando Calderón. New York: Routledge. 40–59.

Ballinas, Victor. 2002. "Persisten desapariciones forzadas y tortura en México: Mary Robinson." *La Jornada*, July 2.

Ballinas, Victor, Andrea Becerril, and Jesús Aranda. 2008. "Si el ejército hace funciones policíacas debe de estar bajo vigilancia civil." *La Jornada*, February 7.

Balz, Dan, and Darryl Fears. 2006. "'We Decided Not to Be Invisible Anymore.'" *Washington Post*, April 11.

Barry, Tom. 2009. "National Security Business on the Border: Former Border Patrol Chief Silvestre Reyes Now a Major Player in New Military, Intelligence, and Homeland Security Complex." Americas Program, Center for International Policy, September. http://americas.irc-online.org/.

———. 2011. *Border Wars*. Boston: Boston Review and MIT Press.

Bauer, H. M., M. A. Rodriguez, S. S. Quiroga, and Y. G. Flores-Ortiz. 2000. "Barriers to Health Care for Abused Latina and Asian Immigrant Women." *Journal of Health Care for the Poor and Underserved* 11: 33–44.

BBC News. 2010a. "Guatemala Fears Mexican Drug Gangs Advancing." Latin American and Caribbean, December 20.

———. 2010b. "Murdered Bodies in Mexico 'Were Migrants.'" Latin America and Caribbean, August 25.

———. 2011a. "Bodies Found as Mexicans March Against Drug Violence." Latin America and Caribbean, April 7.

———. 2011b. "Central America Drug Wars: Clinton Pledges More Funds." Latin America and Caribbean, June 23.

———. 2011c. "More Than 11,000 Migrants Abducted in Mexico." February 23.

———. 2011d. "Mexico Anti-Drug Convoy Crosses Border to Accuse US." Latin America and Caribbean, June 11.

Beaubien, Jason. 2009. "Some Accuse Mexican Army of Abuse in Juárez." *All Things Considered*, National Public Radio, March 13.

Becerril, Andrea, José Antonio Román, Roberto Garduño, and Laura Poy 2005. "Pendientes en México: Respeto de garantías para indígenas y mujeres: Louise Arbour." *La Jornada*, June 30.

Beith, Malcolm. 2010. *The Last Narco*. New York: Grove Press.

Benedek, Wolfang. 2008. "Human Security and Human Rights Interaction." *International Social Science Journal* 59 (Supplement s1): 7–17.

Binford, Leigh. 1999. "A Failure of Normalization: Transnational Migration, Crime, and Popular Justice in the Contemporary Neoliberal Mexican Social Formation." *Social Justice* 26, 3: 123–44.

Blau, Judith, and Mark Frezzo, eds. 2012. *Sociology and Human Rights: A Bill of Rights for the Twenty-First Century*. Thousand Oaks, Calif.: Pine Forge/Sage.

Blau, Judith, and Alberto Moncada. 2005. *Human Rights: Beyond the Liberal Vision*. Lanham, Md.: Rowman and Littlefield.

————. 2006. *Justice in the United States: Human Rights and the U.S. Constitution.* Lanham, Md.: Rowman and Littlefield.

————. 2007. *Freedoms and Solidarities: In Pursuit of Human Rights.* Lanham, Md.: Rowman and Littlefield.

————. 2009. *Human Rights: A Primer.* Boulder, Colo.: Paradigm.

Boli, J., and George M. Thomas. 1999. *Constructing World Culture: International Non-Governmental Organizations Since 1875.* Stanford, Calif.: Stanford University Press.

Booth, William, and Steve Fainaru. 2009. "From Mexico to California, Two Men on the Hunt for Illicit Marijuana." *Washington Post,* October 29.

Booth, William, and Nick Miroff. 2012. "Mexico's President-Elect Wants Close Security Ties with U.S., with Limits." *Washington Post,* July 5.

Border Network for Human Rights. 2003. "The Status of Human and Civil Rights 2000–2003: El Paso, Texas-Southern New Mexico." December 10. http://seymour .textdrive.com/~bnhr/download/bnhr_camp_rpt2003.pdf.

Borunda, Daniel. 2010. "Juárez Nears 5,000 Killings." *El Paso Times,* April 26.

Bouvard, Marguerite Guzman. 1994. *Revolutionizing Motherhood: The Mothers of the Plaza de Mayo.* Wilmington, Del: Scholarly Resources.

Bowden, Charles. 2010. *Murder City.* New York: Nation Books.

Bricker, Kristin. 2011. "Military Justice and Impunity in Mexico's Drug War." Security Sector Issue Reform Issue Papers, Centre for International Governance Innovation 3, October 13.

Broder, Jonathan. 2013. "Citing Oversight Concerns, Leahy Holds Up Aid to Mexico." *CQ Roll Call,* August 1.

Brook, David. 2009. "Retendrá EU apoyo *antinarco*: Evalúa respeto a las garantías." *La Jornada,* Politics Section, July 14.

Brown, Cynthia J., and Wendy V. Cunningham. 2002. "Gender in Mexico's Maquiladora Industry." Working Paper 2002–8, Center for Border Economic Studies, University of Texas-Pan American.

Brownmiller, Susan. 1975. *Against Our Will: Men, Women, and Rape.* New York: Ballantine.

Bruneau, Thomas, Lucía Lammert, and Elizabeth Skinner, eds. 2011. *Maras: Gang Violence and Security in Central America.* Austin: University of Texas Press.

Brysk, Alison. 1994. *The Politics of Human Rights in Argentina: Protest, Change, and Democratization.* Stanford, Calif.: Stanford University Press.

Buff, Rachel Ida. 2008. *Immigrant Rights: In the Shadows of Citizenship.* New York: NYU Press.

Bugarin, Inder. 2007. "Demanda Solana no descuidar DH." *Reforma,* National Section, June 7.

Burgerman, Susan. 2001. *Moral Victories: How Activists Provoke Multilateral Action.* Ithaca, N.Y.: Cornell University Press.

Burnett, John, Marisa Peñalosa, and Robert Benincasa. 2010. "Mexico Seems to Favor Sinaloa Cartel in Drug War." National Public Radio, May 19.

Burton, Fred, and Scott Stewart. 2007. "Mexico: Dynamics of the Gun Trade." *Stratfor Terrorism Intelligence Report*. http://www.stratfor.com/weekly/mexico_dynamics _gun_trade.

Buscaglia, Edgardo. 2009. "Mexico's War on Drugs Is a Sham." Interview by Gardenia Mendoza, trans. Elena Shore. *La Opinión*, Mexico City, June 3.

Bustamante, Jorge. 2002. "Immigrants' Vulnerability as Subjects of Human Rights." *International Migration Review* 36, 2: 333–54.

Cabrera, Luis. 2010. *The Practice of Global Citizenship*. New York: Cambridge University Press.

Caminero-Santangelo, Marta. 2009. "Responding to the Human Costs of U.S. Immigration Policy: No More Deaths and the New Sanctuary Movement." *Latino Studies* 7, 1: 112–22.

Campbell, Howard. 2009. *Drug War Zone: Frontline Dispatches from the Streets of El Paso and Juárez*. Austin: University of Texas Press.

Cansino, César, and Israel Covarrubias, eds. 2007. *Por una democracia de calidad: México después de la transición*. Mexico City: Centro de Estudios de Política Comparada and Ediciones de Educación y Cultura.

Caputi, Jane E. 1987. *The Age of Sex Crime*. Bowling Green, Ohio: Bowling Green State University Popular Press.

Cardenas, Sonia. 2007. *Conflict and Compliance: State Responses to International Human Rights Pressure*. Philadelphia: University of Pennsylvania Press.

Carlin, Matthew. 2012. "Guns, Gold, and Corporeal Inscriptions." *Third Text* 26, 5: 503–14.

Carpenter, Charli. 2007. "Studying Issue (Non)-Adoption in Transnational Networks." *International Organization* 61, 3: 643–67.

Carrasco Araizaga, Jorge. 2012. "El Chapo", eventual aliado de Peña Nieto," *Proceso. com*, December 12.

Castaneda, Jorge. 2010. "De-Narcotize U.S.-Mexican Relations; Focus Should Be on New Binational Development." *New Perspectives Quarterly*, March 25.

Castillo, Eduardo, and Michelle Roberts. 2009. "Mexico's Weapons Stash Stymies Tracing." Associated Press, May 7.

Castillo García, Gustavo. 2007. "Debe definirse la responsabilidad de policías y soldados en operativos: Khan." *La Jornada*, Politics Section, August 4.

Castles, Stephen, and Alistar Davidson. 2000. *Citizenship and Migration: Globalization and the Politics of Belonging*. New York: Routledge.

Cave, Damien. 2012a. "Mexico Updates Death Toll in Drug War to 47,515, but Critics Dispute the Data." *New York Times*, January 11.

———. 2012b. "South America Sees Drug Path to Legalization," *New York Times*, July 29.

Center for Gender & Refugee Studies. 2005. *Getting Away with Murder: Guatemala's Failure to Protect Women and Rodi Alvarado's Quest for Safety*. University of California, Hastings College of the Law. http://cgrs.uchastings.edu/documents/cgrs/cgrs_guatemala_femicides.pdf.

Chavez, Leo. 2008. *The Latino Threat: Constructing Immigrants, Citizens, and the Nation.* Stanford, Calif.: Stanford University Press.

Chavez, Ricardo. 2012. "Mexican Army: Killings in Juarez Down 42 Percent," *El Paso Times,* July 11.

Checkel, Jeffrey T. 2001. "Social Construction and European Integration." In *Social Construction of Europe,* ed. Thomas Christiansen. London: Sage.

CNN News. 2011. "Guatemalan Police Search for 'Massacre' Suspects." *World,* May 16.

Cogan, Neil H. 1989. "Standing Before the Constitution: Membership in the Community." *Law and History Review* 7: 1–21.

Collins, Terry, and Carol Mueller. 2009. "The Measurement of Femicide." Paper at Annual Meeting of the Association of Borderland Studies, Albuquerque, New Mexico.

Collyer, Michael. 2010. "In-Between Places: Trans-Saharan Transit Migrants in Morocco and the Fragmented Journey to Europe." *Antipode* 39, 4: 668–90.

Comisión Civil Internacional de Observación de Derechos Humanos (CCIODH). 2007a. "Presentación del informe de la CCIODH en el Parlamento Europeo." Press Bulletin 19, June 13. http://cciodh.pangea.org/.

———. 2007b. "Presentación del informe de la V visita de la CCIODH por los hechos de Oaxaca ante la oficina de la Alta Comisionada de Naciones Unidas para los Derechos Humanos en Ginebra." Press Bulletin 20, June 21. http://cciodh.pangea.org/.

———. 2008. *Informe de la situación de los derechos humanos en Chiapas, Oaxaca y Atenco: VI visita 2008 30 enero a 20 febrero.* Barcelona: CCIODH. http://cciodh.pangea.org/.

Committee Against Torture (CAT). 2006. *Consideration of Reports Submitted by States Parties Under Article 19 of The Convention: Conclusions and Recommendations of the Committee Against Torture, México.* CAT/C/MEX/CO/4, February 6.

Committee on the Elimination of Discrimination against Women (CEDAW). 2002. *Concluding Comments of the Committee on the Elimination of Discrimination against Women: Mexico.* CEDAW/C/MEX/5, August 23.

———. 2005. *Report on Mexico Produced by the Committee on the Elimination of Discrimination against Women under Article 8 of the Optional Protocol to the Convention, and Reply from the Government of Mexico.* CEDAW/C/2005/OP.8/MEXICO, January 27.

———. 2006. *Concluding Comments of the Committee on the Elimination of Discrimination against Women: Mexico.* CEDAW/C/MEX/CO/6, August 25.

Committee to Protect Journalists. 2011. *Attacks on the Press in 2010: A Worldwide Survey by the Committee to Protect Journalists.* New York.

Congressional Budget Office. 2007. "The Impact of Unauthorized Immigrants on the Budgets of State and Local Governments." Washington, D.C.: U.S. Congress, December. www.cbo.gov/ftpdocs/87xx/doc8711/12-6-Immigration.pdf.

Conroy, Bill. 2009. "Legal U.S. Arms Exports May Be Source of Narco Syndicates Rising Firepower." *Narcosphere*, March 29.

Cook, Collen W. 2007. "Mexico's Drug Cartels." Congressional Report Service, RL34215, October 16.

———. 2008. "Mexico's Drug Cartels." *CRS Report for Congress*, RL32724, May 23.

Cook, Philip J., Wendy Cukier, and Keith Krause. 2009. "The Illicit Firearms Trade in North America." *Criminology & Criminal Justice: An International Journal* 9, 3: 265–86.

Corcoran, Patrick. 2012. "Violence in Mexico 2012: A Halfway Report." InSight Crime, July 16.

Cornelius, Wayne A. 2006. "Impacts of Border Enforcement on Unauthorized Migration to the United States." In *Border Battles: The U.S. Immigration Debates*. Social Science Research Council Series. http://borderbattles.ssrc.org/Cornelius/printable.html.

Cornelius, Wayne A., and Idean Salehyan. 2007. "Does Border Enforcement Deter Unauthorized Immigration? The Case of Mexican Migration to the United States of America." *Regulation and Governance* 1, 2: 139–53.

Cornelius, Wayne, and David Shirk, eds. 2007. *Reforming the Administration of Justice in Mexico*. South Bend, Ind.: Notre Dame University Press.

Cortez, Edgar, and Michel Maza. 2007. "Todos los Derechos para Todos." Personal interview. *Human Rights Network*, Mexico City, October 31.

Council of Economic Advisors. 2007. "Immigration's Economic Impact." Washington, D.C.: Executive Office of the President, June 20.

Council of Europe-Parliamentary Assembly. 2005a. *Disappearance and Murder of a Great Number of Women and Girls in Mexico*. Report, Committee on Equal Opportunities for Women and Men; Rapporteuse: Mrs Ruth-Gaby Vermot-Mangold, Switzerland, Socialist Group (Doc. 10551), May 12.

———. 2005b. Recommendation 1709 (Reply Adopted by the Committee of Ministers on 28 September 2005 at the 939th meeting of the Ministers' Deputies), October 3.

———. 2005c. Resolution 1454, "Disappearance and Murder of a Great Number of Women and Girls in Mexico," June 21.

Counter Terrorist. 2010. "Los Zetas: Massacres, Assassinations, and Infantry Tactics." November 24. http://www.homeland1.com/domestic-international-terrorism/articles/ 913612-Los-Zetas-Massacres-Assassinations-and-Infantry-Tactics/.

Decker, Michele R., Anita Raj, and Jay G. Silverman. 2007. "Sexual Violence Against Adolescent Girls: Influences of Immigration and Acculturation." *Violence Against Women* 13: 498–513.

Del Carmen Sosa, Luz. 2010. "Matan duranate 2010 al doble de mujeres y policies que en ano previo." *El Dario* 20, 42 (December 31).

Delgado, Alvaro. 2010. "'El Chapo' Guzman, el intocable de Calderón" *Proceso*, February 13.

Diaz Briseño, José. 2010. "Prevé EU Retener Apoyo para México." *Reforma*, September 3.

Dirdamal, Tin. 2005. *De Nadie*. Mexico City: Producciones Tranvía.

Doty, Roxanne. 2009. *The Law into Their Own Hands: Immigration and the Politics of Exceptionalism*. Tucson: University of Arizona Press.

Doyle, Kate. 2003. "The Dawn of Mexico's Dirty War." National Security Archive, December 5.

Dudley, Steven S. 2011. "Drug Trafficking Organizations in Central America: Transportistas, Mexican Cartels, and Maras." In *Organized Crime in Central America: The Northern Triangle*, ed. Cynthia J. Arnson and Eric L. Olson. Wilson Center Reports on the Americas 29. Washington, D.C.: Woodrow Wilson International Center. 18–61.

———. 2013. "Police Use Brute Force to Break Crime's Hold on Juarez," *InSight Crime*, February 13. http://www.insightcrime.org/juarez-war-stability-and-the-future/brute-force-breaks-crimes-hold-on-juarez.

Due Process of Law Foundation. 2006. "La situación de los derechos humanos y la crisis del estado de derecho en Oaxaca: Carta dirigida a Santiago Cantón, Secretario Ejecutivo de la Comisión Interamericana de Derechos Humanos." Memorandum, Washington, D.C., October 23.

Dunn, Timothy J. 1996. *The Militarization of the U.S.-Mexico Border, 1978–1992: Low Intensity Conflict Doctrine Comes Home*. Austin: Center for Mexican American Studies, University of Texas at Austin.

———. 2001. "Border Militarization via Drug and Immigration Enforcement: Human Rights Implications." *Social Justice* 28, 2: 7–30.

———. 2009. *Blockading the Border and Human Rights: The El Paso Operation That Remade Immigration Enforcement*. Austin: University of Texas Press.

Durbin, Richard. 2010. Opening Statement, Senate Judiciary Committee Subcommittee on Human Rights and the Law, Hearing "Drug Enforcement and the Rule of Law: Mexico and Colombia," May 18.

The Economist. 2010. "Outsmarted by Sinaloa: Why the Biggest Drug Gang Has Been Least Hit." January 7.

Eisenstadt, Todd A. 2004. *Courting Democracy in Mexico: Party Strategies and Electoral Institutions*. New York: Cambridge University Press.

Ellingwood, Ken, and Tracy Wilkinson. 2009. "Drug Cartels' New Weaponry Means War." *Los Angeles Times*, March 15.

Ellis, Mark. 2007. "Breaking the Silence: Rape as an International Crime." *Case Western Reserve Journal of International Law* 38: 225–47.

Emmot, R. 2008. "Drug Smugglers Bribing U.S. Agents on Mexico Border." Reuters, July 15.

Enloe, Cynthia. 2000. *Maneuvers: The International Politics of Militarizing Women's Lives.* Berkeley: University of California Press.

Ensalaco, Mark. 2006. "Murder in Ciudad Juárez: A Parable of Women's Struggle for Human Rights." *Violence Against Women* 12, 5: 417–40.

Eschbach, Karl, Jacqueline Hagan, and Néstor Rodriguez. 2001. "Causes and Trends in Migrant Deaths Along the U.S.-Mexico Border, 1985–1998." WPS 01-4, University of Houston Center for Immigration Research, Houston. http://www.uh .edu/cir/Causes_and_Trends.pdf.

Espach, Ralph, Javier Meléndez Q., Daniel Haering, and Miguel L. Castillo G. 2011. "Organizaciones criminales y tráfico ilícito en las comunidades fronterizas de Guatemala." Report for Center for Naval Analysis IPR15226, Alexandria, Va. http://www.cna.org/research/2011/organizaciones-criminales-y-trafico-ilicito -en-las.

Estévez, Ariadna. 2008. *Human Rights and Free Trade in Mexico: A Discursive and Sociopolitical Perspective.* New York: Palgrave Macmillan.

European Commission. 2001. *Country Strategy Paper (2002–2006): Mexico.* http://ec .europa.eu/external_relations/mexico/csp/02_06_en.pdf.

European Parliament. 2006. "Delegation to the EU-Mexico Joint Parliamentary Committee: Report by Erika Mann, Chairwoman of the Delegation, on the Visit to Mexico (14 to 19 September 2006) for the Committee on Foreign Affairs." October 16.

———. 2007a. "Murder of Women in Mexico and Central America." European Parliament Resolution of 11 October 2007 on the Murder of Women (Feminicide) in Mexico and Central America and the Role of the European Union in Fighting the Phenomenon (2007/2025(INI)). P6_TA (2007)0431, October 11.

———. 2007b. "Report on the Murders of Women (Feminicides) in Central America and Mexico and the Role of the European Union in Fighting This Phenomenon (2007/2025(INI))." A6-0338/2007, September 20.

Fainaru, Steve, and William Booth. 2009. "Mexico Accused of Torture in Drug War: Army Using Brutality to Fight Trafficking, Rights Groups Say." *Washington Post*, World Section, July 9.

Falcón, Sylvanna. 2007. "Rape as a Weapon of War: Militarized Rape at the U.S.-Mexico Border." In *Women and Migration in the U.S.-Mexico Borderlands: A Reader*, ed. Denise A. Segura and Patricia Zavella. Durham, N.C.: Duke University Press.

Faux, Jeff. 2006. *The Global Class War: How America's Bipartisan Elite Lost Our Future—and What It Will Take to Win It Back.* Hoboken, N.J.: Wiley.

Feldmann, Andreas, and Jorge Durand. 2008. "Die-Offs at the Border." *Migración y Desarrollo* 10: 11–35.

Fernández-Kelly, María Patricia. 1983. *For We Are Sold, I and My People: Women and Industry in Mexico's Frontier*. Albany: SUNY Press.

———. 2008. "Gender and Economic Change in the United States and Mexico, 1900–2000." *American Behavioral Scientist* 52: 377–404.

Finkelhor, David, Richard K. Ormrod, and Heather A. Turner. 2007. "Poly-Victimization: A Neglected Component in Child Victimization Trauma." *Child Abuse & Neglect* 31: 7–26.

Forsythe, David. 2000. *Human Rights in International Relations*. Cambridge: Cambridge University Press.

Foucault, Michel. 1977. *Il faut defender la societé: Cours au Collège de France, 1975–1976*. Paris: Seuil.

Fox, Jonathan, and Luis Hernández. 1992. "Mexico's Difficult Democracy: Grassroots Movements, NGOs and Local Government." *Alternatives* 17: 165–208.

Franklin, James C. 2008. "Shame on You: The Impact of Human Rights Criticism on Political Repression in Latin America." *International Studies Quarterly* 52, 1: 187–212.

Freeman, Laurie, and Jorge Luis Sierra. 2005. "Mexico: The Militarization Trap." In *Drugs and Democracy in Latin America: The Impact of U.S. Policy*, ed. Coletta A. Youngsters and Eileen Rosin. Boulder, Colo.: Lynne Rienner. 263–302.

Fregoso, Rosa Linda. 2006. "We Want Them Alive! The Politics and Culture of Human Rights." *Social Identities* 12, 2: 109–38.

Fregoso, Rosa Linda, and Cynthia Bejarano, eds. 2010. *Terrorizing Women: Feminicide in the Americas*. Durham, N.C.: Duke University Press.

Frey, John Carlos. 2012. "Cruelty on the Border." *Salon*, July 20.

Froehling, Oliver. 1997. "The Cyberspace 'War of Ink and Internet' in Chiapas, Mexico." *Geographical Review* 87, 2: 291–307.

Frontera NorteSur. 2010. "Drug Wars in Tamaulipas: Cartels vs. Zetas vs. the Military." Mexidata, *Frontera NorteSur*, March 1.

Fuentes, Jezmin, Henry L'Esperance, Raul Perez, and Caitlin White. 2007. "Impacts of U.S. Immigration Policies on Migration Behavior." In *Impacts of Border Enforcement on Mexican Migration: The View from Sending Communities*, ed. Wayne A. Cornelius and Jessa M. Lewis. La Jolla, Calif.: Center for Comparative Immigration Studies, UCSD. 53–74.

Galtung, Johan. 2005. "Meeting Basic Needs: Peace and Development." In *The Science of Well-Being*, ed. Felicia A. Huppert, Nick Baylis, and Barry Keverne. Oxford: Oxford University Press.

Garduño, Roberto. 2007. "Fracasa la justicia en México; urge atender la impunidad: AI." *La Jornada*, Politics Section, August 4.

Garduño, Silvia. 2008. "Demanda UE respeto a derechos humanos." *Reforma*, May 14.

Gasper, Des. 2005. "Securing Humanity: Situating 'Human Security' as Concept and Discourse." *Journal of Human Development* 6, 2: 221–45.

Gibler, John. 2011. *To Die in Mexico: Dispatches from Inside the Drug War*. San Francisco: City Lights.

Gibney, Mark, L. Cornett, and R. Wood. 2011. *Political Terror Scale 1976–2010*. http://www.politicalterrorscale.org/.

Gil, Melina. 2009. "Mantiene la entidad el segundo lugar en quejas contra militares y policías federales." *Jornada Michoacán*, July 30.

Gilot, Louie. 2007. "28 Deported After Raid on Chaparral Schools." *El Paso Times*, September 15.

Global Commission on Drug Policy. 2011. *War on Drugs: Report of the Global Commission on Drug Policy*. http://www.globalcommissionondrugs.org/wp-content/themes/gcdp_v1/pdf/Global_Commission_Report_English.pdf.

Goddard, Terry. 2009. "Law Enforcement Responses to Mexican Drug Cartels." Testimony to Senate Judiciary Committee Subcommittee on Crime and Drugs and the Senate Caucus on International Narcotics Control, March 17.

Gonzáles, Daniel. 2011. "Migrant Deaths in Arizona Fell in 2011." *Arizona Republic*, December 29.

Gonzales, Alfonso. 2009. "The 2006 Mega-Marchas in Greater Los Angeles: Counter-Hegemonic Moment and the Future of El Migrante Struggle." *Latino Studies* 7, 1: 30–59.

Gonzalez, Juan. 2010. "Bloody Mexico Drug War Boosts U.S. Gun Shops, Banks." *New York Daily News*, August 20.

González Rodríguez, Sergio. 2006. *Huesos en el desierto*. Barcelona: Anagrama.

Government of Mexico. 2009. "Complementary Response of the Government of Mexico to the Recommendations in the Report of the Working Group on the Universal Periodic Review." A/HRC/11/27. http://lib.ohchr.org/HRBodies/UPR/Documents/Session4/MX/A_HRC_11_27_Add1_MEX_E.pdf.

Grayson, George W. 2010. *Mexico: Narco-Violence and a Failed State?* New Brunswick, N.J.: Transaction Publishers.

Grijalva, Raúl. 2011. "Grijalva Joined by More Than 30 Members of Congress in Calling on State Sec. Clinton to Raise Human Rights Concerns with Mexico." Press release. December 2. http://grijalva.house.gov.

———. 2012. "On International Women's Day, Grijalva Calls on Sec. of State Clinton to Ensure Foreign Law Enforcement Aid Protects Women's Rights." Press release, March 8. http://grijalva.house.gov.

Grillo, Ioan. 2012. "Mexico's Zetas Rewrite Drug War in Blood." Reuters, May 23.

———. 2010. "August 25. Descubre la Secretaría de Marina 72 cadáveres en un rancho de Tamaulipas." Section: Política. August 25. http://www.jornada.unam.mx/2010/08/25/ index.php?section=politica&article=017n1pol. Retrieved April 7, 2011

———. 2011a. "Invita SRE a militares estadounidenses a reunión sobre la frontera México-Guatemala-Belice." April 16.

———. 2011a. "April 15. Localizan 23 cadáveres más en fosas clandestinas en Tamaulipas; ya son 145." Section: Política. April 15. http://www.jornada.unam.mx

/2011/04/15/ index.php?section=politica&article=010n1pol. Retrieved April 19, 2011

———. 2011b. April 16. "Invita" SRE a militares estadounidenses a reunión sobre la frontera México-Guatemala-Belice. http://www.jornada.unam.mx/2011/04/16/poli tica/007n2pol. Retrieved July 9, 2011.

———. 2011c. "July 26. Sistemáticas y generalizadas, las agresiones contra migrantes ." July, May 23.

Guerrero Gutierrez, Eduardo. 2011. "La raíz de la violencia." *Nexos*, June 1.

Guidotti-Hernández, Nicole. 2011. *Unspeakable Violence: Remapping U.S. and Mexican National Imaginaries*. Durham, N.C.: Duke University Press.

Gupta, Girish. 2011. "Mexico's Disappeared Women." *New Statesmen*, February 17.

Haddick, Robert. 2010. "This Week at War: Is Mexico's Drug War Doomed?" *Foreign Policy*, August 13.

Hagan, John, and Wenona Rymond-Richmond. 2008. *Darfur and the Crime of Genocide*. New York: Cambridge University Press.

Harvey, David. 2007. *A Brief History of Neoliberalism*. New York: Oxford University Press.

Haugaard, Lisa. 2009. "The Mérida Initiative, U.S. Responsibilities & Human Rights." Testimony, House Committee on Appropriations, Subcommittee on State, Foreign Operations, and Related Programs. March 10..

Hausmann, Ricardo. 2001. "Prisoners of Geography." *Foreign Policy* 122: 44–53.

Hawkins, Darren. 2002. *Human Rights Norms and Networks in Authoritarian Chile*. Lincoln: University of Nebraska Press.

———. 2004. "Explaining Costly International Institutions: Persuasion and Enforceable Human Rights Norms." *International Studies Quarterly* 48, 4: 779–804.

Hawley, Chris. 2009. "Mexico: Gun Controls Undermined by U.S." *U.S.A Today*, March 31.

Hernandez, Anabel. 2003. "The Sex Trafficking of Children in San Diego: Minors Are Prostituted in Farm Labor Camps in San Diego." *El Universal*, Mexico City, January 11.

———. 2010. *Los señores del narco*. Mexico City: Grijalbo Mondadori, SA.

Heyman, Josiah, ed. 1999. *States and Illegal Practices*. New York: Berg.

Hondagneu-Sotelo, Pierrette. 2008. *God's Heart Has No Borders: How Religious Activists Are Working for Immigrant Rights*. Berkeley: University of California Press.

Hsu, Spenser. 2010a. "Arizona Immigration Law Will Boost Crime in U.S. Cities, Police Chiefs Say." *Washington Post*, May 26.

———. 2010b. "Work to Cease on 'Virtual Fence' Along U.S.-Mexico Border." *Washington Post*, March 16.

Human Rights Committee. 2010. *Concluding Observations of the Human Rights Committee: Consideration of Reports Submitted by States Parties under Article 40 of the Covenant, Mexico*. CCPR/C/MEX/CO/5, May 17.

Human Rights Council. 2009. *Report of the Working Group on the Universal Periodic Review: Mexico.* A/HRC/11/27, March 3.

Human Rights Watch (HRW). 2004. "Human Rights Overview. Mexico." http://hrw.org/english/docs/2003/12/31/mexico7006.htm.

———. 2005. *World Report 2005.* New York: Human Rights Watch.

———. 2006a. *Lost in Transition: Bold Ambitions, Limited Results for Human Rights Under Fox.* Washington D.C.: Human Rights Watch.

———. 2006b. "Mexico: Candidates Should Address Murders of Women." Press release, June 27.

———. 2006c. *World Report 2006.* New York: Human Rights Watch.

———. 2007a. "Mexico: Probe Charges of Police Brutality in Oaxaca; Protestors Allege Serious Abuses by Oaxaca Police." Press release, July 24.

———. 2007b. "Mexico: U.S. Should Include Human Rights Conditions." Press release, October 24.

———. 2009a. "Carta respondiéndole al Secratario de Gobernación de México, Fernando Francisco Gómez-Mont Urueta." November 20. http://www.hrw.org/en/news/2009/11/20/carta-respondiendo-al-secratario-de-gobernaci-n-de-m-xico-fer nando-francisco-g-mez-m.

———. 2009b. "Mexico: U.S. Should Withhold Military Aid." July 13. http://www.hrw.org/en/news/2009/07/13/mexico-us-should-withhold-military-aid.

———. 2009c. *Uniform Impunity: Mexico's Misuse of Military Justice to Prosecute Abuses in Counternarcotics and Public Security Operations.* New York: Human Rights Watch.

———. 2011. *Neither Rights Nor Security: Killings, Torture, and Disappearances in Mexico's "War on Drugs."* Washington, D.C.: Human Rights Watch.

Human Rights Watch/Americas. 1995. *United States Crossing the Line: Human Rights Violations Along the U.S. Border with Mexico Persist amid Climate of Impunity.* New York: Human Rights Watch/Americas.

Huntington, Samuel P. 2004. *Who Are We? The Challenges to America's National Identity.* New York: Simon and Schuster.

InSight Crime. 2011a. "Grupos de poder en Petén: Territorio, política y negocios." July. http://www.insightcrime.org/docs/the-peten-report.pdf.

———. 2011b. "Mexico Should Cut Hype over Drug Gang Arrest." August 5. http://insightcrime.org/insight-latest-news/item/1363-mexico-should-cut-hype-over-drug-gang-arrests.

Inter-American Commission on Human Rights (IACHR). 2002. "La Relatora Especial de la CIDH culmina visita para evaluar la situación de los derechos de la mujer en Ciudad Juárez, México." Press release 4/02, February 13. http://www.cidh.org/Comunicados/Spanish/2002/4.02.htm.

———. 2003. *The Situation of the Rights of Women in Ciudad Juárez, México: The Right to Be Free from Violence and Discrimination,* OEA/Ser.L/V/II.117, March 7.

———. 2006. "IACHR Urges Absolute Respect for Human Rights and an End to the Violence in Oaxaca." Press release 39/06, October 31.

———. 2007a. "IACHR Concludes Its 130th Regular Sessions." Press release 54/07, October 19.

———. 2007b. "IACHR Expresses Its Deep Concern for Violence in Oaxaca." Press release 36/07, July 23.

———. 2007c. "IACHR President Urges Investigation into Acts of Violence in Oaxaca." Press release 45/07, August 16.

———. 2007d. *Public Hearings of the 127*[th] *Period of Sessions*. Video available online at http://www.cidh.org/audiencias/select.aspx.

———. 2008a. "CIDH culmina su 133er período de sesiones." Press release 46/08, October 31.

———. 2008b. "Impacto de las políticas de seguridad pública sobre los derechos humanos en México." Public hearing, October 22. Audio recording at http://www .cidh.oas.org/Audiencias/seleccionar.aspx.

———. 2009. "IACHR Concludes Its 134th Regular Sessions." Press release 13/09, March 27.

Inter-American Court of Human Rights. 2008. *Luz Estela Castro Rodríguez et al. v. Mexico*. PM 147/08, June 13.

———. 2009a. *Case of González et al. ("Cotton Field") v. Mexico: Preliminary Objections, Merits, Reparations, and Costs*. Judgment of November 16, 2009, Series C No. 205.

———. 2009b. *Case of Radilla-Pacheco v. Mexico: Preliminary Objections, Merits, Reparations, and Costs*. Judgment of November 23, 2009, Series C No. 209.

———. 2010a. *Case of Cabrera-García and Montiel-Flores v. Mexico: Preliminary Objection, Merits, Reparations, and Costs*. Judgment of November 26, 2010, Series C No. 220.

———. 2010b. *Case of Fernández Ortega et al. v. Mexico: Interpretation of the Judgment of Preliminary Objection, Merits, Reparations, and Costs*. Judgment of August 30, 2010, Series C No. 215.

———. 2010c. *Case of Rosendo Cantú et al. v. Mexico: Interpretation of the Judgment of Preliminary Objection, Merits, Reparations, and Costs*. Judgment of August 31, 2010, Series C No. 216.

International Organization for Migration. 2010. *World Migration Report 2010—The Future of Migration: Building Capacities for Change*. Geneva: IOM Publications.

Isacson, Adam. 2005. "The U.S. Military in the War on Drugs." In *Drugs and Democracy in Latin America: The Impact of U.S. Policy*, ed. Coletta A. Youngsters and Eileen Rosin. Boulder, Colo.: Lynne Rienner. 15–60.

Isacson, Adam, and Maureen Meyer. 2012. "Beyond the Border Buildup: Security and Migrants Along the U.S.-Mexico Border," Washington Office on Latin America and El Colegio de la Frontera Norte, April.

Jacobson, David. 1996. *Rights Across Borders: Immigration and the Decline of Citizenship*. Baltimore: Johns Hopkins University Press.

Jimenez, Maria. 2009. "Humanitarian Crisis at the Border: Migrant Deaths at the U.S.-Mexico Border." San Diego, Calif.: American Civil Liberties Union of San Diego and Imperial Counties; Mexico City: Mexico National Commission of Human Rights. http://www.aclu.org/files/pdfs/immigrants/humanitariancrisisreport.pdf.

Jiménez, Tómas R., and Laura López-Sanders. 2011. "Unanticipated, Unintended, and Unadvised: The Effects of Public Policy on Unauthorized Immigration." *Pathways*. Stanford University Center for the Study of Poverty and Inequality.

Johnson, Simon. 2010. *13 Bankers: The Wall Street Takeover and the Next Financial Meltdown*. New York: Pantheon.

La Jornada. 2003. "México, Frontera de Represión y Sufrimiento para Migrantes Indocumentados." October 3.

———. 2010. "Descubre la Secretaría de Marina 72 cadáveres en un rancho de Tamaulipas." August 25.

———. 2011a. "Invita SRE a militares estadounidenses a reunión sobre la frontera México-Guatemala-Belice." April 16.

———. 2011b. "Localizan 23 cadáveres más en fosas clandestinas en Tamaulipas; ya son 145." April 15.

———. 2011c. "Sistemáticas y generalizadas, las agresiones contra migrantes." July 26.

Justice in Mexico Project. 2010. "June 2010 News Report." Trans-Border Institute, University of San Diego. http://catcher.sandiego.edu/items/peacestudies/june2010.pdf.

Kagan, J. 2005. "Worker's Rights in the Mexican Maquiladora Sector." *Journal of Transnational Law and Policy* 15, 1: 153–80.

Keck, Margaret, and Kathryn Sikkink. 1998. *Activists Across Borders: Advocacy Networks in International Politics*. Ithaca, N.Y.: Cornell University Press.

Khagram, Sanjeev, James V. Riker, and Kathryn Sikkink, eds. 2002. *Restructuring World Politics: Transnational Social Movements, Networks, and Norms*. Minneapolis: University of Minnesota Press.

Kilmer, Beau et al. 2010. *Reducing Drug-Trafficking Revenues and Violence in Mexico: Would Legalizing Marijuana in California Help?* Santa Monica, Calif.: Rand Corporation.

King, Mary C. 2007. "Even Gary Becker Wouldn't Call Them Altruists! The Case of Mexican Migration: A Reply to Sana and Massey, SSQ June 2005." *Social Science Quarterly* 88: 898–907.

Konrad, Victor. 2011. "Extended Transitions Versus Security Spillover: Building the Trap of Expanded Enforcement." Paper presented at American Borderlands Association Annual Meeting, Salt Lake City, Utah.

Kopel, David. 2009. "Mexico." In *Guns in American Society: An Encyclopedia of History, Politics, Culture, and the Law*. http://davekopel.org/Esanol/Mexican-Gun-Laws.html.

Kopinak, Kathryn, ed. 2004. *The Social Costs of Industrial Growth in Northern Mexico*. La Jolla: University of California at San Diego Center for U.S.-Mexican Studies; distributed Boulder, Colo.: Lynne Rienner.

Koulish, Robert. 2010. *Immigration and American Democracy: Subverting the Rule of Law*. New York: Routledge.

Krikorian, Mark. 2005. "Downsizing Illegal Immigration: A Strategy of Attrition Through Enforcement." Center for Immigration Studies, May 26.

LAND Blog. 2011. "Mexico: Activists File Complaint Against Calderón For Drug War Human Rights Violations," October 12.

Landau, Saul. 2005. "Globalization, Maquilas, NAFTA, and the State." *Journal of Developing Societies* 21, 3/4: 9.Latin American Commission on Drugs and Democracy. 2009. *Toward a Paradigm Shift*. www.cfr.org.

Latin American Herald Tribune. 2011. "ICC Won't Take Up Case of Mexico's Drug War." November 4.

Latin America Working Group (LAWG). 2011. "Congress Weighs in on Human Rights Defenders Protection Mechanism in Mexico." December 18. http://www.lawg.org/action-center/lawg-blog/79/971.

Lavenex, Sandra, and Emek C. Ucarer. 2002. "The Emergent EU Migration Regime and Its External Impact." In *Migration and the Externalities of European Integration*, ed. Sandra Lavenex and Emek C. Ucarer. Lanham, Md.: Lexington Books.

Leahy, Patrick. 2009. Press release, August 5. http://www.leahy.senate.gov/press/comments-on-state-department-and-foreign-operations-on-the-provisions-in-law-that-he-authored-concerning-the-Mérida-initiative.

Lebovic, James H., and Erik Voeten. 2006. "The Politics of Shame: The Condemnation of Country Human Rights Practices in the UNHHR." *International Studies Quarterly* 50, 4: 868–70.

78th Legislature of the State of Texas, H.C.R. 59. (2003). http://texinfo.library.unt.edu/sessionlaws/78thsession/bills/HCR59.pdf.

Leiken, Robert, and Steven Brooke. 2006. "The Quantitative Analysis of Terrorism and Immigration: An Initial Exploration." *Terrorism and Political Violence* 18, 4: 503–21.

Liotta, Peter H. 2002. "Boomerang Effect: The Convergence of National and Human Security." *Security Dialogue* 33, 4: 473–88.

Lipsky, Michael. 1980. *Street-Level Bureaucracy*. New York: Russell Sage.

Livesey, Bruce. 2010. "Trafficking in Power: Narcoterror in Mexico." *National Post*, June 12.

Logan, Samuel, and John P. Sullivan. 2010. "Violence in Mexico: A Bloody Reshuffling of Drug Cartels." Mexidata, *Frontera NorteSur*, April 12.

López-González, Gloria. 2005. *Erotic Journeys: Mexican Immigrant Women and Their Sex Lives*. Berkeley: University of California Press.

López-Hoffman, L., E. McGovern, R. G. Varady, and K. W. Flessa, eds. 2009. *Conservation of Shared Environments: Learning from the United States and Mexico*. Tucson: University of Arizona Press.

Lovenduski, Joni. 1998. "Gendering Research in Political Science." *Annual Review of Political Science* 1, 1: 333–56.

Lumpe, Lora. 1997. "The U.S. Arms Both Sides of Mexico's Drug War." *Covert Action Quarterly* 61: 39–46.

Lutz, Ellen L. 1993. "Human Rights in Mexico: Cause for Continuing Concern." *Current History* 92, 571: 78–82.

Mann, Erika. 2006. "Las relaciones entre Mexico y la Unión Europea." Manuscript. Consulted at http://erikamann.com/themen/transatlantischebe/diebeziehungen dere/SpanischeVersion.

Manz, Beatriz. 2008. "The Continuum of Violence in Post-War Guatemala." *Social Analysis* 52, 2: 151–64.

Marosi, Richard. 2011. "Unraveling Mexico's Sinaloa Drug Cartel." *Los Angeles Times*, July 24.

Martín Alvarez, Alberto, and Ana Fernández Zubieta. 2009. "Human Rights Violations: Central American Immigrants at the Northeastern Mexico Border." In *Human Rights Along the U.S.-Mexico Border*, ed. Kathleen Staudt, Tony Payan, and Z. Anthony Kruszewski. Tucson: University of Arizona Press, 48–62.

Martínez, Óscar. 2009a. "Migración centroamericana, dominio Z." *Proceso*, September 6: 6–11.

———. 2009b. "Nosotros somos Los Zetas." *Elfaro*, August 24. Martínez-Cabrera, Alejandro. 2012. "Juárez Slayings Decreased 59.8% First Half 2012." *El Paso Times*, July 14.

Massey, Douglas S. 2005. "Beyond the Border Buildup: Towards a New Approach to Mexico-U.S. Migration." *Immigration Policy in Focus* 4, 22 (September): 1–11.

———. 2006. "The Wall That Keeps Illegal Workers In." *New York Times*, April 4.

———. 2007. "When Less Is More: Border Enforcement and Undocumented Migration." Testimony (Written Statement) before Subcommittee on Immigration, Citizenship, Refugees, Border Security, and International Law Committee on the Judiciary, U.S. House, April 20.

Massey, Douglas S., Jorge Durand, and Nolan J. Malone. 2002. *Beyond Smoke and Mirrors: Mexican Immigration in an Era of Economic Integration*. New York: Russell Sage.

Mbembe, Achille. 2003. "Necropolitics." *Public Culture* 15, 1: 11–40.

McCombs, Brady. 2011. "Immigrant Arrests Nearing 40-Year Low." *Arizona Daily Star*, September 4.

McConahay, Mary Jo. 2006. "Soldiers on the Border." *Texas Observer*, September 8.

McKinley, James C., Jr. 2009. "U.S. Gun Dealers Arming Mexican Drug Cartels." *New York Times*, December 6.

Mendoza, Martha. 2010. "U.S. Withholding Aid to Mexico over Human-Rights Abuses." Associated Press, September 3.

Menjívar, Cecilia. 2007 "Serving Christ in the Border Lands: Faith Workers Respond to Border Violence." In *Religion and Social Justice for Immigrants*, ed. Pierrette Hondagneu-Sotelo. New Brunswick, N.J.: Rutgers University Press. 104–21.

Merry, Sally. 2006. *Human Rights & Gender Violence: Translating International Law into Local Justice*. Chicago: University of Chicago Press.

Mexico Solidarity Network. 2005. *Femicides of Ciiudad Juárez and Chihuahua*. Washington, D.C.: Mexico Solidarity Network.

Meyer, Maureen. 2011. "Historic Human Rights Reforms Passed in the Mexican Senate; Now State Congresses Should Follow Suit." *Al Día*, March 16.

———. 2012. "Human Rights in Mexico," Testimony before House of Representatives Tom Lantos Human Rights Commission, May 10.

Meyer, Maureen, with contributions from Stephanie Brewer and Carlos Cepeda. 2010. "Abused and Afraid in Ciudad Juárez: An Analysis of the Human Rights Violations by the Military in Mexico." Washington Office on Latin America, September.

Milenio. 2008. "Respalda la permanente el rechazo al plan Mérida." June 6.

———. 2009. "En Mexico ya son 980 zonas de impunidad." June 2.

Monárrez Fragoso, Julia. 2000. "La cultura del feminicidio en Ciudad Juárez, 1993–1999." *Frontera Norte* 12.

———. 2002. "Femincidio Sexual Serial en Ciudad Juárez: 1993–2001." *Debate Feminista* 25: 279–308.

Morales, Maria Cristina, and Cynthia Bejarano. 2009. "Transnational Sexual and Gendered Violence: An Application of Border Sexual Conquest at a Mexico-U.S. Border." *Global Networks* 9, 3: 420–39.

Morfín, Guadalupe. 2004. *Informe de gestión: Noviembre 2003–abril 2004*. Juárez City: Comisión para Prevenir y Eradicar la Violence Contra las Mujeres in Ciudad Juárez, Secretaría de Gobernación (SEGOB).

Moyn, Samuel. 2010. *The Last Utopia: Human Rights in History*. Cambridge, Mass.: Harvard University Press.

Mueller, Carol, and Stanley Buzzelle. 2005. "Feminism Meets Human Rights: The Valentine Day March into Ciudad Juárez." Paper presented at Annual Meeting of the International Studies Association, Honolulu, Hawaii.

Mueller, Carol, Michelle Hansen, and Karen Qualtire. 2009. "Femicide on the Border and New Forms of Protest: The International Caravan for Justice." In *Violence, Security, and Human Rights at the U.S./Mexico Border*, ed. Kathleen Staudt, Tony Payan, and Tony Kruszewski. Tucson: University of Arizona Press. 125–49.

Naciones Unidas—Centro de Información para México, Cuba y República Dominicana (CINU). 2006a. "Condena los actos violentos sucedidos en el Estado de Oaxaca el 27 de octubre de 2006." Press bulletin ONU 06/118, October 28.

———. 2006b. "Llamado a generar un clima propicio en el Estado de Oaxaca que facilite las negociaciones." Press bulletin ONU 06/100, September 11.

Nadelmann, Ethan. 2012. "Drug Legalization Debate Continues to Escalate in Latin America." Drug Policy Alliance, July 30.

Naím, Moisés. 2005. *Illicit: How Smugglers, Traffickers, and Copycats Are Hijacking the Global Economy*. New York: Random House.

Narayan, Uma. 1997. *Dislocating Cultures: Identities, Traditions, and Third World Feminism.* New York: Routledge.

National Drug Intelligence Center. 2008. *National Drug Threat Assessment 2009.* U.S. Department of Justice.

Nef, Jorge. 1999. *Human Security and Mutual Vulnerability: The Global Political Economy of Development and Underdevelopment.* Ottawa: International Development Research Centre.

Nevins, Joseph. 2008. *Dying to Live: A Story of U.S. Immigration in an Age of Global Apartheid.* San Francisco: City Lights Books.

———. 2010. *Operation Gatekeeper and Beyond: The War on "Illegals" and the Remaking of the U.S.-Mexico Boundary.* 2nd ed. New York: Routledge.

New York Daily News. 2011. "27 Killed in Massacre in Northern Guatemala; Farm Workers Beheaded in Lawless Border Region." May 16.

New York Times. 2009. "The Nativists Are Restless." January 31.

No More Deaths. 2008. *Crossing the Line: Human Rights Abuses of Migrants in Short-Term Custody on the Arizona/Sonora Border.* Tucson, Ariz.: No More Deaths. http://nomoredeaths.org/Border-Patrol-Abuse-Report/.

———. 2011. "A Culture of Cruelty: Abuse and Impunity in Short-Term U.S. Border Patrol Custody." http://www.nomoredeaths.org/cultureofcruelty.html.

Nordstrom, Carolyn. 2001. "Out of the Shadows." In *Intervention and Transnationalism in Africa: Global-Local Networks of Power,* ed. Thomas Callaghy, Ronald Kassimir, and Robert Latham. Cambridge: Cambridge University Press. 216–39.

———. 2006. *Global Outlaws.* Berkeley: University of California.

Notimex. 2003. "Proponen abordar muertas de ciudad Juárez en binacional México-EU." October 16.

Nuñez, Guillermina Gina, and Josiah Heyman. 2007. "Entrapment Processes and Immigrant Communities in a Time of Heightened Border Vigilance." *Human Organization* 66, 4: 354–65.

Nuñez-Neto, Blas. 2008. "Border Security: The Role of the U.S. Border Patrol." November 20. Congressional Research Service (CRS) Report for Congress, RL32562, November 20.

Nuñez-Neto, Blas, and Michael John Garcia. 2007. "Border Security: Border Barriers Along the U.S. International Border." Congressional Research Service (CRS) Report for Congress, RL33659. June 5.

Oberleitner, Gerd. 2005. "Human Security: A Challenge to International Law?" *Global Governance* 11: 185–203.

Oboler, Suzanne, ed. 2006. *Latinos and Citizenship: The Dilemma of Belonging.* New York: Palgrave Macmillan.

Ochoa O'Leary, Anna. 2009. "In the Footsteps of Spirits: Migrant Women's Testimonios in a Time of Heightened Border Enforcement." In *Human Rights Along the U.S.-Mexico Border,* ed. Kathleen Staudt, Tony Payan, and Z. Anthony Kruszewski. Tucson: University of Arizona Press, 85–104.

Olivares Alonso, Emir. 2006. "Grave, no indagar las muertes ocurridas durante el conflicto en Oaxaca: CCIODH." *La Jornada*, Politics Section, December 29.

Olson, Eric. 2009. "Police Reform and Modernization in Mexico, 2009." Mexico Institute, Woodrow Wilson International Center for Scholars, Washington, D.C., September. www.wilsoncenter.org/Mérida.

Olson, Joy. 2009. Testimony before the House Subcommittee on State, Foreign Operations, and Related Programs, Hearing "The Mérida Initiative," March 10. http://democrats.appropriations.house.gov/index.php?option=com_jcalpro&Itemid=179&extmode=view&extid=1811.

O'Reilly, Andrew. 2012. "Mexico's Drug Death Toll Double What Reported, Expert Argues." *Fox News*, August 10.

Orrenius, Pia M. 2006. "The Effect of U.S. Border Enforcement on the Crossing Behaviors of Mexican Migrants." In *Crossing the Border: Research from the Mexican Migration Project*, ed. Jorge Durand and Douglas S. Massey. New York: Russell Sage Foundation. 281–98.

Osberg, Carson. 2010. "Inter-American Court Holds That Mexico Violated the Human Rights of Two Women Raped by Mexican Military Personnel." Center for Human Rights and Humanitarian Law, November 16.

Osorno, Diego Enrique. 2012. *La guerra de los Zetas*, Mexico City: Grijalbo.

Papademetiou, Demetrios G., and Elizabeth Collett. 2011. "A New Architecture for Border Management." The Transatlantic Council on Migration, Migration Policy Institute, Washington, D.C., March.

Passel, Jeffrey S. 2005. "Estimates of the Size and Characteristics of the Undocumented Population." Pew Hispanic Center Report, March 21.

Passel, Jeffrey S., and D'Vera Cohn. 2009. "A Portrait of Unauthorized Immigrants in the United States." Washington, D.C.: Pew Hispanic Center.

Passel, Jeffrey S., D'Vera Cohn, and Ana Gonzales-Barrera. 2012. "Net Migration from Mexico Falls to Zero—and Perhaps Less 2012." Pew Hispanic Center Report, April 23. http://www.pewhispanic.org/files/2012/04/Mexican-migrants-report_final.pdf.

Payan, Tony. 2006. *The Three U.S.-Mexico Border Wars: Drugs, Immigration, and Homeland Security*. New York: Praeger.

Pearce, Jenny. 1998. "From Civil War to 'Civil Society': Has the End of the Cold War Brought Peace to Central America?" *International Affairs* 74, 3: 587–615.

El Periódico. 2010. "Enfrentamientos entre narcotraficantes y fuerzas de seguridad genera caos en aldeas de Petén." País. *El Periódico*, October 7.

———. 2012. "Los Zetas dejan mantas con amenazas a la población civil." País. *El Periódico*, March 21.

Portes, Alejandro, and Rubén Rumbaut. 1996. *Immigrant America: A Portrait*. 2nd ed. Berkeley: University of California Press.

Portillo, Ernesto, Jr. 2010. "Cop Had to Take Stand and Fight SB 1070." *Arizona Daily Star*, May 9.

Power, Samantha. 2009. "The Enforcer: A Christian Lawyer's Global Crusade." *New Yorker*, January 19, 52–63.

Prensa Libre. 2011a. "Conferencia Internacional de Apoyo a la Estrategia de Seguridad de Centroamérica. Multimedia." June 22.

———. 2011b. "México, Guatemala y Belice analizan fronteras junto a EE.UU." April 15. http://www.prensalibre.com/noticias/justicia/fronteras-Mexico-Guatemala-Belice-EE-_UU-analisis-seguridad-narcotrafico_0_463153937.html.

Presidencia de la República—Press Room. 2007a. "Joint Press Conference Given by President Calderón and Mr. Romano Prodi, Prime Minister of Italy." June 4.

———. 2007b. "President Calderón Receives Amnesty International Secretary General." Press release, August 7.

———. 2011. "El Presidente Calderón en la Entrega del Premio Nacional de Derechos Humanos 2011." December 9.

Programa Sectorial de Defensa Nacional, Secretaría de la Defensa Nacional. 2007. http://www.sedena.gob.mx/pdf/psdn.pdf.

ProPublica.org. 2012. "The New Border: Illegal Immigration's Shifting Frontier." December 6. http://www.propublica.org/article/the-new-border-illegal-immigrations-shifting-frontier.

Radford, Lorraine, and Kaname Tsutsumi. 2004. "Globalization and Violence Against Women—Inequalities in Risks, Responsibilities, and Blame in the UK and Japan." *Women's Studies International Forum* 27, 1: 1–12.

Radio Netherlands Worldwide. 2011. "Billion-Dollar Pledge for Central America Security." June 23. http://www.rnw.nl/english/bulletin/billion-dollar-pledges-central-america-security.

Ramji-Nogales, Jaya, Andrew I. Schoenholtz, and Philip G. Schrag. 2007. "Refugee Roulette: Disparities in Asylum Adjudication." *Stanford Law Review* 60: 295.

Ramsey, Geoffrey. 2012. "Study: U.S. Marijuana Legalization Could Cut Cartel Profits by 30%." *InSight Crime*, November 5. http://www.insightcrime.org/news-analysis/study-legalization-cut-cartel-profits-by-30.

Rappleye, Hannah, and Lisa Riordan Seville. 2012. "Deadly Crossing: Death Toll Rises Among Those Desperate for the American Dream." NBC News, October 9.

Razack, Sherene H. 2005. "How Is White Supremacy Embodied? Sexualized Racial Violence at Abu Ghraib." *Canadian Journal of Women & the Law* 17: 341–63.

Reuters. 2007. "Indaga AI nuevas denuncias de abusos castrenses." *La Jornada*, Politics Section, June 1.

———. 2012. "Mexico Admits Mistake in High-Profile Drug Case." June 23.

Reyes, Belinda I. 2004. "U.S. Immigration Policy and the Duration of Undocumented Trips." In *Crossing the Border: Research from the Mexican Migration Project*, ed. Jorge Durand and Douglas S. Massey. New York: Russell Sage Foundation. 299–320.

Risse, Thomas, Stephen C. Ropp, and Kathryn Sikkink. 1999. *The Power of Human Rights: International Norms and Domestic Change*. Cambridge: Cambridge University Press.

Robertson, R. 1995. "Glocalization: Time-Space and Homogeneity-Heterogeneity." In *Global Modernities*, ed. M. Featherstone, S. Lash, and R. Robertson. London: Sage. 25–44.

Robles de la Rosa, Leticia. 2009. "Rechazan que EU certifique al país." *Excélsior*, July 29.

Rodgers, Dennis. 2009. "Slum Wars of the 21st Century: Gangs, *Mano Dura*, and the New Urban Geography of Conflict in Central America." *Development and Change* 40, 5: 949–76.

Rodríguez, Néstor. 1996. "The Battle for the Border: Notes on Autonomous Migration, Transnational Communities, and the State." *Social Justice* 23, 3: 21–37.

Rodriguez, Olga R., and Michael Weissenstein. 2012. "Joe Biden Mexico Visit: Calderón Asks Vice President to Stop U.S. Arms, Money Flow." *Huffington Post*, March 5.

Rodriguez, Kat. 2013. Coalición de Derechos Humanos press release. Tucson, March 7.

Roebuck, Jeremy. 2010a. "Authorities: Gulf Cartel, Zetas Gang Up on Each Other as Arrangement Dies." *The Monitor*, March 10.

———. 2010b. "Feds: Pharr Officer Assisted Zeta Kidnapping Ring." *The Monitor*, March 3.

Rose, Amanda. 2012. *Showdown in the Sonoran Desert: Religion, Law, and the Immigration Controversy.* New York: Oxford University Press.

Rosenblum, Mark R. 2012. "Border Security: Immigration Enforcement Between Ports of Entry." Congressional Research Service, Washington, D.C., January 6.

Rubio-Goldsmith, Raquel, M. Melissa McCormick, Daniel Martinez, and Inez Magdalena Duarte. 2006. "The 'Funnel Effect' & Recovered Bodies of Unauthorized Migrants Processed by the Pima County Office of the Medical Examiner, 1990–2005." Border Migration Institute, Mexican American Studies & Research Center, University of Arizona, October. http://www.ailf.org/ipc/policybrief/policybrief/_020607.pdf.

Ruiz Marrujo, Olivia T. 2009. "Women, Migration, and Sexual Violence: Lessons from Mexico's Borders." In *Human Rights Along the U.S.-Mexico Border*, ed. Kathleen Staudt, Tony Payan, and Z. Anthony Kruszewski. Tucson: University of Arizona Press.

Russell, Diane E. H., and Roberta A. Harmes, eds. 2001. *Femicide in Global Perspective.* New York: Teacher's College Press.

Ryerson, Christie R. 2008. "The Human Security Dilemma: Lost Opportunities, Appropriate Concepts, or Actual Change?" In *Environmental Change and Human Security: Recognizing and Acting on Hazard Impacts*, ed. Peter H. Liotta, David A. Mouat, William G. Kepner, and Judith M. Lancaster. Dordrecht: NATO Science for Peace and Security Series C-Environmental Security, Springer.

Rytina, Nancy, and John Simanski. 2009. "Apprehensions by the U.S. Border Patrol." Fact Sheet, June. Department of Homeland Security, Office of Immigration Statistics. http://www.dhs.gov/files/statistics/publications/#4.

Salgado, Agustín. 2007. "ONU: Deben comparecer ante la justicia civil." *La Jornada*, June 13.

Saliba, Armando. 2002. "UN Opens Human Rights Office in Mexico: Asks Government to Fulfill Promises." TheNewsMexico.com, *Reforma*, July 2.

Sampson, Robert J. 2008. "Rethinking Crime and Immigration." *Contexts* 7, 1: 28–33.

Sassen, Saskia. 1996. *Losing Control? Sovereignty in an Age of Globalization.* New York: Columbia University Press.

———. 1998. *Globalization and Its Discontents: Essays on the New Mobility of People and Money.* New York: New Press.

———. 2006. *Territory, Authority, and Rights: From Medieval to Global Assemblages.* Princeton, N.J.: Princeton University Press.

———. 2007. *A Sociology of Globalization.* New York: Norton.

Schatz, Sara. 2008. "Disarming the Legal System: Impunity for the Political Murder of Dissidents in Mexico." *International Criminal Justice Review* 18, 3: 261–91.

Scott, Robert E., Jeff Faux, and Carlos Salas. 2006. *Revisiting NAFTA: Still Not Working for American Workers.* Washington, D.C.: Economic Policy Institute.

Seelke, Clare Ribando. 2009. "Mérida Initiative for Mexico and Central America: Funding and Policy Issues." Congressional Research Service Report for Congress, R40135, August 21.

Seelke, Clare Ribando, and Kristin M. Finklea. 2012. "U.S.-Mexican Security Cooperation: The Mérida Initiative and Beyond." Congressional Research Service Report R41349, February 13.

Segura, Denise A., and Patricia Zavella. 2007. *Women and Migration in the U.S.-Mexico Borderlands: A Reader.* Durham, N.C.: Duke University Press.

Serrano, R. 2008. "U.S. Guns Arm Mexican Cartels." *Los Angeles Times*, August 10.

Shear, Michael D., and Randal C. Archibold, 2013. "Obama Arrives in Mexican Capital to Meet With New Leader," *The New York Times*, May 2.

Shelley, Louise I. 1999. "Transnational Organized Crime: The New Authoritarianism." In *The Illicit Global Economy and State Power*, ed. H. Richard Friman and Peter Andreas. Lanham, Md..: Rowman and Littlefield. 25–51.

Sikkink, Kathryn. 1993. "Human Rights, Principled Issue Networks, and Sovereignty in Latin America." *International Organization* 47, 3: 411–41.

———. 2004. *Mixed Signals: U.S. Human Rights Policy and Latin America.* Ithaca, N.Y.: Cornell University Press.

Simmons, Beth. 2009. *Mobilizing for Human Rights: International Law in Domestic Politics.* Cambridge: Cambridge University Press.

Simmons, William Paul. 2011. *Human Rights Law and the Marginalized Other.* New York: Cambridge University Press.

Simmons, William Paul, Cecilia Menjívar, and Michelle Téllez. Forthcoming. "Violence and Vulnerability of Female Migrants in Drop Houses in Arizona: The Predictable Outcome of a Chain Reaction of Violence," *Violence Against Women.*

Sjoberg, Gideon. 1996. "The Human Rights Challenge to Communitarianism: Formal Organizations and Race and Ethnicity." In *Macro Socio-Economics*, ed. David Sciulli. Armonk, N.Y.: M.E. Sharpe. 273–97.

———. 1999. "Some Observations on Bureaucratic Capitalism: Knowledge About What and Why?" In *Sociology for the Twenty-First Century: Continuities and Cutting Edges*, ed. Janet L. Abu-Lughod. Chicago: University of Chicago Press. 43–64.

———. 2009. "Corporations and Human Rights." In *Interpreting Human Rights: Social Science Perspectives*, ed. Rhiannon Morgan and Bryan S. Turner. New York: Routledge. 157–76.

Sjoberg, Gideon, Elizabeth Gill, and Norma Williams. 2001. "A Sociology of Human Rights." *Social Problems* 48, 1: 11–47.

Small Arms Survey. 2012. *The Small Arms Survey 2012: Moving Targets*. Geneva: Graduate Institute of International Studies.

Smith, Jackie. 2004. "Transnational Processes and Movements." in *The Blackwell Companion to Social Movements*, ed. David Snow et al. London: Blackwell. 311–37.

Smith, Jackie, Charles Chatfield, and Ron Pagnucco, eds. 1997. *Transnational Social Movements: Solidarity Beyond the State*. Syracuse, N.Y.: Syracuse University Press.

Smith, Peter H. 1999. "Semi-Organized International Crime: Drug Trafficking in Mexico." In *Transnational Crime in the Americas*, ed. Tom Farer. New York: Routledge. 193–216.

Smith, Peter, and Melissa Ziegler. 2008. "Liberal and Illiberal Democracy in Latin America." *Latin American Politics and Society* 50, 1: 31–57.

Somers, Margaret R. 2008. *Genealogies of Citizenship: Markets, Statelessness, and the Right to Have Rights*. Cambridge: Cambridge University Press.

Soysal, Yasemin Nuhoglu. 1994. *Limits of Citizenship: Migrants and Postnational Membership in Europe*. Chicago: University of Chicago Press.

Special Rapporteur on Extrajudicial, Summary, or Arbitrary Executions. 1999. *Report of the Special Rapporteur on Extrajudicial, Summary or Arbitrary Executions, Ms. Asma Jahangir, Submitted Pursuant to Commission on Human Rights Resolution 1999/35: Addendum, Visit to Mexico*. E/CN.4/2000/3/Add.3, November 25.

Special Rapporteur on the Independence of Judges and Lawyers. 2002. *Report of the Special Rapporteur on the Independence of Judges and Lawyers, Dato'Param Cumaraswamy, Submitted in Accordance with Commission on Human Rights Resolution 2001/39: Addendum, Report on the Mission to Mexico*. E/CN.4/2002/72/Add.1, January 24.

Spener, David. 2009. *Clandestine Crossings: Migrants and Coyotes on the Texas-Mexico Border*. Ithaca, NY: Cornell University Press.

Stack, Jeremy. 2013. "In the Shadow of the Wall: Family Separation, Immigration, Enforcement, and Security." Tucson: Center for Latin American Studies, University of Arizona.

Staudt, Kathleen 1982. "Bureaucratic Resistance to Women's Programs." In *Women, Power, and Policy*, ed. Ellen Boneparth. New York: Pergamon Press. 263–82.

———. 1985. *Women, Foreign Assistance, and Advocacy Administration*. New York: Praeger.

———. 2008. *Violence and Activism at the Border: Gender, Fear, and Everyday Life in Ciudad Juárez*. Austin: University of Texas Press.

———. 2009. "Violence at the Border: Broadening the Discourse to Include Feminism, Human Security, and Deeper Democracy." In *Human Rights Along the U.S-Mexico Border: Gendered Violence and Insecurity*, ed. Kathleen Staudt, Tony Payan, and Z. Anthony Kruszewski. Tucson: University of Arizona Press. 1–27.

———. Forthcoming. "Bordering the Other in the U.S. Southwest: El Pasoans Confront the Sheriff." In *Keeping Out the Other: Immigration Enforcement Today*, ed. Philip Kretsedemas and David Brotherton. New York: Columbia University Press. 291–313.

Staudt, Kathleen, and Irasema Coronado. 2003. *Fronteras no Más: Toward Social Justice at the U.S.-Mexico Border*. New York: Palgrave U.S.A.

———. 2007. "Binational Civic Action for Accountability: Antiviolence Organizing in Cd. Juaréz-El Paso." In *Reforming the Administration of Justice in Mexico*, ed. Wayne A. Cornelius and David A. Shirk. Notre Dame, Ind.: University of Notre Dame Press.

Staudt, Kathleen, and Zulma Méndez. 2014. *Courage, Resistance, and Women in Ciudad Juárez: Transnational Challenges to Militarization*. Austin: University of Texas Press.

Staudt, Kathleen, César Fuentes, and Julia Monárrez Fragoso, eds. 2010. *Cities and Citizenship at the U.S.-Mexico Border: The Paso del Norte Metropolitan Region*. New York: Palgrave.

Staudt, Kathleen, Tony Payan, and Z. Anthony Kruszewski. 2009. *Human Rights Along the U.S-Mexico Border: Gendered Violence and Insecurity*. Tucson: University of Arizona Press.

Staudt, Kathleen, and Rosalba Robles. 2010. "Surviving Domestic Violence in the Paso del Norte Metropolitan Region." In *Cities and Citizenship at the U.S.-Mexico Border: The Paso del Norte Metropolitan Region*, ed. Kathleen Staudt, César Fuentes, and Julia Monárrez Fragoso. New York: Palgrave. 71–90.

Stohl, Rachel, and Doug Tuttle. 2008. "The Small Arms Trade in Latin America." *The Defense Monitor: The Newsletter of the Center for Defense Information* 37, 3: 8–9.

Sullivan, Mark P., and June S. Beittel. 2008. *Mexico-U.S. Relations: Issues for Congress*. Congressional Research Service, RL32724, December 18.

Tancredo, Tom. 2009. "Why the Lies About Guns Going to Mexico?" *Human Events*, April 30.

Tanfani, Joseph, and Brian Bennett. 2013. "Border 'Surge' Plan would be Financial Bonanza for Private Firms," *Los Angeles Times*, July 8.

Thomas, Daniel C. 2002. "Human Rights in U.S. Foreign Policy." In *Restructuring World Politics: Transnational Social Movements, Networks, and Norms*, ed. Sanjeev Khagram, James V. Riker, and Kathryn Sikkink. Minneapolis: University of Minnesota Press. 71–95.

Thomson, Adam. 2007. "U.S. Must Help More in Drug War, Says Calderón." *Financial Times*, January 18.

Tilly, Charles. 2008. *Contentious Performances*. New York: Cambridge University Press.

Tlachinolan Human Rights Center. 2012. "Ejército se opone a una sentencia histórica en materia de derechos humanos." Press release, January 29.

Tom Lantos Human Rights Commission. 2012. Hearing notice. http://tlhrc.house.gov /hearing_notice.asp?id=1229.

Toro, María Celia. 1995. *Mexico's "War" on Drugs: Causes and Consequences*. Boulder, Colo.: Lynne Rienner.

Torres Ruiz, Luis Bernardo. 2011. "Mexican Maquiladoras: Evidence from Plant-Level Panel Data." Ph.D. dissertation, University of Colorado at Boulder.

Towns, Edolphus. 2009. Opening Statement, Committee on Oversight and Government Reform, Hearing "The Rise of the Mexican Drug Cartels and U.S. National Security," July 9. http://oversight.house.gov/images/stories/documents/20090709093736.pdf.

Turner, Bryan S. 1993. "Outline of a Theory of Human Rights." In *Citizenship and Social Theory*, ed. B. Turner. London: Sage Publications. 162–90.

———. 2006. *Vulnerability and Human Rights*. University Park: Pennsylvania State University Press.

———. 2009. "A Sociology of Citizenship and Human Rights: Does Social Theory Still Exist?" In *Interpreting Human Rights: Social Science Perspectives*, ed. Rhiannon Morgan and Bryan S. Turner. New York: Routledge. 177–99.

Turner, Heather, David Finkelhor, and Richard Ormrod. 2006. "The Effect of Lifetime Victimization on the Mental Health of Children and Adolescents." *Social Science & Medicine* 62, 1: 13–27.

Ugarte, Marisa B., Laura Zarate, and Melissa Farley. 2003. "Prostitution and Trafficking of Women and Children from Mexico to the United States." *Journal of Trauma Practice* 2, 3/4: 147–65.

United Nations. 2008. *World Drug Report 2008*. Vienna: UN Publication Office.

UN Human Rights Commission (UNHRC). 2005. "Set of Principles for the Protection and Promotion of Human Rights Through Action to Combat Impunity." http:// derechos.org/nizkov/impu/principles.html.

———. 2008. *Report of the Special Rapporteur on the Human Rights of Migrants*, U.N. Doc. A/HRC/7/12/Add.2, March 5 (prepared by Jorge Bustamante, Mission to the United States of America).

UN Office of the High Commissioner of Human Rights (UNHCHR). 2003. *Diagnóstico sobre la situación de derechos humanos en México*. Oficina del Alto Comisionado de las Naciones Unidas para los Derechos Humanos en México.

U.S. Bureau of Justice Statistics (BJS). 2007. *Criminal Offender Statistics*. August 8. http://www.ojp.gov/bjs/crimoff.htm

U.S. Central Intelligence Agency. *2012 World Factbook*. https://www.cia.gov/library /publications/the-world-factbook/geos/mx.html.

U.S. Commission on Civil Rights, Arizona, California, New Mexico, and Texas Advisory Committees. 1997. *Federal Immigration Law Enforcement in the Southwest: Civil Rights Impacts on Border Communities*. Los Angeles: Western Regional Office.

U.S. Congress. 2008. FY 2008 Supplemental Appropriations Act (P.L. 110-252).

U.S. Customs and Border Protection, Department of Homeland Security. 2009. "Securing American's Borders: CBP Fiscal Year 2009 in Review Fact Sheet." News release, November 24.

U.S. Department of Homeland Security. 2010. "Budget-in-Brief, Fiscal Year 2011." www.dhs.gov/xlibrary/assets/budget_bib_fy2011.pdf.

U.S. Department of Homeland Security. Customs and Border Protection. 2013a, "United States Border Patrol; Border Patrol Agent Staffing by Fiscal Year," http:// www.cbp.gov/linkhandler/cgov/border_security/border_patrol/usbp_statistics /usbp_fy12_stats/staffing_graph2.ctt/staffing_graph2.pdf.

U.S. Department of Homeland Security. Customs and Border Protection. 2013b, "Enacted Border Patrol Program Budget by Fiscal Year," http://www.cbp.gov/xp/cgov /border_security/border_patrol/usbp_statistics/usbp_fy12_stats.

U.S. Department of State. 2007. *2007 Country Reports on Human Rights Practices: Mexico.* http://www.state.gov/g/drl/rls/hrrpt/2007/100646.htm.

———. 2008a. *Country Reports on Human Rights Practices: Mexico.*

———. 2008b. "President Bush Attends Council of the Americas." Office of the Press Secretary, news release, May 7.

———. 2010. "Mexico-Mérida Initiative Report." September 2.

———. 2012. "Mexico-Merida Initiative Report." August 30.

U.S. Government Accountability Office (GAO). 2006. "Illegal Immigration: Border-Crossing Deaths Have Doubled Since 1995; Border Patrol's Efforts to Prevent Deaths Have Not Been Fully Evaluated." GAO-06-770, Washington, D.C.

———. 2009. "Secure Border Initiative: Technology Deployment Delays Persist and the Impact of Border Fencing Has Not Been Assessed." GAO-09-896, September, Washington, D.C.

U.S. House of Representatives. 2009. "Conference Report to Accompany H.R. 3288." Report 111-366, December 8, 1487. http://frwebgate.access.gpo.gov/cgi-bin/getdoc .cgi?dbname=111_cong_reports&docid=f:hr366.111.pdf.

U.S. Library of Congress-Federal Research Division. 2008. *Country Profile: Mexico.* July. http://memory.loc.gov/frd/cs/profiles/Mexico.pdf.

U.S. Northern Command. n.d. "Joint Task Force North." http://www.jtfn.northcom .mil/subpages/mission.html.

U.S. Office of Border Patrol. 1994. "Border Patrol Strategic Plan 1994 and Beyond: National Strategy." July.

———. 2004. "National Border Patrol Strategy." U.S. Customs and Border Protection. Department of Homeland Security, September. http://www.customs.gov/linkhan dler/cgov/border_security/border_patrol/national_bp _strategy.ctt/national_bp_stra tegy.pdf.

U.S. Office of National Drug Control Policy (ONDCP). 2008. *Drug-Related Crime.* March. http://whitehousedrugpolicy.gov/publications/factsht/crime/index.html.

El Universal. 2007. "Advierte AI de uso de fuerzas armadas en combate a crimen." National Politics Section. May 23.

Vélez Ascencio, Octavio. 2007. "Amnistía, 'escandalizada' por el 'ciclo vicioso de abuso y violencia en Oaxaca.'" *La Jornada*, Politics Section, August 1.

Vila, Pablo. 2000. *Crossing Borders: Social Categories, Metaphors, and Narrative Identities on the U.S.-Mexico Border*. Austin: University of Texas Press.

Villareal, Andres. 2002. "Political Competition and Violence in Mexico: Hierarchical Social Control in Local Patronage Structures." *American Sociological Review* 67, 4: 477–98.

Washington Office on Latin America (WOLA). 2006. *Youth Gangs in Central America: Issues in Human Rights, Effective Policy, and Prevention*. Special Report, Washington, D.C., November.

———. 2007. "U.S. Lawmakers Urge Calderón to Fight Violence Against Women." Press release, August 9.

———. 2009. "Mexican and U.S. Human Rights Organizations Call on the U.S. Government to Withhold Mérida Initiative Funding for Mexico." July 16.

———. 2010. "Congress: Withhold Funds for Mexico Tied to Human Rights Performance." September 14.

———. 2011. "Members of U.S. Congress Urge Secretary Clinton to Raise Human Rights Concerns with Mexico." March 3.

———. 2012a. "U.S. Congress Calls on Secretary Clinton to Request Information Related to Human Rights in Mexico." July 5.

Washington Office on Latin America (WOLA), et al. 2012. "Memo to the U.S. Department of State," June 25. http://www.wola.org/sites/default/files/downloadable/Mexico/2012/Merida%20Memo_June%2025%202012%20FINAL.pdf.

Washington Valdez, Diana. 2006. *Harvest of Women: Safari in Mexico*. Los Angeles: Peace at the Border Publishing.

Watkins, Thayer. n.d. *Economic History and the Economy of Mexico*. San Jose University, Department of Economics.

Weisman, Jonathan, and Charlie Savage. 2012. "Eric Holder Found in Contempt of Congress." *New York Times*, June 28.

White, Marceline. 2004. "Look FIRST from a Gender Perspective: NAFTA and the FTAA." *Gender & Development* 12, 2: 44–52.

White House, Office of the Press Secretary. 2009. "Press Conference by President Obama, President Calderón of Mexico, and Prime Minister Harper of Canada, Cabanas Cultural Center, Guadalajara, Mexico, August 10."

White House Press Office. 2007. "Remarks by President Bush, Prime Minister Harper of Canada, and President Calderón of Mexico in a Joint Press Report." August 21.

Wilkinson, Tracy. 2008. "'El Chapo' Has Left the Building." *Los Angeles Times*, November 3.

Williams, Phil. 2009a. "Drug Trafficking, Violence, and the State in Mexico." Strategic Studies Institute United States Army War College. http://www.strategicstudiesinstitute.army.mil/pubs/display.cfm?pubID=913.

———. 2009b. "Illicit Markets, Weak States and Violence: Iraq and Mexico." *Crime, Law and Social Change* 52 (3): 323–36.

Wright, Melissa W. 2001. "A Manifesto Against Femicide." *Antipode* 33, 3: 550–66.

———. 2004. "From Protests to Politics: Sex Work, Women's Worth, and Ciudad Juárez Modernity." *Annals of the Association of American Geographers* 94, 2: 369–86.

———. 2007. "Femicide, Mother-Activism, and the Geography of Protest in Northern Mexico." *Urban Geography* 28: 401–25.

———. 2010. "Feminism and a Feeling of Justice." *Progress in Human Geography* 34: 818–27

———. 2011. "Necropolitics, Narcopolitics, and Femicide: Gendered Violence on the Mexico-U.S. Border." *Signs: Journal of Women in Culture and Society* 36, 3: 707–31.

Zepeda, Eduardo, Timothy A. Wise, and Kevin P. Gallagher. 2009. *Rethinking Trade Policy for Development: Lessons from Mexico Under NAFTA*. Washington, D.C.: Carnegie Endowment for International Peace.

Alejandro Anaya Muñoz is Associate Professor in the International Studies Division of the Center for Research and Teaching in Economics (Centro de Investigación y Docencia Económicas, CIDE). His publications include articles in such journals as *Human Rights Quarterly, International Journal of Human Rights,* and *Journal of Latin American Studies.* His most recent book is *El país bajo presión: Debatiendo el papel del escrutinio internacional de derechos humanos sobre México.*

Luis Alfredo Arriola Vega is a researcher at El Colegio de la Frontera Sur, Mexico. His current work focuses on border and migration studies. He earned a doctorate from the University of Florida and has worked among rural populations in Guatemala and southern Mexico. His most recent book is *Human Agency and the Making of Territoriality at the Frontier: A Case-Study from Northern Petén, Guatemala.*

Timothy J. Dunn, Professor in the Sociology Department at Salisbury University, Salisbury, Maryland, has researched and written about the U.S.-Mexico border, immigration, and human rights for over twenty years. He has published two books, *Blockading the Border and Human Rights: The El Paso Operation That Remade Immigration Enforcement* and *The Militarization of the U.S.-Mexico Border, 1978–1992: Low-Intensity Conflict Doctrine Comes Home,* as well as several journal articles and numerous anthology chapters. He lived on the border in El Paso, Texas, in 1994–1999 and earned his M.A. and Ph.D. from the University of Texas at Austin.

Miguel Escobar-Valdez, Consul of Mexico (retired), Mexican Foreign Service, has a background in journalism and education. He is also a writer and a lecturer whose fictional works have earned several literary awards in Spain and Mexico. He has written numerous essays about immigration. His latest book is *El muro de la vergüenza* (The Wall of Shame).

Clara Jusidman is Economist and Founding President of INCIDE Social, a Mexican NGO working in public policy promotion based on research in social development, democracy, social dialogue, economic, cultural, and social rights, and social determinants of violence.

Maureen Meyer is Senior Associate for Mexico at the Washington Office on Latin America (WOLA). Her work focuses on U.S.-Mexico security policies and their relation to organized crime-related violence, corruption, and human rights violations in Mexico. She also carries out advocacy work regarding U.S. security assistance to Mexico and the impact of U.S border security policies on migrants. Before joining WOLA in 2006, she lived and worked for five years in Mexico City, primarily with the Miguel Agustín Pro Juárez Human Rights Center.

Carol Mueller, Professor of Sociology and former Director of the School of Social and Behavioral Sciences at Arizona State University, is best known as a social movements scholar, with particular attention to the international women's movement. She has published books on social movement theory (with Aldon Morris), *Frontiers of Social Movement Theory*, *The Politics of the Gender Gap*, *The Women's Movements of the United States and Western Europe* (with Mary Katzenstein), and *Repression and Mobilization* (with Chris Davenport and Hank Johnston), as well as dozens of articles and book chapters.

Julie A. Murphy Erfani is Associate Professor of Political Science in the School of Social and Behavioral Sciences at Arizona State University. Her research interests include violence, overkill, and the posthuman condition in the Americas. Her article "Selling SB 1070: Anti-Immigrant Rhetoric Harms Arizona's Image and Self-Interest" appeared in *AZTLAN: A Journal of Chicano Studies*.

William Paul Simmons is Associate Professor in Gender and Women's Studies and Honors Interdisciplinary Faculty at the University of Arizona. His research is highly interdisciplinary, using theoretical, legal, and empirical approaches to study social justice and human rights issues. His books include *Human Rights Law and the Marginalized Other* and *An-Archy and*

Justice: An Introduction to Emmanuel Levinas' Political Thought. He has published in such leading journals as *Philosophy and Social Criticism*, *Yale Human Rights & Development Law Journal*, *Perspectives on Politics*, *Journal of International Human Rights*, and *Social Sciences Quarterly*.

Kathleen Staudt, Professor of Political Science at the University of Texas at El Paso, teaches courses on public policy, democracy, women and politics, and borders. Besides more than a hundred academic articles and chapters, she has published seventeen books, including *Women and Violence at the Border*, and served as lead editor of *Human Rights Along the U.S.-Mexico Border* and *Cities and Citizenship at the U.S.-Mexico Border.* Her forthcoming volumes include *A War That Can't Be Won: Binational Perspectives on the War on Drugs* (with Tony Payan) and *Courage and Resistance: Civil Society Activism in Ciudad Juárez* (with Zulma Méndez).

Michelle Téllez, an interdisciplinary scholar, teaches in the School of Humanities, Arts and Cultural Studies, and the M.A. in Social Justice and Human Rights program at Arizona State University. Her writing and research seek to uncover the stories of transnational community formation, migration, and resistance.

INDEX

ACKNOWLEDGMENTS

This volume has gestated over many years, and we are grateful for our many colleagues and friends who have supported us through this process. Dean Elizabeth Langland and Associate Dean Thomas J. Keil of the New College of Interdisciplinary Arts and Sciences at Arizona State University provided necessary funding and logistical support as did the Mexican Consulate in Phoenix, especially former Mexican Consul General to Phoenix, Carlos Flores Vizcarra and former Program Director, Susana Ibarra-Johnson.

Our colleague Julie Murphy A. Erfani was very helpful in brainstorming about the direction this volume ultimately assumed. We are grateful to numerous colleagues at Arizona State University who provided helpful insights into these complex binational human rights issues, including Luis Cabrera, Stan Ackroyd, Kristin Koptiuch, Alejandra Elenes, Ed McKennon, Lisa Kammerlocher, and Michelle Téllez. We also learned a great deal and benefitted from the seemingly endless energy of a special group of students including Rebecca Coplan, Sarah (Grace) Daniels, Francisco Flores, Zeenat Hasan, Emily Taylor, Michael Gardiner, Courtney Anderson, Marla Conrad, Katie Norberg, and Layal Rabat.

We would like to recognize the vibrant intellectual and creative atmosphere created by ASU's annual Border Justice events, which have included public art, film screenings, theater performances, panels with activists, scholars and writers, activism, and musical performances.

Several artists and activists in Phoenix, including Marco Albarran, Judy Butzine, Melanie Ohm, Malissa Geer, Stella Pope Duarte, Laura Ilardo, and James Garcia, played important roles in our Border Justice events and in helping us to better understand the human rights implications of U.S. policies. We learned a great deal from performances by Jeffrey Solomon and the Houses on the Moon Theatre Company and presentations by Iliana Martinez, Marisa Ugarte, Olivia Ruiz, Isabel Garcia, and Lindsay Marshall.

At the University of Pennsylvania Press, Peter Agree showed great faith in this project early on and shepherded us through several rounds of revisions. The anonymous reviewers for Penn provided numerous helpful suggestions, big and small, for improving the manuscript. We thank them for their very close and informed reading of the work. We are deeply appreciative of the patience and diligence of our contributors who revised and updated their chapters in a timely fashion, and for their faith in this project.

Bill is especially grateful for the love and support of Monica, Mason, and Delaney, who are constant sources of inspiration and make all the difference. Carol is very hopeful that this volume's publication in the University of Pennsylvania Press series on human rights will help people living beyond the border states to better understand the complicity of U.S. politics in the ongoing tragedies and complexities described here.